# CHRISTIAN ETHICS

## *An Introduction for College Students*

BY

REV. LEO R. WARD, C.S.C.

B. HERDER BOOK CO.

15 & 17 SOUTH BROADWAY, ST. LOUIS 2, MO.

AND

33 QUEEN SQUARE, LONDON, W. C.

1952

*NIHIL OBSTAT*

*Arthur J. Hope, C.S.C.*
*Censor Librorum*

*IMPRIMI POTEST*

*Theodore J. Mehling, C.S.C.*
*Superior Provincialis*

*December 15, 1951*

*IMPRIMATUR*

✠ *John F. Noll,*
*Bishop*

*Fort Wayne, Ind., January 19, 1952*



*Vail-Ballou Press, Inc., Binghamton and New York*

# PREFACE

This introductory study of Christian ethics aims to combine a study of the moral order with a study of cases. The emphasis in the first part is on order and standards, or norms; in the second part, cases are considered in the light of these standards. The standard affirmed above others is man, or human nature. In this way the book would bypass both Kant, who holds that human nature does not matter, and such a man as Sartre, who holds that human nature does not exist. This work tries to use the ideas of St. Thomas, who has considerable respect for human nature and for man, and that of Maritain, who says that man is great enough and sacred enough to serve as a measure for all the goods of this world. In considering man, order, standards, and numerous empirical cases, the author would honor, as integral to Christian ethical study and life, the evangelical concern for humanity.

By utilizing many sociological materials and by being willing to be taught by Christ, by great thinkers past and present, we may hope at last to begin a bridging of the gap between scientific progress and ethical lag.

The general position taken is Aristotelian; but we think that ours is a baptized and democratized Aristotelian humanism.

## Chapter 1

# NATURE OF AN ETHICAL PROBLEM

Among the problems with which every person is obviously confronted are health problems, economic problems, and moral problems. We cannot escape these last; they show themselves at every turn and in every context. Above all, they are problems of the manner in which we use our freedoms; they are not, in any direct and proper way, problems of our minds, bodies, or external goods. It is possible to state in several ways how it is that these ethical problems arise. The way chosen here is an inductive approach: from cases and experience. Consider the following enumerated instances, familiar to everyone.

1. A man or a group tears up a treaty: it is a scrap of paper. People say that the action is wrong and intolerable; they say that the man or group should not act in that way.

2. A small, local group of druggists and pharmacists refuses to sell comics till these are purged. They say that comics drug and dope child minds, lead to gang mentality and to juvenile delinquency. The druggists and pharmacists assume that we have not the right to promote or allow such effects.

3. In spite of, even on account of, a decision of the Supreme Court in 1948, people say that if religion and education are separated, the child's understanding of nature and man and society is stunted. They say we have no right to suffer such separation, and that on this question a neutral government, backed by a neutral Constitution, is an impossibility, and that we ought to change either the decision or the Constitution, or, as will at least pro tempore be done, we ought to disregard them.

4. Some people say that nations that fall and surrender in a war have rights, and that their peoples have rights.

5. Some people say it is wrong to drink liquor; some say that under such and such conditions, changing with circumstances, drinking is not wrong. Some say it is wrong to dance, wrong to smoke, wrong to play cards, wrong under any and all circumstances.

6. People say it is wrong to scandalize anyone, especially a child. They say we have a responsibility to give good example and that some have a greater responsibility than do others.

7. Most people in industrial nations now say that workers have the right to strike.

8. Some people say that, because of the public good involved, workers in vital key industries have no right to strike, or have the right to strike only under specifiable conditions.

9. Some people say that industrial plants, taxed at a much lower percentage than are other properties, should be taxed in all states on the same percentage of their face value as are the other properties.

10. Some people say that nonprofit, nonincome businesses, should, along with profit or income businesses, pay income tax.

11. People say that Americans, as do any people, have the duty (a) to train men for foreign consular and diplomatic service; (b) to look to national defense; (c) to work perpetually for peace with all nations; (d) to learn soil conservation techniques and habits of conserving water, timber, oil, coal, and iron; (e) to develop science, and a grasp of science and its place in modern society, especially in youthful minds; (f) to build, out of our freedoms, intelligence, and great resources an economic structure that will give every family the chance to get the economic reserve for normal living; (g) to integrate religion and life; (h) to integrate practical economic and political life with science, history, philosophy, and theology; (i) to learn again, by the hard process of doing, what the unity, even under

present difficult conditions, of marriage and the family means for persons and society.

The list might mount to hundreds, but is enough to show that the world is running over with ethical problems. Whenever we exercise our freedoms we most likely enter the realm of moral good or bad, of right or wrong conduct and responsibility for our acts. We say "most likely," since we can freely look at the wall, drink more or less water, rise at six or at seven, and yet possibly encounter no moral problems thereby. The realm of our freedoms: this is the realm and the only realm of ethics. As the enumerated list suggests, we can exercise our freedom on any of a thousand things. It is not possible to exercise it on the end of existence; this we must desire and seek, or so the Scholastics have consistently held. Means to the end, in a complex, variegated, and beautiful world, are innumerable, and on any of these million and their multimillion possible combinations we can exercise our freedom. Evidently people need to develop the virtue of knowing how, in many different circumstances, to manage the means in relation to the end. The virtue of this know-how, technically called *prudentia,* is the subject studied in ethics. Our effective freedom regarding some possible means is almost nil, and in our circumstances the choice of some others could not make more sense than could crying for the moon.

The general situation is that we can do good or evil. By nature we are good and desire to do good; at least that is the position explained and defended in this book. But we can be confused regarding what is good, and this in two senses: we can be confused as to whether it is good to kill this man in these circumstances; whether it is really evil to take part in a war, in some particular war, or in any war; and we can be perplexed as to what is the basic difference between good and evil. To be confused is the evil of intellect and not of the will; that is the reason why it is an intellectual and not a moral evil. To be a muddled man is one thing; to be a bad man is another; and we cannot reduce intellect to will or will to intellect, though Socrates thought that the only good is intellectual good and the only evil, intellectual evil. We know good things, but we do not always do them; each of us, along with St. Paul and Horace, has encountered this fact.

We are fallible on fact, on principle, and in reasoning; we are susceptible to error, a condition that is basically intellectual.

Also, at times we refuse to do what we see we ought to do, or we do what we see we ought not to do. Action against the light is morally bad action. Of course, ethics takes account of the fact that knowledge or lack of knowledge affects freedom and thus affects conduct.

If man were God he could not know good and yet do evil, and if he were an ox or turnip or a pot of gold he could not intellectually know, would not be free and would not be subject to knowing good and doing evil. He is free and is like God, but has a limited intelligence and a limited freedom. He is a person, an individual being with intelligence and freedom, but an imperfect person. He is good and is determinately set in the direction of good; that is, he has not the slightest taste for, or tendency toward, nonbeing; on the contrary, he has tremendous inner dynamism and demand for goodness, and yet, given the fact that he is not finally confirmed in good, he can lapse in a particular act or lapse as in a habit, which is an inner state of possessing and having himself, in an acquired way, toward these good things or away from those. He is good and demands good, but his intellect is both limited and darkened, and his will, limited and weakened. If a person does not say this on grounds of faith, he must admit it on grounds of experience.

We are so used to judging in terms of good and bad and so used to doing what we take to be good or to be bad—and, as this book will claim, usually being correct in judgment and action—that it is as if we knew all about good and evil, and about how moral problems arise. It is an oversimple view which holds that we really comprehend them. If we were to take them as the child takes them, as what he is told is right and wrong, it would be simple, since some children in this sense know many things as right or wrong before they know right from left. But if we raise the question, which is at least as old as Plato, whether right and wrong are somehow rooted in the universe and possibly depend on the will of God; and, if we consider that we can take the way to the sanctity of a St. Francis or to the perversions of the gangster, dictator, profiteer, or sodomist, we see that the childlike view, so proper to man, is inadequate. For this reason ethical studies are made.

In place of the foregoing cases, anyone may substitute hundreds out of his own experience, and may offer substitutes for the following materials. We have found it useful with classes in ethics to begin by asking students to read some current, perhaps popular, article in a magazine or a news weekly and to state the ethical problems raised. In this way the mass effect, with twenty to forty students in a class, is to make emphatic and real the kind of ethical problem that people in the nation at a particular time encounter and must try to handle. Then we ask students to find some of the problems raised fifty or a hundred years ago, and, if possible, to see in the light of what principles the author of this or that article takes his stand on ethical questions. We also use materials out of ancient ethical studies, chiefly Aristotle's *Ethics,* and out of some medieval and later studies. The student sees the recurrence, almost the constancy, of particular problems relative to various types of dictatorship, to rights and responsibilities, to sex and family life and education, to charity and justice and ownership, to slavery in various forms and degrees, to privilege, to work, to worship.

Here are some materials reported by students in September 1948:

1. Abortions to save Jewish and other women from death at the hands of the Nazis: *Time,* September, 1948.

2. "Brave New World," an article by Julian Huxley: *Life,* September, 1948.

3. Sacrifice of Mass Humanity in War.

4. "Hogs on the Highway."

5. "Must we change our sex standards?" *Readers Digest,* September, 1948.

6. "Are Strikes Inevitable?" *Irish Digest,* August, 1948.

7. "The Hickman Case," *Harpers,* August, 1948.

8. "Should Religion be taught in our Schools?" *Ladies Home Journal,* September, 1948.

9. "Parasites on the UN," *American,* September, 1948.

10. "Youth and the Comics," *America,* September, 1948.

11. "Color and race discrimination," *New Republic,* September, 1948.

12. "The Ethics of Capitalism," *Newsweek,* September, 1948.

This simple list is given to show how students can, at any moment, readily pick up in every sort of magazine, materials that raise ethical problems. The following lot of magazine articles, with references in some cases indicated, covers some materials for several previous years: "Can the Communist Party be outlawed?" "Revenge costs too much" (*Harpers,* May, 1946). "Problem of the Catholic Writer" (*Commonweal,* February 13, 1948). "Should the U.S. Admit 100,000 DP's?" Stimson on the Decision to Use the A-Bomb (*Harpers,* February, 1947); this article is an apology. Is it an effective one? To what standards does Stimson appeal? "These Russians" (*Forum,* 1930); articles of great interest. A school coach was fired and thereby deprived of a livelihood: Is the problem fundamentally a cultural one? an athletic one? an economic one? an ethical one? Who is responsible for the frequent deaths from boxing? the public? the MD's in the cases? the commissioners? the managers? or the promoters? A few persons get rich quickly; e.g., the McCabes of Minnesota have allegedly realized $40,000,000 from grain elevator transactions and grain milling; others have suffered, to balance the account: Is this good national and regional policy? What would be the completed syllogism showing that such policy and practice should, if it should, be abolished? In that case, who should stop it: the State? public opinion? action of a nonpolitical sort on the part of the people?

Men in political high places deal in commodity markets and thereby trade in human misery, exploit their fellow citizens, disrupt the economy and betray the trust of the people. Are the citizens of a democracy guilty, along with these men?

Suppose the monopolist or the monopolist-politician scalps the people: is this not a free country, and can we have free enterprise without some monopoly and some dirt even in politics? After all, this is not heaven, and we should not expect all-white politics or economy. Should we therefore simply ignore evil? Does NAM's free enterprise bless the monopolist, the commodity-trading politician, the employer and the landlord who practices discrimination? Take a local case. Mr. X refuses to rent an apartment to a GI couple with children: is not his action that of a free man in a free country? What is moral or immoral about it?

Here are other materials. Must we try world government or must we forget it? Must we establish an international community? Are we ethically obliged to retain teachers who are Communists, or are we ethically obliged to fire them? "Palestine Partition," "Bankrupt Britain," "There's Nobody to Relieve Us," "Must America Save Europe?" If the boss is your friend and offers you a job not otherwise coming to you and properly coming to another, should you accept it? Is the giving of gifts to make business contacts unethical? How about test-tube babies? Is virginity unethical? How should we feel about the denial of rights to the Negro despite the Constitution? What of the refusal to admit Negroes, in many northern cities, into Catholic schools? What is to be thought of indiscriminate bombings? How evaluate the case of an airman coming home from a raid and unloading on farmers and villagers his extra ammunition without orders to do so? What should we think of the secret rebate on eyeglasses? Was Gandhi justified in his hunger strikes? "Confessions of a used-car dealer." College life vs. morality: fraternities and week-end house parties. "Fifty Years of Movies—for What?" (*Atlantic Monthly,* September, 1947).

It is also pertinent for our consideration to go on a tour of ethical problems faced by people fifty or a hundred years ago; results such as the following are easily achieved.

"Work and Wages," *Nation,* August 16, 1883.

"The Ethics of Political Lying" [in England], *Nineteenth Century,* 1889.

"The State, the Church and the School," *Atlantic Monthly,* June, 1889.

"The Genesis of the [Boy] Gang," *Atlantic Monthly,* 1889.

"Imprisonment for Debt," *Gentleman's Magazine,* 1789.

"Substitution for Hanging," *Nation,* 1873.

"The New World and the New Man": *Atlantic Monthly,* 1858; most interesting: on the discovery of a new world, and the ethical problems of men living far from home under new conditions.

"The Good and the Evil in Industrial Combinations," *Atlantic Monthly,* 1897.

"War as a Moral Tonic," 1903.

"Euthanasia," *Catholic World,* 1896.

"Labor Unions and the Negro," *Atlantic Monthly,* 1898.

"Let's Keep Marriage a 'Pretiosum,' " *Harpers Magazine,* September, 1895.

"What Shall the Public Schools Teach?" A series of debates; *Forum,* 1888.

"The Scientific Moralists vs. the Theists," by W. H. Mallock; *Forum,* 1886–7.

"What is the object of life?" W. H. Mallock; *Forum,* 1887.

"Divorce and some of its results," *Catholic World,* 1880.

"For whom should one vote?" *Nation,* May 23, 1872.

And so the never-ending list goes on.

Ethical problems arise in every sort of context, and in relation to all sorts of matter, wherever man has effective freedom as an individual person or a member of a group, in education and science and art, in family life, in economic and industrial relations, in the small community, in the production, processing, and selling of food, as a workman, as a teacher, a priest, a professional man, in the field of political life and the field of religious life.

Since all normal persons have ethical problems, it is possible to take as a starting point the common experience of "ought": I ought, you ought, and so on. People, to the extent they are influenced by the Hebrew-Christian tradition, are strong on the "ought," stronger in some ways than Oriental and Near East peoples. The Hebrew tradition is a tradition in the moral order, not in the scientific or intellectual. Compared to the Greek tradition, it is moralistic. The Law and the Commandments are, at their core, moral and not intellectual, and the Greeks and the Romans have nothing properly comparable to them. A Christian intellectualism was later to develop; but, in essence, the Christian tradition is a moral tradition, and certain movements have accelerated it, for example: the Protestant movement, which was much more markedly moral than intellectual; the Albigensian movement; and, in relation to developments in the United States, the Puritan moralistic tradition. Blue laws, written or unwritten, have always been characteristic of American life, and it is difficult for us to understand that other peoples might be good men without our taboos, or to understand how the ancients, to say nothing of the Russians, could do some of the things attributed to them, and seemingly do them without reference to moral judgments.

A second note is that ethical problems, in some form or other, rise up again just as if they had not been answered a hundred times. Old problems come up in new circumstances, and dressed in new headlines they look like new problems; and in a moralistic nation like ours with Hebrew-Christian and Puritan backgrounds, people want to hear about moral problems: witness the circulation success of magazines like *Coronet,* the *Post, Time, Newsweek,* the *Atlantic,* with their perpetual appeal to moral issues. Note how Mencken boomed to big circulation with the *American Mercury* in the "twenties," partly on the appeal of caustic, "we've-left-all-that" criticism, but partly on the ground of an anti-moral moralism. It would be more difficult to publish these articles in Russia or in ancient Greece; but the problems come up among all peoples. Men want moral questions discussed; they thrive on them.

Circumstances vary widely, and matters on which we exercise our freedom vary. It is now the slaves, and now the slaves presumably set free. It is now the enemy, and now the fallen enemy. It is now our enemy, now, after all, our ally. It is now the white and now the Negro, now the craftsman and now the machine, and the factory workers and the proletariat. It is now youth, now adults, now the aged. Problems of sex are not novel, nor are problems of justice and charity, though occasions for doing good or evil are, in many matters and in many ways, new: housing, cars, work, bombs, capitalistic and corporation control over economic goods.

Still one more note. In passing, we mention some romantic notions about man's freedom. First, we take it as an absolute, which means that man is absolute. Secondly, we suppose therefore that nothing is to interfere with it; whatever would, thereby would be fascist and dictatorial. Thirdly, we imagine that the research man, for example, has a total freedom, not bound or limited in any basic way by his own nature, by the common good of the nation or humanity, or in an immediate way by the people who financially or politically back his work. Fourthly, we imagine that the American child has, as a volume in sociology is advertised to say, a "perfect freedom" and the wife "enjoys with her husband equality and partnership in all family affairs and property rights and is even entitled to separate domicile and independent citizenship." In short, we, especially we in the colleges, are dominated by the romantic liberalism of the late nineteenth century: much science, some conceivable though ill-defined progress, a generally humanitarian goodness.

It is better to accept at the start the fact of great, if somewhat limited, freedoms in man and a corresponding great and limited responsibility. There is no point in taking as true what our everyday practice makes clear is untrue. Vast possibilities are in man. Otherwise he would not have reached the heights he now and then has reached in persons and groups. In particular matters of freedom and intellect and thus of ethical, scientific, and artistic achievement we cannot say *what* is man's limit; but we must say that he has limits, of which we are painfully aware in ourselves and in current events and in history.

An interesting fact about moral experience is that in it the ordinary man, though rarely conscious of this, reasons and follows an argument in deciding that, here and now, "X" is to be done or "Y" to be avoided. He has the general principle that only good is to be done, in the ethical or any field, and that evil is always to be avoided. This he knows when he knows the meaning of the words, and it is his major premise. Then in the light of whatever moral standards or norms he employs, he sees that to do such and such kind of action is good and may, or even should, be done by a man in such and such circumstances, and that to do another kind would be evil. But then he sees that here and now he is a man in just those circumstances, and that he may or should do the act, or that in his circumstances he should not do an act of the second type. Thus:

Major: Good is to be done and evil avoided.

Minor 1: But for a man to do this kind of act in these circumstances—actions occur only in particular circumstances—would in the light of my standards be good and may be done; or evil. . . .

Minor 2: But I am a man in just those circumstances.

Conclusion: Therefore I am here and now to do the act; or not to do the act.

Men scarcely notice this reasoning, and because they do not notice it we may think highly of their moral life; they are attuned to loving good and hating evil, are keen in the use of standards, and run through the process quickly in a subconscious way. Once in a while a man adverts to the standard; e.g., when he says, "Why should I do this?" Or, "Why should I not do that?" A reply can be made only in the light of some standard, justified or unjustified. Having intelligence, he can see what to do and with freedom he can ordinarily do it. But as a limited person he can fail to see the light or fail to follow the light he has and in that way do what he takes to be, and what may objectively be, evil.

It is inevitable that man, being what he is, will have moral problems.

## CHAPTER 2

# DETERMINANTS OF THE MORAL ORDER

AN OVERDOSE of order is a dangerous thing, producing the Puritan, the dogmatist, the fascist, the rigid classicist, and tending to kill development and creative ability. Yet we must have order if we are to do anything in science, in art, in society. It is odd that so few study "order." It is as if people would rather, in theory and practice, try to muddle through. For the sake of clarity it is best to ascertain, at the start, the determinants of the moral order. We wish to know each determinant, to know them all in their possible integration, and afterwards to see them applied to concrete matters such as the family, property, population, and resources.

Other words for the determinants of the moral order are the "causes," the "elements," or "principles."

To know moral order we must first know order, and the procedure will be the following. First, we shall consider some simple and familiar instances of order. Secondly, we shall find the elements or causes in any order. Thirdly, we shall point out the two radical kinds of order and their interrelationship. Lastly, we shall define "order" and, at the end of this chapter, give a tentative definition of the "moral order."

To operate as men we have to order many things. We order things in traffic, in national and international affairs, in finance, in the kitchen and menage and the family, in our religious life, at work and at play. Order, as we know it from experience, falls under two main heads, which we state with illustrations.

A—Order in the life of our wills; this is largely in the relation of man to man, and demands a know-how called "prudence."

1. In traffic.
2. In family or domestic life.
3. In finances and economics.
4. In ownership, assemblies, and associations.
5. In religious life.
6. In national life.
7. In international life.

B—Order put by us into things outside us, demanding a know-how called "art."

1. In the use of words, written and oral: speech, rhetoric, drama, fiction, poetry.
2. In the use of sounds: music.
3. In architecture: the use of varied materials.
4. In sculpture.
5. In machines.
6. In the culinary art.

Evidently the series of illustrations under "A" and also under "B" can be prolonged almost without end, and each can justly be broken down under many subheadings. This shows how well acquainted people are with "order."

Besides the practical order, at all levels of culture people have known something about the order of nature. In our times it is easy to make a long list of particular "orders" discovered by man, orders presumably "there" in nature and to some degree known to us. It is sufficient to name half a dozen and to assume that they have some relation besides that of contiguity to "A" and "B."

C—Order that man (presumably) has found and progressively finds.

1. The biological order.
2. The physical order.
3. The (formal) logical order.
4. The metaphysical order.
5. The mathematical order.

Whether the formal logician or the mathematician studies a real order or beings dependent on the mind for their being, is here irrelevant.

Is "order" in things, or merely in the mind? We have the idea of order, said Kant; but he asked whether it is merely a handy and regulative idea that helps us with our thinking, or an idea conceived by us because order is implanted in all things. We here assume a positive reply: we find order in things; in the first place we find things, we find "a world" and do not make it. This world, with its great variety of things and persons, imposes itself on the mind. Of course, it is obvious that in human matters such as family life, political life, and the arts we impose order on things.

If people are so familiar with at least the order they make, it is apropos to inquire into the elements present in any order of this type. To make this inquiry is to attempt to give a breakdown of order, but not to define it.

Take any simple case under "A" or "B." The traffic order has many elements, as moving vehicles, and people, and, above all, human wills; and these things are to be ordered. Here we combine them as the material cause of order: the stuff, the materials. Left to themselves they are as likely to effect disorder as an orderly movement of traffic. We need someone to order them, some person or persons; the city fathers, traffic policemen, and the people who are being ordered and who simultaneously help to do the ordering. The people who so order constitute another cause, usually called the "agent" or "efficient cause." Still, suppose the people do not desire or do not effectively desire traffic order. Such order will not then result. Commonly people wish traffic order, and wish it as a means to safety and convenience and to expedite traffic. (This order, as any other, is also beautiful.)

Thus far, we have found three "causes" of traffic order, the materials, the agents (or persons), and the ends. These are insufficient, since persons often seek ends and have materials at hand and yet achieve little order. How are things put together so as not to make merely a pile or a mess?

The answer is that order depends also on another principle, or cause, usually called the "form," or the "formal cause." This fourth cause of traffic order is that according to which the persons line up the materials for the sake of the ends, and, evidently, it is the traffic law in the present instance.

This law is an obvious example of the formal cause used by men to achieve order, and is all the more interesting because, till 1915, no city needed a complicated traffic law.

Wherever we impose order on things or on our acts or on combinations of things and acts, the same four causes team up to form order. Consider order effected by us in sports: on a baseball or basketball team. We must have "materials"; we must have persons or agents, such as coaches, captains, and players; some commanding end or ends in view, such as fun or glory or money; and some strategy, or plan, according to which the agents use materials to reach the ends. So it is in case after case: in the work of the cook, of the architect, of persons that work together for national order and peace. National order requires materials—and surely some nations have gotten along well on scanty materials; national order requires persons with prerequisites of intelligence, freedom, and goodness; national order requires ends, such as national good, freedoms, security, peace: "in order to form a more perfect union"; and all the materials are marshalled into one order and unity by the persons, for the end, according to some pattern, elaborate or simple, written or unwritten, democratic or monarchic.

Hence we add two important remarks. One remark is that the pattern must allow for developments, in the case of any dynamic order; not in the order of this poem, this piece of music or sculpture or painting, where pattern and materials are permanently integrated, and room for further freedoms and developments is not needed. In a dynamic order, such as the order in sports or in traffic, in a church, a family, or nation the requirements differ. Here things are perpetually being ordered, and the pattern, the materials, the agents, and perhaps the end, too, must allow for many eventualities. People who do not allow for change and who want to sew up everything into never-to-be-changed completion do not help much in a world of change. Such people achieve static and man-killing order. In politics, their order amounts to too much order: it is all law, no liberty, and we call it tyranny and totalitarianism, whether communistic or fascistic. In the arts, men with fixed laws and formulas are extreme classicists, and their era usually is not noted for development in the arts. In morals, the all-laws, no-liberty men are puritanic and rigoristic.

However, the case for confusion and disorder is not so strong as confused, all-liberty people assume. With Henry James [1] we say, "The effort really to see and really to represent is no idle business in face of the constant force that makes for muddlement." People who suffer from too much order need not bolt for impressionism, lawlessness, and revolution. Would one extreme be good because the other is evil?

Now follows the second remark that we referred to above: the four causes must be integrated, to obtain order. Two or three or the four of these causes lying alongside one another amount at most to potential; they must operate together. The old axiom is that persons are the orderers: *Rationis est ordinare,* which means that the orderers must have intelligence and freedom and an active good will. Otherwise they scarcely are persons and cannot effect order. If boys do not wish to win games, they are likely to lose. Their purpose must command their energies and stamina, along with their intelligence. But if they have not "materials," that is, good players, the will to win is not enough. And they must have a good supple plan. The four causes must be operatively possessed and the four must match. An end or goal that is too high for boys to aim at will not help them win games. So in other cases. If the orderers are not interested in safety,

[1] *The Art of the Novel,* p. 149.

disorderly traffic will result; so, too, if the traffic policemen, though interested and concerned, are ineffective, or if the traffic law is awkward, incomplete, or badly conceived.

In a household, many things are to be ordered by the persons according to some understood rules and regulations and for the happiness, peace, and order of the members; in general, for their good. Economic goods are to be ordered by some person or persons, by the household, by the nation for the economic security of the people and according to monetary laws—it is for economists to say whether any such exist—and according to banking and fiscal regulations and familial and personal rules for making, saving, and spending wealth.

Always in man's life there are things to be ordered, by men, for men's good, and according to standards more or less clearly seen and used. This statement holds for the mechanical and fine arts, which are so important for man and society, in his moral life, his family life, and all public affairs.

Why do we not achieve and maintain international order? The Lord knows we desire it! Both by nature and by our own conscious willing, we desire peace and order, as St. Augustine says.[2] Let us try to state the basic order-principles without which this good is impossible. First, things are to be ordered, such things as shipping and armies and bombs and oil and patents and colonies and empire and whatever has any considerable bearing on international relations. That is one cause, and though it keeps changing, it is always roughly given. Men and not angels are to do the ordering. That is cause number two; cause number three is the end, mentioned a moment ago. The fourth is the formal cause, or principle. It is some usable pattern according to which all these things could be ordered and possibly kept ordered by ourselves to the end and good of world order.

Why, then, do we have such uproars and threats of wars? Not because we lack materials. The Russians and British and Americans and Chinese would not like to say it is because we

[2] *City of God,* Bk. 19.

lack intelligence and freedom and are short on scientific development. The end seems great enough to command everything. Do we not have patterns for peace, a usable, "according-to-which" principle, such that, using this, we, the intelligent and admittedly emancipated, could bring things together for the great good of peace? It is easy to growl and say we have never had a workable plan. But it is likely that some of the old standbys, such as the League, the UN, the World Court, or Wilson's Fourteen Points are sufficient on their part to effect the work.

At least one factor lacking is part of number two, the efficient cause. To order things a person is required, but a person can also be destructive of order; with intelligence and freedom, he needs what Kant called a good will. It is enough to say that a good will is a will that in spite of the cost is directed to the end; not (says Augustine) to the end by which we are destroyed, but to that by which we fully are. To desire an end in terms of someone's tantrum and not in terms of objective human good can only make trouble; to want peace in a willy-nilly fashion is not the road to peace. In the concrete, this means to want the end and yet to want what cancels it out; for example, empire, prestige, power, and revenge.

Persons and nations must be ready to pay for the good of international order. So long, Aquinas says, as each seeks his own, there will be war. So far as the occasion and times demand, the nation must be ready to trim down its old sovereignty.

Our purpose is only to illustrate the elements in any order and thus to explain these elements or causes:

| | |
|---|---|
| To build a house or a city hall | materials<br>persons<br>ends in view<br>blueprint |
| To maintain national order | materials<br>persons<br>ends in view<br>law: the Constitution |

| | |
|---|---|
| To prepare a dinner | materials<br>persons<br>ends in view<br>recipes |

It is a nice question why some are much better orderers than others. With poorer or relatively the same materials they get up a better dinner, have a more equilibrated national order, build an all-round better house. Is it a matter of intelligence, of freedoms, possibly of good will, of disciplined intellect or will? Or is it a matter of set determination toward ends? A matter of blueprints and recipes? Or is it a matter of knowing what counts?

It is interesting to notice the rules children follow in games and how they eliminate one who does not keep the rules; how they shift from pretense to the real, and again to pretense, and how the strong boy or bully changes rules without consultation.

Some artists put a blueprint on paper. Some writers do this, and some composers; but most do not. Materials, persons, ends, whether fun and expression or glory or money, are required, and then the elusive formal factor.

Next we state the two kinds of order in the universe. There is the order made by man and not found by man, the man-made order. The ancients called it the work of "art"; it is not found in nature, but made by man's art and therefore is "artificial." The medievals said it is the work of "will"; it is a work effected by our freedoms, either properly within the will of persons and social bodies or in external materials on which we impose blueprints and recipes, and, directing materials according to these for our ends, we effect an order not directly given in nature.

Secondly, there is the order found by man and not made by man. The biologist finds order, he does not make it; so, too, of the physicist. The formal logician, and to some degree any logician, is bound by laws somehow given by nature for right reasoning and not set up arbitrarily by the logician. The case of mathematical science may be basically the same. The metaphysician wishes to find, for example, the natural relationship between essence and existence, and Jewish and Christian theologians and philosophers say they have found this. Essence is that by which a thing is what it is; existence is that by which it is. These theologians and philosophers say they have found that in one being, and in only one being, essence and existence are really the same.

The second kind of order is the order of "nature." In this man-found kind, human intellect merely knows. In the other kind, it knows and makes order; the human intellect patterns the order and achieves it, whereas, relative to the order of nature, its utmost is to find the order and the plan of the order.

In a way we have a third kind, an order perpetually achieved by man and nature. For instance, when man builds a bridge, he and not nature builds it, but he does not build it contrary to the order of nature. The same is true in many, if not all, arts, mechanical and fine, and we shall contend that a combination of nature's order and of order made by man holds true also of the order effected by man in his moral life.

To balk at "order in nature," as Kant did, is to doubt that things exist except for our thinking. In this nonepistemological study we take the position that things exist with particular natures and tendencies towards ends. At the outset, with regard to the moral order, it is enough to note that people classify some acts as good and some as evil. In that way people have, justifiably or not, introduced a moral order; they have classified some acts "before" and others "after," and they have done this, consciously or not, according to some formal principle and standard. Hence we do not assume a moral order, but observe that some sort of moral order exists in fact.

We return to the causes of order, so as to prepare the way for the definition. It was remarked that the available instances of order known to us are innumerable. We also know much about the formal principle, the most elusive of the four. In different areas of human experience we have special, more or less technical, names for it. We call it a form, a formula, a formal cause, a blueprint, a recipe, a pattern, a design; and we know its function. It is that according to which persons arrange and order materials for the sake of ends. The orderer puts some things before others, "before" and "after" getting their sense and meaning, in the particular case, from their relation to the formal principle. According to the traffic law, fire trucks have priority, that is, they get the go-ahead sign in traffic. Materials for a house already built or being built are not thrown into a pile, but arranged according to the blueprint. According to the "system" or "formation" used, the guard goes before the center on this play and after the center on that play, the terms in this case, "system," "formation," "zone defense" and a "five-man line," being largely nontechnical, and in one sport mainly applicable to defense and in another to offense.

Even in a matter as simple and arbitrary as a game, the pattern cannot be altogether what we will, but depends in part on the ends in view, the materials, and the adequacy of the agents. So too, and more strictly, in building, in designing, in ordering matters in family life and national and international life. Only the rampant pragmatist and individualist-impressionist thinks that good depends primarily on his likes, vagaries, and desires, and that the world must take the shape he pleases.

Each cause is necessary, but the final and the formal are the most decisive. The end is king among causes, above all in the practical realm; it is the cause of causes. Such a pattern is used as is likely to help achieve the end, only such stuffs are eligible as material cause, and it is only for the end that the person is interested and becomes an orderer at all.

In the things that men do and make, the end sets limits within which the pattern or form must operate. If the form will not assist in leading to the end, the form is useless. Because, in making a table, I have in view both usefulness and decoration, I must blueprint to match these ends; if I restrict the end to one, the blueprint must accordingly be restricted. That is the sense in saying that form follows function, "F. F. F." The more practical the order, the more evidently the end dictates. Hence the Aristotelian-Thomist axiom that in operative matters the end is the first principle.

Even so, the formal principle is the most elusive, and though easy to identify in traffic order and international order, it is difficult at times to see and apply it in the moral order and in the artistic order.

With Aristotle we may say that the end is a quasi-formal cause. A thing is not formally and definitively its total self until the end is reached. The boy is and is not a man, the oak is and is not "all there" in the acorn.

With this background of illustrations and of the causes, we define "order." Aristotle often remarks that order is a series, a line-up, as in an army or a battle-line. St. Augustine's fuller statement, in his *City of God,* Book XIX, is famous. Order, he says, is "the distribution of things equal and unequal which allots to each its place." St. Thomas says that good as Augustine's definition is, it omits the decisive formal principle. How do we know "the place" of each ordered material? From what point of view are we to know, and perhaps justify, the "before" and "after" implied in Aristotle's series? The definition must include not only the things ordered and the distribution of "before" and "after," but also the principle according to which things are arranged and ordered and have their "place" and, arbitrarily or from nature, are "before" and "after." Hence the definition:

*ORDER is the relationship of "before" and "after," among distinct things, according to some fixed principle.* This last is the formal cause of order. It is the plan which is followed, the formula, the rule and law and measure of the things ordered, the standard, the recipe, the design. Since each of us is familiar with these terms and has effectively used what they denote in achieving order, it is clear that everybody knows much about the formal principle. St. Thomas often calls it *ratio ordinis,* which means the measure and ground of the particular order, and he designates law as *ratio operis,* which means the measure and ground of some particular dynamic and operative order.

Thus we have stated the form and matter of "order," the matter naturally being the "distinct things" or "materials." Any law that men make is a guide and formal principle for action. A law of nature (said George Henry Lewes about 1870) as formulated by man is a description and report—a transcript, to use Arthur Compton's word—of the paths nature takes in going to her goals. Our assumption is that if there is any law of nature, it is "really there in nature," whether transcribed or not.

How "fixed" is the principle mentioned? In children's play it is as fixed as they make it; children say a child does not play fair when he breaks the rule. In civil law it is much more fixed, though relatively; many features of "the law" or Constitution may need to be made over with the times. In the order of nature, we have reason to suppose that the principle does not change, and later we shall inquire whether moral standards belong in any way to nature; whether the moral order belongs in any way to the natural order. Take the simple case of traffic order. Man makes and remakes the form of this order, and yet the end to be served by this order, namely, the social good, is stipulated by nature, and with that end demanded, the traffic law made by him must be kept within limits that serve that end. It is conceivable that some features of moral order likewise are stipulated by nature. Look at the strong statement of nature, limits, and ends made by Dewey and Tufts [3] in 1908: "Biological instincts and appetites exist, not for the sake of pleasure, but as activities needed to maintain life—the life of the individual and the species. Their adequate fulfilment is attended with pleasure. Such is the undoubted biological fact."

In spite of this realistic declaration by Dewey in his heyday, he was saying then, and for a generation afterward, that natures, ends, and forms do not exist. Nature and the order of nature,

[3] John Dewey and James Tufts, *Ethics,* 1908, pp. 270–71.

he kept saying, are figments of philosophers' and theologians' minds. The most he would allow was that if the order of nature exists, it is useless; it would not be made by us and, for that reason, any knowledge of it would be merely theoretic. In a word, for fifty years Dewey's pragmatism resisted the facts. An order made by man: yes, of course; and on this point everyone has always been in agreement. But an order found by man and accepted by man: no.

From about 1905 that was Dewey's ultrapragmatic position, which would throw out Copernicus, Einstein, and the basic work of all scientists. Man's theoretic and pure-science task is to discover order, and his practical task, to make order. Dewey's position, however, was what Maritain has described as a titanic demonism. The art of acceptance, Dewey said in *The Quest for Certainty* (1929), is antiquated: modern man's art is the art of control, and we feel control "passing into our hands."

Though the ultrapragmatist is out of date, it is difficult for the secularist, whether pragmatist or not, to accept forms, principles, and ends given in nature and to accept any order of nature. The Communist is a revolutionary secularist.

Next we formulate a tentative definition of the moral order. In the moral order as in other orders we have the four causes, but they are specific to moral order and not to order in traffic or in a machine. The materials must be "moral" ones; the agent must be specifically a moral agent; the end, a good not directly given in good traffic or good finance, but in a good human life; and the form, or standard, must be such that this type of agent, using this type of materials, can achieve a corresponding end, order, and good.

The materials and the agent are named with relative ease. In no direct way is the act of a man's eye or foot or hand moral or immoral. His eye sees well and that is its business and excellence; his feet walk well and are good; his hands grasp well and are accordingly good; or, rather, using eye and feet and hands, he is, thus far, good. But at that, he could be quite immoral. Neither is the act or habit of his intellect ever in a direct way moral or immoral; it is right and true or crooked and false; to reach reality and be true as a plumb line is its good. Only the will can be morally good or bad; yet, as a thing given in nature, the will is good both in its being and its direction.

It is the act of the will that is morally good or bad, and also the resulting habits and dispositions in persons and groups. Only here do we have materials for moral order or disorder, though anything on which the will can operate and which it can make its object, can come indirectly into the moral order or disorder. In this indirect way, anything can serve as material cause, unless evil is excluded; since it is only in fiction that man's will can say, "Evil, be thou my good."

The thing to be ordered is the act of the will, then the habit, then the disposition. At least, for convenience, we take habit and disposition in that sequence. For example, a fellow may have a bad habit, but be doing everything to get rid of it; another has the same habit and does not care. The latter has a bad disposition.

We may also say that a social body, national, religious, cultural, occupational, familial or racial, has a good or bad disposition. The English claim to have great respect for the law in England, and though Englishmen break the law in England, the claim is by and large justified. Their being regularly disposed to keep the law is a considerable factor in moral order; given the disposition, the moral order is in some measure already achieved. In certain families, it is understood that certain things are done; in short, the members of a family have the constant disposition to particular good acts and habits; which is a big installment on its maintenance of moral order.

If the will's act is to be ordered, what is the orderer? Man himself in his intelligence and freedom; that is, man as a person.

A human person exercising freedom is the efficient cause, and the act of this exercised freedom is the material cause, the main thing to be ordered.

Final and formal cause are more difficult to identify, and much space is given to them in moral theory. Material and efficient cause are relatively so evident that many take them for granted. But what is the end for which men exercise freedom? Is there any such end? May we make it any end we wish? Again, what is the form of the moral order? May men make it anything they wish? The formal principle is definitive and specifying; along with the matter it goes into the formula to give the definition of any being or any order; it makes being or order specific: it gives us exactly and specifically the being or order we get. What the final and the formal causes of the moral order are, will be taken up in later chapters; at present we wish only to know what kind of thing each is. The end is the result of the ordering and is that for which the ordering is done. The form and specifying cause is the principle according to which we achieve order. The phrase "according to which" expresses the function of the form: "according to which," no doubt, translates the Latin *secundum quod,* and this may also be translated as "following which."

Hence the present, incomplete definition: *the MORAL ORDER is the relationship of "before" and "after" among the acts of our freedom and the resulting habits and dispositions in persons and groups, according to the moral standard.* This last, the formal cause of the moral order, is commonly called "standard"; other words for it are "norm" and "criterion." Until we identify the standard we cannot complete the definition. "Before" and "after" originally are space-time terms, and "above" and "below" might be substituted for them. But reflection shows that when we rate goodness "before" and badness "after" or rate goodness "above" or "below" knowledge, or ask whether, to take Graham Greene's case in *The Heart of the Matter,* mercy is preferable to truth, we are effectively operating on a world not bound by space-time limitations.

This chapter concludes with a case, that of national political order, to review the causes of order and likewise of the moral order.

## THE CAUSES

1. Material: What is ordered?
2. Efficient: By whom?
3. Final: For what?
4. Formal: How?

Causes of the Moral Order

1. Our free acts
2. Persons in their freedom
3. The end of our freedoms
4. The moral form, or standard

Causes of the National Order

1. Things and persons to be ordered
2. We the people through our rulers
3. National order and good
4. The Constitution

Chapter 3

# ARISTOTLE CONCERNING THE END

In a work on morals in 1909, Ralph Barton Perry said that for a long time we have "shunted the deeper problems of ends and purposes." Sir Richard Livingstone in his work on education in 1944 said that to do this is to try to deprive man of direction, with the result that we are muddled people without ideas on ends, not in possession of but possessed by endless and meaningless means.

It was this meaningless result that many, under the influence of the evolutionary naturalistic idea, say from 1859 to 1909, thought the true issue of thought and action. For instance, John Dewey said (1922) that ends are endless, which, he declared, is to say that there is no end. He said life has no purpose, but living men have many and varied purposes (1930).

The problem is always real. Which is it: some end, or many man-chosen ends, or means upon means and, after all, no end?

What, if anything, is man's life for? What does it finally add up to? The question is radical, and it is no reply to duck our heads under our wings and say with the activist and evolutionist that ends are endless or, with impressionists and vitalists such as D. H. Lawrence, that we loathe goals, that goals are jails.

On basic questions, it is good for Hebrew and Christian democratic students and philosophers to dive for a while into non-Hebrew and pre-Christian Grecian waters. Plato wishes man to reach the good life, which seems, as with most Grecian thinkers and doers, to be a life exclusively belonging to the State. What do we expect of "mere pagans," anyway? Whatever we expect, we find doctrine paying great honor to man and his nature. So far as concerns setting ethical problems in a vital and open way, above all the problem of means and ends, Aristotle has not been surpassed. His main treatise on ethics may well seem to thoughtful minds the best work ever written on the subject. It consists of ten short chapters or "books," and the first (perhaps not written first) expresses a marvellously integrated and balanced doctrine on human conduct. Anyone who reads our present chapter should read, both before and after it, Aristotle's first book. The teachings of Aristotle's first book relative to the end and purpose of human life can, with little transposition, be stated in "a teachable form" almost like a lesson in arithmetic.

1. By a tendency native to it or imposed on it, every art and every knowledge and every activity and act of choice moves in the direction of good. That is what each is "for." This tendency and direction is natural to each or it occurs by a kind of second nature. That is why "good" is well described as that toward which things by their nature tend.

2. Perpetually in our experience and observation, thing is subordinated to thing. There is no argument on this score. We could not live if we did not order things and put some before and some after. We subordinate industry to war, war to victory, and victory to the goods of peace. Within the total series of end seeking, any given series has its own series of means leading to an end. The shipbuilding art is subordinated to other ends, but the work and good of shipbuilders precisely in their own line is to build ships and to build good ones.

3. The question is whether all seeking is merely a seeking and in the long run is unavailing, or whether man has some last end that is simply an end. If so, it would be advantageous to know the fact and more so to know if possible what that end is. Then like archers with their eyes on the mark, we could direct our lives and be "more likely to hit what is right."

4. In fact there is and must be such an end. Why say so? First, because if not, our going comes to nothing, and we do not get anywhere because there is nowhere to go. In Aristotle's word,

our going and our life are "in vain," an untechnical phrase to say that in that case we must write off any hope of purpose and optimism for man. Our life, then, is useless, pointless, has not by nature any end or goal. Aristotle thinks the supposition false, and therefore supposes that life has some end. Next, there are "means," and try as we will we can find no meaning for these unless there is ultimately an end that is not a means at all, but simply an end. With means given, an end is also given (a conclusion merely implied in the text). Lastly, everyone says there is an end. Everyone is agreed on the matter, and Aristotle often uses the principle that when everyone is agreed there must be something to the matter on which all are agreed. The basis of the argument is belief in man or the social-democratic principle, and odd as it is for Aristotle, a confirmed social aristocrat, to use it, he does so.

We must say, then, that human life has an end that is truly an end. All men say so, and "all" here means those with refinement and privileges, and also the many, the masses, "the people." All agree also in calling it *eudaimonia,* a term we leave in the literal form so as to see from its use what it means.

5. People agree on the word, but not on its content. Literally it would mean something like "the condition of being prosperous as man." But when is a man prosperous? This is to ask: What is the end and in what does *eudaimonia* consist?

If we look at the question empirically, from actual cases of what different persons and groups seek as if it were the end and as if *eudaimonia* consisted in it, we get a diversified and heterogeneous reply. Some people in their way of living declare that *eudamonia* consists in having money, some in effect say it consists in pleasure, some seem to say that if they had prestige and glory they would be prosperous. These are the commonest types, Aristotle thinks: the lover of money, the lover of pleasure, and the lover of glory; and everybody has known persons possessed by lust for power in these forms. Are we accordingly to say that *eudaimonia* must consist in getting these or some combination of these? Of course there are endless instances of smaller gauge that appear nevertheless to fall within the three general types. Take for example the youth at school who, to judge from his actions, lives for the sake of winning a monogram; from the moment he stirs in the morning, this emblem is the center of his thoughts. Or consider the girl who follows a boy across the continent, as if catching him were the crown of existence.

We could not make sense out of the data contained in end seeking if we were to use merely this positivistic, case-by-case approach. And then after we have collected instances, must we try to show which are defective and which properly justified as ends for man? This will be a big undertaking and demand principles on which to base our judgment. For example, honor is too superficial to qualify as the inner-possessed good for man and is, besides, more like a means than an end. Money is evidently a means and not an end. Still, to proceed in this way, finding the myriad cases and approving and disapproving, is a long and roundabout method of attempting to say what is the end and chief good for man. Aristotle's conclusion is that positivistic method would be endless and also useless in this matter.

6. We had better take a different approach. As an installment on saying what "the end" is, we note some of its characteristics. It is altogether an end and not a means at all; it is self-sufficient once it is obtained; and it is incommensurable; that is, it is not merely ten times or one hundred times as good as some particular means, but is incomparably good. How can we discover and identify such an end?

The way to do this is to use the functional approach, and ask, "What is the work of man?" Let him do that work whatever it is, and the doing of it through a lifetime is the achieving of *eudaimonia* and the end. That is the whole of the argument.

The meaning of "functional approach" is evident in common instances supplied by modern as well as by Grecian convictions. What is the function of the eye? To see, and only to see. A "blind eye" is no more functionally an eye than is the eye of a statue. The justification and meaning of the eye are found in its function; and either an eye sees or it does not exist at all. So of any organ; the hand has a function, and so have the ear, the lung, the heart, the stomach, the mind, and the will. Each has an *ergon,* or work, to do, and the doing of that work is its end. (We would illustrate from machines, but the Greek was closer to nature.) The same holds for artisans and professional men. The cobbler precisely as cobbler is to cobble shoes and his excellence as cobbler consists in his cobbling and in his cobbling well. As lawyer the lawyer has a work to do. As surgeon the surgeon has a work to do. As priest the priest has a special work to do. As pilot the pilot has a special work to do. Let each do his work. His excellence and his being in that line consists in his doing his work. It may be that the specialized work and end of priest or cobbler or surgeon is properly a means, subordinated to some farther end. This possibility need not now be explored, and the fact remains that as priest or cobbler or surgeon the being of the man can be defined by his function. Though this functional approach is intelligible to all peoples and is used by all, we may call it "Greek" because the Greeks looked on a man's profession or occupation as his by inheritance and birth.

So much for the illustrations from particular organs and from men in particular capacities. The basic question concerns man's work as man. The reply is manifest, says Aristotle, "once man's work is grasped." "It would seem to be the same with man, if there is any work proper to him." Whereas the carpenter or cobbler has a work and some activity to perform, has man none at all? Is he left by nature unemployed? Each organ has a work. Are we to say that man as man and quite beyond special organs and professions has no work to do? Aristotle presumes that it is proved that man has some work. But if so, what is it?

7. That work is whatever is proper and specific to man. It cannot, therefore, be such an end as nourishment and growth, since this is common even to plants, and we are in search of the end and work for man. Nor is it the life of sensation, since this

goes with horse and ox and every sort of animal. The function proper and specific to man is the activity of reason or the logos. This life of reason has two aspects or phases; one aspect is the direct exercise of reason and the other is activity subordinated to and obedient to reason. Which of these is more truly proper Aristotle inquires later. The life of man precisely as man is the life of the logos, and the work of man is a functioning of the soul in line with the logos or at least never in opposition to the logos. We have said that the work of any genus is identical with its good and excellence; for example the harpist plays the harp and plays it well; this is the harpist's work and virtue and excellence, and is the end for him as harpist. He cannot qualify as harpist unless he does this, and to do it in finished style is truly and fully to be a harpist, since the end of anything that has work to do is the first principle and a quasi definition of that thing.

Functioning in line with the logos is the good of man. It is concurrently the end for man, and *eudaimonia* for him, to develop fully and precisely as man and always, of course, in accordance with the logos or what is man-defining in him.

*Eudaimonia* equals the end. This equals the proper functioning of man throughout a lifetime. This equals his excellence and virtue. We could justly give the same equations for the *eudaimonia* of the eye as eye or the cobbler as cobbler, so long as we allow for the proper function in each case. Hence the inadequacy of translating *eudaimonia* into our elusive word "happiness." *Eudaimonia* is the condition of prospering precisely as, and functionally as, eye or cobbler or man.

8. To function in line with the logos for just one act is, so far, to live as man, and this is what we are called by nature to do. So far it is good, but life thus abbreviated is incomplete. It is not one day or a short while that makes a man blessed and happy.

9. Many are the prerequisites, too, though these could not possibly constitute the end for man. But merely because the end and good is within man, an excellence of his soul, we may not conclude that external goods are wholly beside the point.

They are needed to support man while he achieves the end, and it is not easy if at all possible to work out our characteristic human excellences, literally, "to do lovely deeds," when we are without supplies; many things are done with the help of instruments, friends, money, and political power. Besides, to be short on some things mars our blessedness, e.g., to lack good birth, good and noble children; and the homely fellow, the solitary and friendless man, the childless or bereaved person are less likely to succeed with the functioning in which *eudaimonia* consists. Of course, the asides must not overshadow the functionings themselves.

10. On the one hand, pleasure is not the end and purpose of human life, since pleasure enjoyed under certain conditions must be condemned, whereas the end is never to be condemned. On the other hand, to live in line with the logos or what makes us men can hardly be unpleasant. In Greek, the pleasant is literally the sweet, and what could be more unpleasant and sour for any being than to go against the form, such as the logos in man, which gives it its being, its end, and good? Aristotle says that to most people the things that are pleasant are in conflict, a condition that results from seeking things not pleasant by nature, whereas if a man loves lovely and noble deeds, he loves and does what is pleasant by nature. And if a person gets pleasure out of what he is fond of, such as horses or food or shows, how could going with his nature be an unpleasant experience? Such is his task and assignment, and it is most truly pleasant.

11. The characteristic functioning of man is to go with the logos, the principle of reason in him. He goes directly with it whenever, and so far as, he exercises reason; and he does this when his intellect grasps anything and knows it as it is. Intellect then reaches truth; this is what it desires to do and is its good. Man functions according to reason also when his will obeys reason and conforms in its act to the light of reason. Then the will is right and good, and man does good.

By repeatedly doing good acts of intellect or of will, we get good habits, a matter that Aristotle treats in the second book of the *Ethics*. Good habits result from good acts, and also result in good acts. Or we may turn the terms around and say that good acts result from good habits, and result in good habits. But what is "a good habit"? The Greek word *hexis* means an inner perfection, a condition and state of being, an interior possession such that once a person has it he can more readily do the acts that go with it and with his natural tendencies and toward his whole development as man. When we get a set of good habits, of habits conforming to the logos and of habits directly perfecting the logos in us, we are good and, so far, perfect men, and we are at least on our road to *eudaimonia*. This doctrine of human development by way of many varied perfections, excellences, or virtues within us, as members of society and generally as persons, may be expressed in the following chart (the materials are mostly furnished in Book VI).

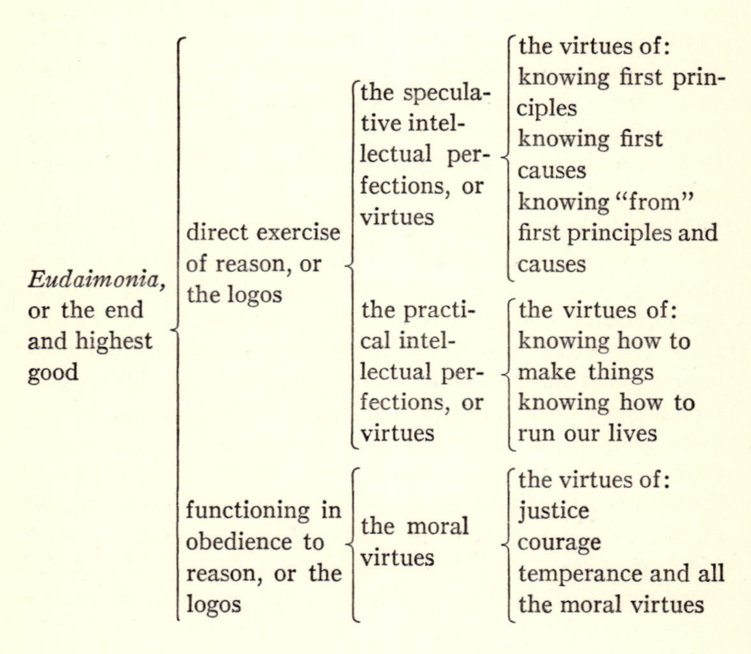

Aristotle is profoundly wise and a person of balance and common sense. The problem is to live according to what man is and according to what man is to be. In other words, man is to respect his being and destiny. It is meaningless to talk about "duty," "ought," and "right" on any other ground. This consideration takes us close to the center of Aristotle's ethical doctrine. Man's nature and his end set limits for him, and these are inner or immanent limits, not imposed from without by any sort of dictator; and at the same time man's nature and end give him direction and make demands on him. Man does not reach the end by random and hit-or-miss acts, but by such judicious discipline as will keep him up to his nature. The basic reason for these limits, and for the end itself, is the nature of man: he is not a nondescript, but precisely this kind of being; hence the end must match his being, and the road and standard be of such a kind as leads that given nature to that end. This takes us all the way to the center of Aristotle's ethics, and it is the central and primal doctrine of any ethics, ancient or modern, that believes in man. Democracy depends entirely on it,—an interesting point, since Aristotle is not a democrat—all properly human development, whatever the type of government, depends on it.

All that has been said may be restated in the famous phrase of Aristotle, "Man is made for virtues." This implies that he is made for *eudaimonia,* for the development of himself through the development of the characteristic human virtues, which in Greek go by the better name of excellences or perfections. Man is by nature commanded to go in this direction, and with this elementary premise of his life given, it is like a detail, though an immense addition, to say that to reach this consummation man must learn to perfect the means, must perfect the social forms such as the familial, the economic, the political, and the religious life, and all the levels of education, and many arts and sciences.

12. In Aristotle's first book several details are included. He twice says that what he writes on moral problems cannot be

stated according to mathematical formulas; the matter does not lend itself to such treatment. He says that young persons cannot readily grasp truths in the field of ethics, since this learning presupposes a doing or at least is accompanied by a doing, and young persons have not yet had the opportunity for the wealth of experience required. Of course, everyone beyond childhood has some of the needed experience, but boys and girls of sixteen do not have so real a comprehension of the practical good as will be possible for them after another ten years of ordinary vital knocks.

The Greek world in Aristotle's time was being wrecked by an excess of individualism. But bad as it was then, individualism was not of such long standing or such general acceptance in ethics, religion, economics, and art as it has been in modern times. We must concede that individualism has set the major body of problems in modern society, such problems as capital and labor, the proletariat, and Communism. When we individualists read Aristotle on "the end," we suppose that he has in mind merely the development of rugged individuals. It would be more correct to say that Aristotle goes to the other extreme and tends to fall into collectivism, subordinating persons to the State. At any rate, in the *Ethics* and its sequel, the *Politics,* he explicitly develops a theory of social good.

13. Later formulated is a law for the psychology of conduct, a law not of how we ought to act, but of how we do act, a law important in itself and also for us, since in modern thought till Freud this fundamental law was neglected.

Aristotle's teaching is this: As a man is, so he acts, and "such things" seem good to him. The first half of the statement is a law of being, and not only of human being: As a being is, so it acts; and the order of the parts may be interchanged to read: "As anything acts, so it is," "Actions speak louder than words." The second half brings in the human mind and its evaluations. As a man is, so he acts: action is like agent; and things like the agent and his actions are the things that he comes to approve and proclaim as good. If a man acts in a particular way relative to a particular matter,—say, he is perpetually a liar—he will tend to say eventually that such action is justified and that his way of acting is the proper way; he will tend to proclaim it a law of nature and of the universe. An example is found in Rousesau, who in morals was a vagabond, and he came to preach that such a way of life is natural and the original direction for man. His way, he said, was the way for all men to live: "Live as I live, and you will live according to nature." This is a hard law to escape in its subconscious workings, and it holds in the lives of families, nations, races, religions, and all sorts of human groups; the way any of these is and lives, it tends to proclaim as law for human life. As a man is, so he does, and goods like himself and his actions he comes to approve as the proper and supreme goods. So too for a family, a nation, a religion: a law useful for understanding human events, past and present.

The reader must first read Aristotle's *Ethics* for himself and discover questions that will help him to read it a third and fourth time. Not that it is abstruse, but classics are inexhaustible.

As we have taken logos, in the usual sense, it clearly is a moral standard. It might be differently translated. In various passages of Aristotle, logos has a dozen meanings, depending on the context. Yet to consider it in Book I, not as "reason" or "the power of reason," but as a nice calculating done by the aristocratic class is unfair to the text.

The second book is a remarkable introduction to many issues in moral philosophy; among them the relation of the intellectual to the moral virtues, the relation of art to scientific knowledge and to morals, and the formation of habit. The main problems are "virtue" and "the mean" as a standard, and by rereading parts of Book I and reading the first lines of Book VI, the reader must discern for himself the relation of the logos as standard to the mean as standard. We suggest questions on Book II, questions taking the form of posers; the reader must determine from the text Aristotle's reply to them:

1. Every virtuous action is a mean between excess and defect.

2. Is the mean applicable to all actions or not? If not, why not, in Aristotle's view?

3. The mean is relative. Explain Aristotle's teaching on this point.

4. Does art fall within the mean? Explain.

5. If the mean does not apply to actions X, Y, Z and to passions A, B, C, what standard, if any, does Aristotle apply to them?

6. What are the relations of the mean to pleasure and pain?

7. What is Aristotle's basic standard: the mean, the gentleman's and aristocrat's conduct, the logos principle?

8. Good is finite; evil is infinite.

9. Pleasure debases man.

10. In Aristotle's view, in what matters, if any, do Americans go to extremes? On the nationalistic spirit? Materialism? Imperialism? Externalism and activism? Mechanism? "Gadgetism"? Braggadocio? In the use of liquor? In seeking pleasure? In lust for getting money? In spending?

11. What does this signify: "to go to extremes"? Is the mean, in Aristotle or in fact, to be tested by any other standard? That is, the mean is or is not a primary standard. Which is correct?

12. According to Aristotle, virtue in art and in morals is that level at which nothing is in excess and nothing is lacking. Does he hold this? If so, how, according to him, are we to know when we reach that level?

## CHAPTER 4

# THE END AND A CHRISTIAN PHILOSOPHY

IT IS all the same whether we say that Aristotle's ethics is teleological, which means that, in his view, by freely choosing means to various goals man has not chosen and cannot choose the end, which is set by nature, or whether we say that Aristotle accepts freedom and nature as limited.

To say that man has a nature means, for Aristotle, only that man exists and is of a determinate kind. Man is not simply any indiscriminate and nondescript kind, in which case he would not be at all. He is the determinate human-nature kind.

To exist at all as a real being, a being must be determinate. Man is determinately free and determinately fixed: free regarding means, and fixed regarding the end.

All this makes sense to a Christian. That man as he freely acts should respect human nature is the primary law of human existence; and Aristotle states this law without compromise. That man by nature has a given end to seek is the second law of human existence; and Aristotle also states this law. Concerning the nature of that end Aristotle, perhaps, is not far wrong, at least as a pagan. But Christians find fault with Aristotle's identification of the end; and even when the end is studied only as temporal, the Christians, in whose thought freedom and a radical democracy are implied, cannot regard the end as totally subordinated to the end of political society. Such subordination to the state is not true to nature and works out badly, opening up the way to totalitarianism in education, science, art, philosophy, theology, and in religious life.

The greatest constructive development in Christian thought in the 20th century is the reaffirmation of "Christian philosophy." An expression of this is available in Etienne Gilson's works, and is most understandably stated in *The Spirit of Mediaeval Philosophy*. The question arises regarding the relation between reason and Revelation. Gilson says that he will call Christian any philosophy that, while keeping the two orders *formaliter* distinct, nevertheless considers Revelation an indispensable auxiliary to reason.[1]

Many things we believe and afterwards know; and, in some cases, belief is an indispensable aid to knowledge. In no case is knowledge necessarily invalidated merely because we first believe. Any grown person can name a dozen instances to verify what we have just said. But does believing ever certainly help us to know?

Famous theologian-philosophers in the Middle Ages thought that believing sometimes helps us to know. *"Fides quaerens intellectum"* is an immortal formula for the relation of faith based on the Scriptures to philosophical knowledge, as is the other formula: *"Credo ut intelligam."* This latter may be translated: "I believe in order to understand," or "Believing, I will be able to understand." The person with faith desires, if possible, to understand, and he is better able to understand. The greatest distinction between the medieval theological philosopher and the modern philosopher, whether the latter is of a religious and theological turn or not, is that the former integrates theology and philosophy and the latter dissociates them and assumes that they have nothing to do with each other. The most he will allow, and some Christians who are philosophers allow only this, is that Revelation and theology can be only a negative norm for philosophy: Revelation says that some things are not true and we take it on faith that to try to prove them would be to go down a

[1] *The Spirit of Mediaeval Philosophy* (London and New York: Sheed & Ward, 1944), pp. 33 ff.; by all means memorize the prayer of the Christian philosopher (here, Duns Scotus), pp. 51–52.

blind alley. The Christian philosopher claims there is also a positive relationship between reason and Revelation. Certain things believed, perhaps time out of mind, are finally proved. The belief is not a proof, but in some historical cases it has been a lead in the direction of proof. If you had not believed, you would not have known.[2] Believing, you may possibly, in time, come to understand. With an "iron curtain" of unbelief, it will be much more difficult.

Still, we do not and cannot reduce belief, as belief, to understanding, or Revelation to reason. Reason and Revelation are not separated—separation is the great error since Descartes's time (1596–1650)—but reason and Revelation are at once distinct and integrated. What we know and understand after having believed it for ten years or ten centuries is the subject of philosophy. Outside of all such belief in the Scriptures, man could prove the same truths and embody them in philosophy. But in fact he did not. The theistic Plato and Aristotle did not arrive clearly at a knowledge of one God, and we have little reason to believe that any pagan, great as some were, arrived at the identity of essence and existence in one and only one being. This truth could have been reached by the unaided, unbelieving mind of man. As a matter of fact it was not thus reached; likewise other truths, including some in the theory of ethics.

The human race believing God's word is more likely to come to theoretical truths X, Y, and Z and to practical truths A, B, and C, than the human race not believing God's word.

That is what we mean when we say that a Christian philosophy was potential in Isaiah, St. John, and St. Paul, and is actual, at least to some degree, in the Fathers and Doctors of Christianity. Christian philosophy was stock in trade for Bede, for Rabanus Maurus, for Anselm, for Aquinas, to name only a few. Beginning in the 1890's, it has had expression and defense in such men as Blondel, Gilson, Maritain, Garrigou-Lagrange and

[2] Cf. Isa. 7:9; familiar to St. Augustine from the Septuagint as: "Nisi credideritis, non intelligetis."

their disciples and co-workers in many lands. In England, E. I. Watkin, M. A. D'Arcy, and Christopher Dawson are affected by a genuine Christian philosophy; in Germany, Josef Pieper; [3] in the United States, such men as Virgil Michel and Anton Pegis.

To begin to work out the concept "Christian philosophy" and to find the riches of this notion for theory and practice, has been the problem and achievement of the group. The weakness of some devotees has been to overstate the privileged position and to belittle truths learned by ancient pagans and to neglect and, at times to belittle, truths in modern and contemporary science and philosophy. True, Christian philosophy has long been neglected; it is important.[4] Many Christians and all secularists are opposed to it, exaggerations are at times used for rhetorical effect, and there is a limit to what any group can do. But Christian philosophers will be more effective when they get over silly assertions, such as "Aristotle knew no metaphysics" and "Aquinas learned nothing from Aristotle," and integrate their thought with the dynamism and totality of human thought. We suggest integration, and neither isolation nor theological and philosophical snobbery.

In Christian moral philosophy, the basic problems are two: whether moral philosophy is possible for a Christian who has a moral theology based in part on supernatural grounds and who is to practice supernatural virtue; and whether any natural end is available for the Christian.

We hold that the Christian is not allowed to neglect the knowledge of nature and human nature, and that human nature exists. If the Christian is required by nature to try to know the natural, in himself and outside himself, and is required by nature to try to develop nature in himself and outside himself, a Christian ethics is demanded.

[3] See Josef Pieper, "On the Christian Idea of Man," *Review of Politics,* XI (January, 1949), 3 ff.

[4] See Gilson's revealing and overlooked work: *Pour un ordre catholique* (Paris: Desclée, Brouwer, 1934).

In short we hold that nature exists in man, that it can be known, and is to be respected in our conduct.

Aquinas says in the treatise on "Charity" and in that on "Evil" that supernatural charity is a kind of superform. He does not say that the natural forms or standards have therefore ceased to be, and in fact he has treated three of them with care. The first standard is "reason," into which we suppose he translates Aristotle's logos. The second is "natural law," which may be the same as "reason," but is not shown to be the same. The third is the means, which few persons take to be a primary and radical standard.

Aquinas is evidently making a place for natural standards and in that way for a Christian ethics. Why not? Would it not be unrealistic as well as catastrophic for Christians to stand by and cease to investigate human nature and its rights and responsibilities?

Regarding "nature," Aristotle remains on three counts inadequate. First, the end as he sees it is for men of his class only. No commoners need apply. He says that no one would think of the slave as capable of enjoying *eudaimonia,* which means that for most people of that society the end as understood by Aristotle has no meaning or existence. It is for people of Aristotle's social class, an elite, the privileged few.

He says some are slaves by nature. They cannot reach the end, the possession and enjoyment of which supposes, and in part consists in, the exercise of freedom. By nature they are slaves, not free, not persons with any right or chance to attain the end, not merely due to social and historical chances, but because of nature.[5]

The pot must not call the kettle black. Persons who have lived in a foreign land know that nations are nationalistic and are taught no great love toward outsiders. But granting setbacks,

[5] Aristotle's view is intelligible but not defensible. Winston Ashley's attempt to defend natural slavery, in *Theory of Natural Slavery according to Aristotle and St. Thomas,* Notre Dame, Ind. (1941), is unsuccessful.

we have made progress toward belief in man. The main social movement in the Occident since 1600 has been the establishment of individualism, until the present century, when the movement is toward collectivism. Yet the demand for democracy has not been totally on the defensive since James I. The English, the American, and the French revolutions have been mass efforts; each got results, and the American achievement, though qualified, is taken by many as the model. Government of the people and by the people and for the people is at least the ideal, and if the result is spotty, precarious, and not peculiar to modern times, yet each is something, the ideal and the qualified result.

We take political democracy to mean at a minimum that every normal adult is helping to rule the tribe; economic democracy to mean at a minimum that every family has a chance to secure the economic wherewithal to live a reasonable life; and social democracy to mean that everyone is respecting every man.

Progress in political democracy is not half the story. We can begin to think of something like economic democracy. The ideal is nebulous, whether in state capitalism, state socialism, communism, or fascism; but the ideal has a minor embodiment in distributism, though this has made no marked headway, and in people's cooperatives, so far as these have been developed. We do not readily believe, as the Greeks did, that economic goods and the freedoms conditioned by them are "by nature" for a few.

We believe also in the dignity and worth of every person. Not that the belief is consistent or effective, but in spite of greed, discrimination, imperialism, and wars, belief in man's dignity has become a mark of society. It may in time be impossible for us to believe war propaganda even during a war: we may refuse to disbelieve in man.

Why is this belief in man so nearly automatic with us, whereas so great a mind and humanist as Aristotle lacked it?

Through Christ we have come to comprehend that man is sacred and inviolable, and this in spite of qualifications and compromises in Christian lives; when we go secularistic we remain indebted to the Christian light. To be Christian means seeing Christ as the God-man, and man as close to God. Man's task has always been to be what he really is, the image of God, but we see this task better now and can better do it. In communities and nations where this vision has long been effective, man's life, granting that it remains man's and is not an angel's, is on a new level.

It is this difficult new level of a universal social democracy that Plato and Aristotle could not envision. Here is radical social democracy. Slavery should never be, and we should work, even if slowly and patiently, toward political freedom for all, food and health for all, education for all, respect and economic freedom for all. Have schools and teachers, at least in the Occident, a right any longer to inculcate ends contrary to these, and have students a right to be in college for contrary ends? The question arises whether we have leave to write off the two most basic things learned about man; a) that he has a nature of a logos and rational kind, and b) that he is now intimately related to God. Hence no slavery, no peons, no serfs; all are men.

In Aristotle the logos principle that specifies man is the standard of good, and the development of man is the end. If the statement is amended to read, "any and every man," and not merely the aristocracy, the statement is one of the wisest and most basic on human conduct and its evaluation. We wish some treatise on ethics by Hebrew or Christian, given the light of Revelation, would match Aristotle's treatise, given his light.

The second point on which his ethics is deficient is massive. It is this: Aristotle's doctrine is secularist and temporalist, has no overt reference and perhaps is meant to have no implicit reference to God, Providence, or immortality.

In the *Phaedo,* Plato has Socrates argue that a man's soul is immortal and at the end of the *Republic* he expresses in an allegory the retribution of the heroes after death. In Aristotle this kind of doctrine does not appear, and in his ethics we find no hint that belief in immortality has anything effectively to do with how we live, or that God knows or cares. In Book III of his treatise "on the soul," Aristotle argues that something in the soul is eternal, but nowhere does this doctrine seem to have leverage on how man is to live. It is as if he said, "The aristocrats live in a rational way and thereby in fact achieve *eudaimonia*. If there is God and Providence and personal immortality, the way of living leading to that end is the way the human world is, and if only some or none of these exist, that is still the way."

The Christian philosopher claims that man can naturally know that God is, that He rules by an over-all plan, part of which is a knowable blueprint for human conduct, and that we can know that man's soul is immortal.[6]

The third point is that any end set by nature, and thus by God, is for all men and is fully attainable only in a life of personal immortality. On all these points Aristotle's teaching is deficient.

It is thus incomplete even on the natural level. As to the supernatural we must not expect a pre-Christian to have any teaching. We wish next to show how the revealed word completes Aristotle's doctrine on the end of human life.

Man's destiny is a question for both nature and grace. With tremendous insistence nature says that any living thing is in order that it may be and that it may fully be. Nothing falling under the natural light is clearer: we are to preserve our being and to develop it. Not merely some man or group, but every man is made with this nature and consequent immanent demand. Sometimes the conditions will not let us be with any proper fullness, and that is why with intelligence and freedom we must try, as far as possible, to make conditions fit to allow man fully to be. On this matter John Dewey's statement is perfect. He said we must work out such conditions as will allow every man the chance to reach the full stature of his possibilities. It is true that man's intelligence and freedom are limited, but we cannot

[6] See A. E. Taylor's closely reasoned *The Christian Hope of Immortality* (New York: Macmillan, 1947).

see the limits of them.[7] This social, temporal end, often neglected by Christian moralists, includes education and cultural life, and, surely in the land of Jefferson and Lincoln, it includes political, economic, and social democracy.

The full stature of persons and societies is not the demand of some philosopher or sociologist, but of nature.

This is knowable on the strictly human level. Christians hold that we also have a new vision and dimension for man's life in the revelation of a supernatural end. Nothing is more constant in Christian theologians and philosophers than that through Christ we are raised to a new life and a new destiny. I cannot see that this abrogates any truth won by great thinkers, but simply goes beyond them.

At least since Moses the Jews knew men could not of their own power come directly into the company of God. "Man shall not see Me and live" (Exod. 33:20). The Lord tells Moses (Exod. 19:21) not to let the people come too close "lest they should have a mind to pass the limits to see the Lord, and a very great multitude of them should perish." If they passed the natural limit, they would not only break a law, but would perish.

Yet Christians say man is to come to see God face to face. Of his own nature he cannot do it, and yet he is to do it; this doctrine is everywhere in the New Testament. St. Paul says our destiny, of directly seeing and loving God, is an immortal one. "We see now through a glass in a dark manner; but then face to face. Now I know in part; but then I shall know even as I am known. And now there remain faith, hope and charity, these three; but the greatest of these is charity." [8]

Later (II Cor. 12:1–6) St. Paul tells of his vision of heaven, a vision which he says he had "in Christ, . . . (whether in the body, I know not; . . . God knoweth), such a one [was] caught up to the third heaven. And I know such a man (whether in the body, or out of the body, I know not; God knoweth) that he

[7] See Joseph Buckley, *Man's Last End* (St. Louis: Herder, 1949).
[8] I Cor. 12:12 f.; cf. II Cor. 5:1–8; Matt. 18:10; I John 3:2.

was caught up into paradise and heard secret words, which it is not granted to man to utter. For such an one I will boast; but of myself I will glory in nothing, but in my infirmities. For though I should have a mind to glory, I shall not be foolish; for I will say the truth."

He also says (I Cor. chap. 2) he speaks a wisdom not of this world, "the wisdom of God in a mystery, a wisdom which is hidden, which God ordained before the world, unto our glory: which none of the princes of this world knew." The end is more than we can comprehend with natural powers: ". . . eye hath not seen nor ear heard, neither hath it entered into the heart of man, what things God hath prepared for them that love him." [9]

St. John saw man's final destiny: "I, John, saw the holy city, the New Jerusalem, coming down out of heaven from God, prepared as a bride adorned for her husband. And I heard a voice from the throne saying: Behold the tabernacle of God with men, and he will dwell with them. And they will be his people; and God himself with them shall be their God" (Apoc. 21:2 f.).

Such passages say the end for every man is an association and fellowship with God in immortal life.

The cheap objection is that this is too good a doctrine: "pie in the sky when I die." The reasonable reply is: "Who says it is too good to be believable?" "And on what ground is this said?"

Immortal life, a supernatural society with God, this for every human person: such is the completion by Christians of Aristotle's excellent doctrine on human destiny.

St. Thomas says that even on the natural level our everyday series of means and ends demands a beginning not dependent on anything else and also an end not dependent on any other end. This is true wherever there is "essential subordination" of event to event.[10]

This is to say that world process must have a beginning and an

[9] The thought is nearly the same in Isa. 64:4; but that is natural, since St. Paul knew the Old Law practically by heart.

[10] *Summa theologica,* Ia IIae, q.1, a.4.

end. But has nature, and again supernature, set any end for man? First, we know it goes with man's nature to seek ends and guide himself toward them, since to be a man is to have the capacity for reason and will. But exercising reason and will, what does man radically desire? Anything desires its being and perfection, and thus man desires what would totally round out his being, that by which he would be completed so that he would fully be, as Augustine and Aquinas declare, that "fullness of being" which is an open and quasi-limitless end.

We expect St. Thomas to rate riches and power and pleasures as means and not the end. Nor does he see man, even in his perfected being, as the end. "It is evident that man is subordinated to something as his end: since man is not the supreme good." The possession and enjoyment of the end is within man, and the object which man is to possess and enjoy and which meets the demands of his striving is God. The fulfillment is called "blessedness," in some sense an equivalent of *eudaimonia*. "In that state of blessedness, man's mind will be united to God by one unbroken and everlasting operation." [11]

". . . This is eternal life: That they may know thee, the only true God . . ." (John 17:3). "The Philosopher, placing man's blessedness in this life [*Ethics,* 1098$^{b}$–1099$^{b}$] says it is imperfect and after much discussion concludes: 'We say that men achieve *eudaimonia,* as men.' But a perfect blessedness is promised us by God when we will be as the angels in heaven, as Matthew says (see Matt. 22:30)." "The Philosopher speaks of imperfect blessedness such as can be had in this life." "It is said (I John 3:2) when He shall appear we shall be like Him and shall see Him as He is. . . . Final and perfect blessedness can consist in nothing less than the vision of the divine essence," the intellect demanding to go beyond knowing that God is and to know in a direct way what God is.

[11] Unless otherwise specified, matters to the end of this chapter are from the treatise on "beatitudo," *Summa theol.,* Ia IIae, q.2, a.4, 5, 7; q.3, a.1, 2, 3, 5, 7, 8; q.4, a.6.

Theologians hold that we must be raised to a supernatural level to be able to see God. Strictly speaking we do not qualify for this end, but only qualify to be qualified.

Our life at present has a foretaste of the end and the more so when its operations are one and unbroken as contemplative acts can be, and though in such circumstances as a flood, acts of the external order are preferable, as a general rule (*Contra Gentes,* III, c. 37) acts of the practical order are to be subordinated to the goods of contemplation. For the blessedness of the present life, welfare of the body is ordinarily required as a good in its own right since "beauty of body and keenness of perception belong to man's perfection" and since perfection of the lower part is presupposed for perfection of the higher, and at the resurrection the body and the bodily senses will, as an overflow from the higher life, be perfected in their operations (as Augustine says). "It is natural for the soul to be united to the body" and "impossible for the perfection of the soul [speaking here of its ultimate fulfillment with God] to exclude its natural perfection." For perfect blessedness the perfection of the body, both in our temporal life and in the resurrection, is required. A person also needs friends, that we may do good for them and delight in seeing them do good and be helped by their comradeship in works of the active and contemplative life.

To sum up the completion of Aristotle regarding the "end":

1. The end is for the human person and therefore for all men.

2. It is achieved in part, but only in part, in our temporal life, and since man is naturally immortal, the end demanded is beyond this life.

3. In the present life and in immortality on the natural level, the end is imperfect and incomplete and is to be perfected and surpassed by a supernatural destiny of human association with God through direct knowledge and love. The doctrine on a supernatural end, based on Biblical texts, is evidently theological.

4. Aristotle's theory is one of essences and as such could be

wholly true, but is incomplete and deficient because it is temporal, secularistic, and antidemocratic. Besides, Aristotle does not write of man's de facto existence, taking no account of man's fall or redemption or supernatural destiny. These words from Claudel are post-pagan: "There is no such thing as perfect and integral development, unless this be proportioned to its end, and this, for mankind, is God." "I came that you should have life and have it more abundantly" refers to more than is supposed in Aristotelian metaphysical biology. Christ came that the law, embodied in nature and written in the Old Testament, should be fulfilled.

Practical matters in ethics are better seen once we believe and have learned to live a Christian life. The will of God, hard to accept, is less difficult for the believer who has for several years tried to accept the will of God, for example, in the loss of spouse, parent, brother, child, than for the unbeliever who has never tried to think whether there might be a will of God. Droughts, floods, epidemics, pestilences and wars are less final and catastrophic, as Rosalind Murray shows in *The Good Pagan's Failure,* for people who believe in God than for people who think they do not believe in any divine will and providence.

In 1930, when Protestants first made way in principle for birth control, Rev. J. M. Lloyd-Thomas wrote [12] an attestation to the power of faith over conduct. He did not like the Roman Catholic Church and said it was too ready to lay down the law, yet he said we can all be magnanimous enough to say that Rome holds in a uniquely tenacious manner not only to the mysteries, but to the moral witness of the Christian Church. "The supreme attraction of Rome is to be found not in its devotions or ceremonialism or the absolutism of its intellectual foundations. It is to be found in its ethical rigorism, in that very sphere which Puritan Protestantism thought to be its own: Rome, whatever its past or present laxities of practice, is seen to be the one un-

[12] Rev. J. M. Lloyd-Thomas, "Lambeth and the Wider Outlook," *Hibbert Journal,* XXVIII (1929–30), 649–63.

compromising corporate witness to that moral code of Christianity which preserves Western Civilization from final collapse. It represents the last loyalty of the human race to its own highest moral standards." Others are rock-firm for Christian ethics, but can commit nobody but themselves. "There is no authoritative moral theology which can tell us what is the final judgment of Anglicans and Free Church men on questions such as marriage, divorce, birth control, companionate experiments, abortion, euthanasia, suicide. Only Rome speaks with one voice on such themes, and these are the issues of life and death, of the survival or decline of the West." The attraction of Rome is "its moral challenge to a high temperance, chastity and self-control."

The points of the present chapter are three. First, Aristotle's statement of the end needs emendation. Secondly, to be a believer makes a negative difference to philosophical theory about God, man, and the universe, and often a positive difference also. Thirdly, to live as Christians helps us to understand many moral matters we could scarcely otherwise know. Believing and living as Christians, we may at last come to know that humility and sacrifice are good, that universal brotherhood and charity are good, that spiritual childhood is a road to prudence and wisdom.

CHAPTER 5

# SHAPING MODERN ETHICAL THEORY AND PRACTICE

THE physicist or mathematician may skip most modern movements and institutions. Not so the student of ethical theory and practice. It makes little direct difference to a knowledge of what men think in physics whether the Reformation occurred and whether the proletariat exists. Each of these makes a big and direct difference to how we live and to our judgment on how to live, since in many ways it conditions thought and practice. We shall detail some modern revolutions not properly philosophical which have great effect on conduct and moral theory.

1. The first modern movement was the Renaissance, which was launched and perhaps established in Italy by 1374, the year that Petrarch, great among Italian humanists, died. In 1499, Erasmus, Dutch priest and the humanist greatest in repute, went to England for the first time to meet English humanists, including St. Thomas More, who was martyred in 1535 for refusing State dictatorship over religion. These dates, names, and nations suggest the time when Renaissance humanism was well under way in various countries.

Positively, the movement was a revival of interest in the civilizations of Greece and of Rome. People began to study these almost exclusively, and the knowledge acquired was destined to influence education and man for many generations, even to our own day.[1] Negatively, the former theological interest,

[1] See T. Corcoran, S.J., "The Education of Peoples since the Renaissance," in volume VI of Eyre's *European Civilization.*

in its day almost exclusive, tended to be dropped, as a reaction and in part due to new engagements. Loyalty to the new humanism tended to take the place of theological preoccupation. Less and less would there be taste for theology, and more and more immersion in ancient learnings. In Petrarch, Erasmus, and More these learnings were broad and deep. But in time, with theological and metaphysical studies less pursued, educated men with less ability and less faith in learning came to study mainly the rhetoric and eloquence in Cicero and the same as proposed by Quintilian, and by the time the present author went to school the hope at most was to read Greek and Latin: hardly a student in American schools thought of mastering the ancient civilizations.

What has this to do with ethics? The humanists, whether of Renaissance days or of ancient days or now in a kind of organized way in America [2] or scattered here and there always in Western nations, belong together on human values. The ancients as humanized with the emphasis on man, and their modern counterparts of early modern times or of today, with the same emphasis and with refinement gained by living into established learning, have always tended to rounded learning and to tolerance, avoiding extremes and aiming at the mean. "Nothing too much" is their recurrent formula, not only for arts, but generally for human life. *In medio stat virtus* means that virtue, strength, goodness resides in the mean. When we go to extremes we likely depart from human goodness. Pascal's is the great modern eloquent expression of this view (in his *Pensées,* or *Thoughts*), and somewhat more than representative is Irving Babbitt's statement: "for most practical purposes, the law of measure is the

[2] See, e.g., the many works of Irving Babbitt, or of Paul Elmer More, or T. S. Eliot, or Norman Foerster, and the work *Humanism and America* (edited by Foerster, 1928); and the last chapter of Louis J. A. Mercier's, *The Challenge of Humanism* (New York: Oxford Univ. Press, 1933); and his "Half-way House of Humanism," *Commonweal,* May 28, 1930. A work enriched by this tradition is Richard Weaver's *Ideas Have Consequences* (Chicago Univ. Press, 1948).

law of life, because it bounds and includes all other laws." [3] The development toward extremes in early modern art and morals was not directly a humanist development.

The old and also our current American humanists are against the uncritical popular standard, "The bigger the better." They do not believe that the more economic goods, the better; the more machinery, the better; the more speed and gadgets, the better. If men do not tend to extremes, at least they go to extremes. So the humanists judge; it is difficult to remain in the mean, difficult to mediate between extremes, but good and even necessary if we would be truly human. In the light of this principle some humanists [4] scold what they consider overemphasis on physical science, the economic motive, and utilitarian and pragmatic drives, from Francis Bacon till our day. If man's place is in the middle and if extremes are generally bad, then the Renaissance and later humanists have served a great purpose.

On the other hand, humanists are not likely to show, at short range, the hard, driving, pioneering virtues, nor likely to be fond of war or to make war in an obtrusive way. They have also commonly tended to the aristocratic. The Renaissance humanism was a cultural and educational movement, and I do not think it allowed, or that our American humanists have clearly allowed, for a humanistic culture that would reach and enrich the people. Here they are one with Grecian humanism. This is the great defect of humanism as we have had it, but possibly not an inherent and necessary defect; a later chapter gives attention to Maritain's Christian democratic humanism, and in the author's view these three, Christian, democratic, and humanist, naturally go together.

It is remarkable that the Renaissance humanist movement, quiet as it was, amounted to a revolution in thought and life, and the dynamic early modern thinkers were notably influenced

[3] Irving Babbitt, *Literature and the American College* (Boston: Houghton Mifflin, 1908), p. 23.

[4] See Irving Babbitt's *Democracy and Leadership,* and *Rousseau and Romanticism.*

by it. In fact, modern times, say from 1500 to 1900, are characterized as the age of the Renaissance.[5]

The Renaissance quite unconsciously started us toward secularism: toward the position, in theory and practice, that man is totally on his own. This view proceeded by way of deism and secularistic liberalism and has left man a kind of Atlas, trying to manage and operate the world.

2. Geography should make little difference to thought and life, but the discovery of America was another revolution. For the first time, Europeans, who form nearly all our ancestors, saw men and nations vastly different from themselves. The Europeans called them savages, in part because they found them so different; they even had a strange color. The story was incredible and was as if a plane arrived today from Mars with the story of red, white, and blue men. The color, though superficial, astounded people; and so, too, the languages. But the mores, the customs! Here were people who had ways of judging conduct and ways of living that were not European. *Tempora et mores!* Something was wrong; it was as if "man" had lapsed from the only prototype, the European as known to the European. This was an affront, and "proved" what comparative ethical studies were afterward to "prove": that ethics is all relative. People got queer notions of how the Indians lived. Hobbes wrote as late as 1651 that some Indians were without law or government; in his *Essay* of 1690 Locke said they had neither religion nor first principles; and Rousseau a century later said that these people were in a paradise, without law or government, and even after 1800 Chateaubriand, follower of Rousseau, came to America to see these lawless, tribeless people. The point is that if men of distinction were strangely influenced in their thinking and were not saved by the new learning, the New World, or the new science, the masses must occasionally have fallen into such superstitions and been affected in thought and action.

3. A third immense influence on conduct and ethical judg-

[5] Cf. N. Berdiaev, *The End of Our Time* (tr. 1933).

ments was the Reformation. Negatively this meant the splitting of the Christian Church in two, and not just taking off a slice or splinter, or splitting it for a generation. Positively, it meant a quickening of the inner spirit, and in terms of dogmas the declaration that not works, and not faith and works, but faith in the Bible as privately interpreted is the Christian religion. In the sequel it resulted in wars, such as the Thirty Years' War, and never any full, genuine peace and understanding, but truce accompanied by feeling and bad will on religious questions. It gave rise to some new judgments on ethical matters, because Scripture was differently interpreted. The Catholic Church is more an assembly of worshipers with common understandings on crucial matters and with authority to define teachings for members of this assembly; hence the Catholic is more obedient to and reliant on authority, and less independent. The Protestant, so far as a private interpretationist, has less authority and more independence. Whether the Catholic is therefore more likely to submit to unworthy political rule and to a worthy but aristocratic rule, is a question raised, though not easily answered. The Protestant, at least in an immediate, obvious sense, is more open to the freedoms, more demanding of them; at the same time, he falls more surely into individualism, and the Protestant principle of every man a Bible and religion to himself is a major force in early modern times making the individualistic movement and era.

On ethical standards the Catholic tends to say that the more firm and stable the rule the better, and the Protestant to say that the more independent the ruled the better. Each tends, as always happens with church members, to accept his church's teachings on many matters of conduct, but the Protestant can more successfully buck his church's teachings, since these are less definite and declared and authoritative than with the Catholic.

We have cited three early modern revolutions and have only started. These three, the cultural-educational, the geographical (and, one might almost say, the anthropological), and the religious, begin to influence each other. The Renaissance can promote the Reformation, and be helped and hindered by it. The discovery of a new world raises problems of a missionary kind for religions, and occasions the best work of Vittoria who, in the face of wars for conquest and empire, took up the rights of the oppressed Indians and the possible right to make war and became the father of international law and has thereby done what is perhaps to date the best treatise on the ethics of war and the rights of postwar victims.[6]

4. The glamor revolution is the fourth, which is modern science. Science had existed before, but it had never been, even in fiction and imaginative leaps, anything like what it now is in extent, and besides, though hypothesis and experimentation had been used, the value of these for discovery had not been vividly seen, much less exploited. Copernicus died in 1543, and that year appeared his famous work, *De Revolutionibus Mundi,* dedicated to the Pope. He emphasized the hypothesis plus the principle of logical economy. Soon after 1600 we have many great names in sciences and many discoveries: Galileo, Kepler, Gilbert, Toricelli, Harvey, Boyle, and Newton (whose *Principia* appeared in 1688). The development of science has since gone by leaps and bounds, and more crucial than particular discoveries is the method by which we suppose, if man survives normally, we can make endless discoveries not now predictable.

For men to know is a good thing; intellect by nature desires to know, and science progressively explores the unknown. But what has that to do with ethical theory and practice? Nothing, in a direct way. In a direct way, science like any knowledge is the good of intellect.

Many ethical problems indirectly arise. The knowledge as used can (a) protect and develop people, or (b) it can destroy people. It can have effect "a" or effect "b" on intellect, on morals, on health and on life; it can preserve, or destroy: as used in war,

[6] See Vittoria's lectures (1532) on "The Right of War" and the rights of the Indians.

in therapy and surgery, in education, and in the economy of persons and groups. Cars, movies, planes, radios, television, and a hundred scientific products have every kind of complex good and bad effect. The good of knowledge in physics, biology, history, and economic statistics, is the good of intellect, but indirectly, and in an accidental way and not because it is an intellectual good, it is used well or ill by mankind, and thus becomes, in its use, an occasion and implement of moral good or moral evil.

Old-time romantic progressivists have long been overpowered by the sentimental and precritical view that knowledge in physics must be an absolute human good, and when we suggest that as knowledge it is good, but that as used knowledge it may or may not be good, they are sure we want to hoax them. The fact is that gadgets, technological products, and bombs are excellent to know; in them we know nature and know how to make things; but the Lord knows what use we shall make of them.

An interesting by-product, not predictable by a Copernicus, Newton or Einstein, is that it is thought that science must furnish moral standards. What science cannot do, cannot be done. Science furnishes knowledge of nature, the know-how of mechanics and of surgery; it is our great modern constructive work, a less ambiguous good than democracy, which in the political field is subject to challenge and reverses and, in the economic and social fields, has had no extensive existence. Democracy gets pushed around and set back. Not so science. If totalitarian countries cramp science, this is local and temporary, and even such governments, along with wars, step up some scientific developments. In short, the one modern achievement of which we are proud and confident is modern science.

Surely it may be assumed that science will or does furnish standards of good and evil. It is derogatory to our greatest modern good to say that it does not, or to doubt that it does; therefore it does.

Such deduction is made, especially by extreme naturalists, for example, by John Dewey in *The Quest of Certainty.* Science does; science will. If science does not or will not, what does or will?

That is argument number 1: Science does, or will. If science does not, what does? [7]

Here is number 2: People assume that anything made possible by science, our most indubitable modern achievement, must be good. Process X is now scientifically possible. Therefore process X must automatically be good. Contraceptives and artificial insemination are accepted partly on this basis. Another way to state this argument is to mix two standards; (a) the mores: what people at a particular time and place do, and (b) science.[8] Then the argument runs: You do not do X. But it is modern and scientific, and you are out of date and unscientific if you do not. Therefore, you had better! Advertisers perpetually combine these two appeals.

Argument number 3: In 1859, after years of research, Charles Darwin announced his theory of evolution. How did this raise ethical problems? First, it raised the question of man's origin and thereby the question of his nature and destiny, since origin, nature, and destiny should match and be consistent with each other; and any view of man's nature or his destiny is a principle determining conclusions relative to conduct. Secondly, among derivatives of evolutionary theory were studies in comparative religion and comparative ethics. These studies were hurriedly made on the presumed premise that the later stages were the better and that primitive men were immoral and ourselves the advance types of what the moral life ideally should be; and they raised, more effectively than did the discovery of America, the old theory that all morals are simply the mores or simply what people at a particular time and place take to be good and what they take to be evil.

[7] Cf. John Dewey, *The Quest of Certainty,* 1929, chap. 4.

[8] See Louis T. More, *The Limitations of Science* (London: Constable, 1915), chap. 7, "Science as Arbiter of Ethics."

5. Out of positive and negative influences from politics, economics, and religion came the capitalistic revolution which was full-fledged by 1723, the year Adam Smith was born. The revolution arose in England, with background in Italy and Holland. After two centuries we hear of it mainly in terms of "profit" and "free enterprise," and some assume that capitalism is synonymous with Christianity and democracy. For working purposes we use Max Weber's description of "the spirit of capitalism" as the spirit that dominates an age whose chief dynamic is profit and ever-increasing profit, gained with the help of theoretically free labor.

Capitalism is an economic movement, and its study belongs within the history and theory of economics, and not within those of ethics. But any economic system raises ethical problems, since man as a getter, holder, and spender of economic goods is basically subject to ethical laws. Economic goods are means subordinate to the ends of human life; it is ethics and not economics that studies these ends. In terms of justice and charity, economic goods enter daily into the life of every mature person. The system of ownership and the status of ownership condition the exercise of freedoms: of employment, speech, the press, religion, education, and political life. If some man or group controls most of the economic goods, people's freedoms amount to little. Whoever owns is sure to control and dictate. We all learn this, in the classroom, in the pulpit, on the stage, and on the air. We need not, perhaps, hold that all problems in economics, except problems of bare factual statistics, are rooted in ethical problems; but we must hold that at most turns of human life economic factors raise ethical problems. This is evident among primitive peoples or among peoples reduced to primitive conditions, as the Germans were after World War II. But it is patent when production has been the biggest in the modern industrialized nations. Witness the problems, always close to ethical problems, of housing, of employment and unemployment, of health, of wasted resources, of mothers working out of the home, of usury, of political wars, of labor-ownership conflicts, of economic, political warfare over rubber, oil, and the atom and hydrogen bombs.

What is odd is that capitalism has raised the problem of moral standards. What is good is what is productive. Better conduct is what produces more goods and profits. The bigger is the better: the bigger the turnover, the better; the bigger the sales, the bigger the school or factory, the more miles goods are shipped back and forth, the better. The best man is the man who makes most money. Is not the wealthy man "well off"? What poor man or what poor Western nation does not, along with the wealthy, say this? The nation with the biggest crops, biggest oil reserves, biggest empire, is most loved by God. Is it not most blest? In general the more capital goods, the more business, the more profits, the better the person, the family, the group, the nation. Often it is said that the more freedom to pursue profit, the better; free enterprise in practice commonly means this freedom to make more and more profit. The business man's business, as we in the Occident conceive it, is to make profit, and even in the heat of a war, when others must face the guns, the business man will function only in view of profit.

Hence our slogans: Money talks. Business is business. We know on which side our bread is buttered. To feather one's nest. Every man has his price. As good as gold. A sterling character. Time is money.[9]

If a problem of our times is to get over individualism, in economics, in religion and in politics, we shall have in the long run to coin, out of post-individualistic life, slogans as effective as these, as much employed and as native to the new era as these to the old.

The profit motive in isolation and as a law to itself has raised many ethical problems, such as the following: what the effect

[9] See Léon Bloy, "Four Comfortable Sayings," *Colosseum,* II (1935), 257 f., a translation from Bloy's *L'exégèse des lieux communs;* and Christopher Dawson, "Catholicism and the Bourgeois Mind," *Colosseum,* II (1935), 246–56.

is on persons who think this way, who believe that profit may be sought in isolation and as a law to itself, an effect not limited to rich men, since many without property are capitalistically minded. Next, what the effects are, in terms of social conflict and on human freedoms and welfare. Lastly, what problems follow for the political, economic, cultural, and religious life of man, problems outlined in part in many studies.[10]

6. The industrial revolution came after capitalism was established and Adam Smith was buried. Capitalism used the new steam power along with applied science to make profit; the marriage was silently accepted by political democracies, and the excesses and inhumanities of early industrialism-capitalism were possible only because Christianity was ineffective and inert and capitalism had become a dictator to religion.

Industrialism raised ethical questions by the dozen. This was because, besides money power and political power, it gave man new instruments by which to use men for his interests. Along with capitalism, industrialism raised the labor-ownership problem with its many interesting ramifications. It helped to implement capitalism, and gave more people, at least in the Occident, a chance to live more comfortable lives and either more human or less human lives.

We doubt whether industrialism raised in an independent way the problem of ethical standards unless for persons who think that the more machinery and gadgets the better.

7. All this time, say from 1600, the modern struggle for democracy had proceeded. In minimum terms, political democracy means that each normal adult is allowed to and encouraged to help rule the tribe; the modern struggle for this type began at least as early as the reign of James I of England (1601–1625),

[10] A. A. Berle and Gardiner C. Means, *The Modern Corporation and Private Property* (1932). R. J. Tawney, *The Acquisitive Society* (1920), and *Religion and the Rise of Capitalism* (1926; reprinted in various editions, including a 35 cent edition). Christopher Dawson, *Enquiries into Religion and Culture* (1933), Introduction. F. Hayek, *The Road to Serfdom* (Chicago Univ. Press, 1944).

and the struggle in England has continued in quiet though effective ways; other movements are the American Revolution, the French Revolution, and many uprisings in nations which have declared themselves for freedom. Struggle for social democracy is less explosive, and has had its most marked results in the United States and Canada, where it is possible for almost any man to speak to almost any man on somewhat equal terms and not merely "if your Honor permits." The high hat has not much glory any longer in Western society. Still, this is the hardest and most basic kind of democracy to carry out, the kind that supposes that the human world properly is one world, that one man is basically as good as another. It is primarily on this foundation that the other forms rest, on the radical, simple notion that man is man.[11] As minimum requirement for economic democracy, we must try to achieve in society such conditions that every family will have the opportunity to obtain the economic means for living in a human way.

Aside from the question of particular goods and evils promoted by the three forms of democracy, standards are to some degree set. A new emphasis on man is sponsored and urged by the modern struggle for democracies and by the achievement, even if hamstrung, of de facto democracies. Not mere public opinion and the vox populi, but man back of these has gained, in many crude ways, new consideration, a social consciousness, and a new social significance. Man is important, man is to some extent in the saddle. Man decides things. This is perhaps the major good of modern developments.

Of course, this vital result is crossed by qualifying factors. Things also are in the saddle and ride mankind: with new wonders and conveniences, man tends to go bourgeois, sinks to acceptance of good things, and is no longer vitally their creator.[12] Even more seriously, man tends to make a paradise and to take

[11] See Chesterton's tremendous statement of it. *Orthodoxy,* chap. 4.

[12] See Ortega y Gasset, *The Revolt of the Masses* (New York: Norton & Co., 1932), chap. 7.

means, often playthings, as the end, as Steinbeck so powerfully says in *Grapes of Wrath* (chapter 15). Besides, democracy is challenged, the totalitarian rulers using its vocabulary and even its techniques, to turn things to undemocratic ends.

To say this is to emphasize the axiom that eternal vigilance is the price of freedom. Man remains the standard, as man to some extent has always been the standard among all peoples. But democracy as an ideal helps people better to take man as standard, and some techniques worked out to achieve political democracy, and some which help toward economic democracy, such as labor unions, participation of labor in ownership and control, cooperatives and credit unions, give people ways to make man more effectively the standard; ways of the peoples justly coming to own and of recovering a sense of ownership, are steps toward economic, political, and social democracy, and to the reaffirmation of man as the basic moral standard.

8. Next is the proletarian revolution. Many people in rich America own little and depend on wages. If employment and wages fail, they depend on the state, that is on some form of collectivization. These people are the proletariat, and their condition is proletarian.

Karl Marx, prophet of the proletariat, since 1848 tells them they are enslaved, which neither they nor we can well deny. He tells them their condition is intolerable. He tells them to unite, which to some degree they were already doing. He tells them they will be free. This is said to be the revolution *of* the proletariat, and presumably by the proletariat and for the proletariat: thus it is the masses, the people, man in revolt, in the act of breaking the chains.

Many questions have arisen in the course of a century. Marx stated unforgettably that the condition is intolerable. He was not the first to attempt this, but the first to do it. But in fact whose revolution is it? Who engineers it and for whom? Is the proletarian condition necessarily ethically indefensible? Is anyone wrong, and if so who is wrong, in the situation condemning so many to be without property and any other than state security? Does the Communistic revolution liberate men or enslave them? Was the sacrifice of twenty million Russians by the Russian military and political leaders (up to 1945) intended for the people's good and liberation? Does it effect any such end?

In terms of standards, the movement as it has worked out is a cross between the principle that the end justifies the means and the principle that the totalitarian dictator's will is always right.

This mention of some chief nonphilosophical events and movements helping to shape thought on ethical problems is not a history of ethics; but when matters are thus sketched, it is remarkable how far, at least seemingly, we may disregard the philosophers. Nearly all matters outlined continue to influence thought and action, and recent wars, economic troubles, international sparring, and scientific discoveries add little except intensifications either to the welter of standards or to good and bad practice. To make the picture complete, one would have to consider the thinkers and consider the Grecian-Roman and the Hebraic-Christian backgrounds, for these carry over inevitably into the present. A more basic factor must be allowed, the natural direction and demand of all life and being, and especially of human life and being, for good.

## CHAPTER 6

# STANDARDS OF MORALITY

IN THE light of some principle, human actions are good, and, by failing to square with this norm of morality, actions are evil. In general they can be right in no other way and wrong in no other way. To seek that principle is the task of this chapter, and to find it is to find the key to lesser questions in ethics.

We saw John Dewey's statement regarding the end, worthy to be a formula for Christian social democracy. This is surprising, since he was not a Christian and since he often said there is no end. On historical questions, Dewey had less precision and sympathy. In August 1944 an article of his in *Fortune* asserted: "According to medieval theological philosophy, the basis of all ultimate moral principles is supernatural—not merely above nature and reason, but so far beyond the scope of the latter that they must be miraculously revealed and sustained."

What is bad about this statement is how far it is from truth. The Christian philosopher, old-time or recent, consistently says that nature is the standard of human conduct. The standard is man, is human nature, is reason, is the law of nature as known by man and enforced by man on himself.

Any action that is *contra naturam* is an evil action and is evil just so far as it is *contra naturam*. We cannot go against our nature and thereby do good. This is evident to the Christian philosopher. What is unnatural cannot be good.

The reason, not hidden from Plato and Aristotle or the Stoics, is that we believe in man's nature, in its goodness and dignity. Not that we believe that every pervert gangster measures up to what man by nature is to be; but so far as any man in his actions comes up to human nature, he is good and right. He who rejects "human nature" as standard has to say that human nature is evil and that we ought not to respect it or try to live up to it. On his view, we ought to take some puritanic, antihuman and man-hating principle as a standard of human goodness; and go with those who enslave and liquidate men under pretense of perfecting them.

The standard is the very being of man, a proper and adequate standard. God could not make a better law for man, and if God has created human nature it is God who has made this the standard and law for man. Our teaching boosts man as the measure, not of all things, since it is not in line with man's blueprint that all things exist and have their natures, and man is not the measure of human nature, since obviously he has not made this. But human nature, and in that sense man, is the measure of the goodness in human action, a measure and pattern designed by whatever forces have given us human nature as measure and pattern.

To preserve and develop human nature, we can never do better than go with human nature, and to deflate and wreck it we can never do better than to turn on it and counter it. To go with it is good; to go against it is sin. The pirate, the unjust, the impure, the liar, the gangster, and the dictator go against it and tend to destroy it. "Be a man!" That is what nature asks of the human person, and that is all it may ask. We have the saying, "Let that child be!" What heaven and earth say to our species is, "Let man be!" Here the word "be" means what it says: it means to be and fully to be. The pirate, gangster, dictator, does not accept this primary law. As a result—it is like subtraction in arithmetic—such a man is not all there. A. G. Hebert [1] put it remarkably:

". . . A bad man is less of a man than a good man. After

[1] *Introduction to God and His Works* (selections from the *Summa Theologica*).

all, a drunkard or a coward is a poor creature. . . . The same is true of every type of clever and successful but selfish humanity; whether the profiteer, the 'ideally unjust man' of Plato's *Republic,* or the Unjust Steward of our Lord's parable . . . the question, What is man living for? shows that one region of his manhood is hollow, where it should be solid. These men, clever and strong as they are, are antisocial types; they have failed to grow into the form of real manhood. They are not good men, because they lack the fulness of manhood; they are 'deformed.' " Not all there. Not truly expressing the form of man; not good for man.

That is what we say of any action, habit, or disposition that is evil for man, and we must say the same, so far, of the man. Respect for nature is the law. It is the road for him; following it as the principle, persons and societies by continued effort can keep erect the edifice of human goodness. Otherwise they cannot. Any justified law is a plan for action: the traffic law, for instance, and the Constitution interpreted by the courts. But the deepest plan for man is within and is his nature and is not imposed on him by the mayor or the founding fathers. On the contrary, laws passed by legislators, no matter how democratic, must square with our nature and perfect it. If they do not, they are unjust and we may refuse to obey. That is why people are anti-Hitler and anti-Stalin. The right of governments to exist and of men to be rulers derive from the status and needs of man's nature.

The law is man's nature. That is the measure and standard. To use Dewey's tautological phrase, "the basis of all ultimate moral principles" is nature.

That is why men in both pagan and Christian times have always spoken of a natural law. This means that if nature exists, man's nature is law and standard. The idea is implied in Aristotle's *Ethics,* Book I, that the good man lives up to reason or the logos principle, and this idea is often repeated in the doctrine that it is hard to live up to what man is. In the Stoics, the notion reappears as "nature," and in Marcus Aurelius the affirming of nature as standard, though it lacks creative punch in theory and practice, is remarkable. In Cicero, "nature" or the "logos principle" is reasserted as "natural law," the Romans, by that date, being famous lawgivers.

In the medievals the two notions of reason and of law are kept. Reason is perpetually affirmed as standard. "Nature" in man is "law" for man, and the notions combine as "natural law." In the light of facts this was inevitable, because:

First, the Christian world developed within a world ruled politically by Roman law, and the Romans are to date man's greatest lawgivers.

Secondly, even more influential was "The Law," that is, the Old Testament, with its tremendous impact on Hebrews and Christians.

Thirdly, Hebrews had believed time out of mind that all is in the hand of God, and this doctrine of Providence, expressed in the parable of the lilies of the field, means that all is ruled by God's eternal law.

Natural law is the law of human nature, and is human nature. To go with one is to go with the other. The only relevant questions are: Have we a knowable nature and can our conduct go with it? If we must say "no," human nature as standard is out, and no further questions on human conduct make sense and it does not matter what we do.

Forces have combined to make us deny nature as law. First, individualists are against all law. Secondly, the sceptical deposit left by Hume and Kant and brought up to date by positivists and existentialists has made us ask: Can we know the nature and essence of anything? Thirdly, evolutionary theory, turned philosophical, tended to say that since species change, no species or natures exist. Fourthly, the ancient relativist mores theory was reaffirmed by discovery of a new world, by evolutionary philosophy, rapid communications, and world wars. Fifthly, some Catholics, and many Protestants, believe that through original sin man's nature is totally evil; [2] and can we not do better than take evil as law?

That it does make a difference what we do is basic to this book. It makes a difference naturally, the nature of man being the center of reference. That is also the verdict of mankind. We naturally revolt against tyrants and, if we dare, we openly revolt; not because we find revolt pleasant or our Church tells us to revolt, but because our nature makes certain demands. I am against tyrants because they are against man. I am against unjust men and detractors because they are against man. If they were for and with man, certainly I would be "wrong," a biological freak, to be against them. Some actions are with man's nature and can be known to be with it; for example, respect for life and for man; and other actions can be known to be humanly destructive.

This is the fundamental sense in holding, as people implicitly do, that there is a natural law, and of believing with Emerson that there is a law for man and a law for thing.

That is the basic sense in saying that rule must be by law, not by the wish of some top man or elite, not by the accidental position of one or many, but by the universal nature of man. This is evidently the democratic standard.

Let us see how Christian thinkers of today restate this old standard, so clearly a "natural" one.

First Christian thinker. The human-nature theory is expressed vigorously by Gilson who says: "if this ought to be is not inscribed to begin with in that which is, no artifice of dialectics can put it there. To discover what each thing ought to be or to do, it is enough to state the definition of that thing and to ask it to realize itself."

Second. This thought is lucid in *Moral Values* by W. G. Everett who says: "Moral law is just as real as human nature, within which it has its existence. Strange, indeed, if man alone of all living beings could realize his highest welfare in disregard

[2] For fuller treatment of this point see below, pp. 116–18.

of the principles of his own nature! And this nature, we must remember, is what it is, is always concrete and definite. Indeed the sceptic nowhere else assumes the absence of principles" and expects, in spite of disregarding the natures of things, that the highest form of life will, perversely, be attained; he does not expect the lily or polar bear to thrive under any and all conditions. Just as sure "must be the failure of man to realize, in disregard of the laws of his being, the values of which he is capable. The structure of man's nature, as conscious and spiritual, grounds laws just as real as those of his physical life, and just as truly objective."

Third. Interesting is the tentative statement of A. K. Rogers: "if there is such a thing as a generic human nature, it will in an intelligible sense supply an objective standard," in the sense that correct judgments on right and wrong have "this common backing."

What we are, says Gilson, that is what we are to live up to; our own nature, say Everett and Rogers, is the standard of morals. Among many others who have stated and elaborated this democratic, human-nature standard in recent times, we mention Michael Cronin, John A. Ryan, and Virgil Michel, and give a separate chapter to Maritain's statement of man as standard.

Fourth. In *The Science of Ethics* (Volume I, chapter 5) Cronin works out what he calls "the standard of human nature." He says that when man in his freedom directs an act to the ultimate end of human life, the act is good. Of this there could be no doubt. But since we do not know the end in any particular way, how are we to know when an act is directed to the end?

Cronin's reply is that, if in the use of freedom we tend through our acts to the immediate natural end of a particular faculty, such as sight or speech or the power to reproduce, and at the same time respect the natural order of the faculties, we tend to the ultimate end. This means that so far we have acted according to our nature and have done good. The primary test is the natural objects or ends of the appetites; it is "the natural," since this is sure to be in accord with our natural demands and needs. "The rule not to use a faculty in such a way as to oppose the realization of its natural end is universally and absolutely valid. There is not a single exception to it. To use a faculty in such a way as to make its natural end impossible of realization is intrinsically unnatural and bad. There could be no more direct and unequivocal violation of nature than this. It is the complete perversion of nature's purposes and needs."

"The violent and unnatural blotting out of Reason" in drunkenness cannot be morally good; the natural order of faculties is inverted, the demand for physical pleasure getting precedence over the demand of Reason to let its light shine in the person's life. Sex sins are perversions, since the natural direction of the faculty is perverted.

Cronin says that (what we here call) the pragmatic standard is a just one; because, if rightly understood, it is seen to manifest the basic standard. It comes to this: Any act which, raised to a general line of conduct, works evil for the race, cannot be with the way of nature; for example, lying, stealing, hating, the intermarriage of close relatives, antinomianism, and nihilism.

The fact that often it is difficult to discern the natural line of conduct does not argue that there is no such line or that we are not obliged to try to discover it. By our nature we are obliged to try to know and respect our nature; that is the center of this doctrine on the standard. The institutions we set up, such as a given state or a family, must be indeed natural, but only in the sense that they are in accord with the laws of nature; so too of our making and using machines, spectacles, and hair ribbons: making and using must accord with our nature; otherwise the action is unworthy of us, fit perhaps for a mouse or an angel, but not for us.

Fifth. A compact statement of human nature as standard is

made by John A. Ryan. Degrees of approach to the end are degrees of goodness, and an act leading toward the end is good; but in the great complexity of personal and social life, the relevance of a particular act to the end is not seen. A standard closer to us is needed. Ryan declares for the standard acclaimed for centuries, namely, ourselves.

Man must be respected in his complete and composite nature. Body must be respected, protected and developed, because, unlike money and houses, it is part of man. Soul must be respected and nurtured for exactly the same reason, but soul as rational gives the type "man," specifies man and is accountable for *homo sapiens*. Rational soul or "reason" must dominate, and on occasion must rule the body. When there is conflict between rational and animal factors, the rational, formal factor has precedence. Otherwise we do not live as man, do not operate on the level of our species. That is why we condemn such acts as drunkenness and solitary vice.

We cannot go toward the end of human life if our action is below the level of our nature.

We also have to respect the relationship essential to us as men. On a par with us is any and every man. The man we speak of is not a hypothetical man cut off from mankind; he lives among men who in essential, basic needs and demands are one with him. Rights and duties of justice and charity rest on this community of nature.

Man's natural relation to "things," to animals, plants, and minerals, is that of natural lord. They are means for his good and enjoyment and may be sacrificed to his health, knowledge, and love, even if it takes centuries to get the mastery due to him.

Above man is the absolute being whom man in his wisdom can know and in his life recognize.[3]

[3] John A. Ryan, "The Basis of Objective Judgments in Ethics," Proceedings of the Sixth International Congress of Philosophy (1926), and Proceedings of American Catholic Philosophical Association, II (1926); elaborated as *The Norm of Morality,* defined and applied (Washington, D.C., N.C.W.C., 1944).

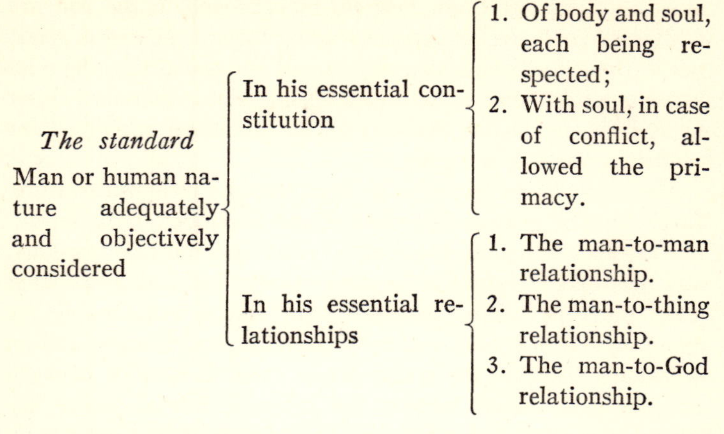


Sixth. Virgil Michel's chapter on standards in *Philosophy of Human Conduct* [4] is called "human nature as norm," and this title as well as the treatment of the subject makes it clear that Dewey's "miraculously revealed" assertion is deductive and unreal. Michel says inadequate theories on standards are not totally false, not simply "contrary to our nature or the nature of things"; they are false if they "harmonize with only a partial aspect of our nature," ignore other aspects and "overbalance or exaggerate the true nature of things." Human nature is wonderfully rich and complex, and scientific study "must mean more rigorous examination, at the start, of human nature in all its complexity, in its properly proportioned totality, and in its manifestations over the whole extent of human existence."

What is "natural" in man? All actions and reactions of the human system below the level of human decision, replies Michel,

[4] Burgess Publishing Co., Minneapolis, 1936. The American humanists searching for standards of good in the arts, were forced to seek standards of moral good and all good. Though they affirmed "the mean" as the standard, Babbitt went deeper in *On Being Creative,* p. 23: creative work needs "to be disciplined to some truly human norm. Such a criterion may seem difficult and elusive, but it is the only one that is finally valid." See also T. S. Eliot, *The Sacred Wood,* close of Preface to 1928 edition.

as well as the determinations fulfilled through choice.[5] It is natural for reason and will to rule the senses and feelings; no other procedure is natural for man, since man is man by the gift of reason and consequent will. Hence two conclusions; first, to have any meaning, ethics must honor "natural reason; it must be amenable to rational scrutiny and investigation and to consistent formulation by human reason"; secondly, it must be grounded in the nature of things, above all "in human nature itself."

Michel's statement of the standard is: "Human nature taken in its broadest sense is then the norm to which human conduct must conform to be morally good." This is a particular application of a general law: what is good for any being is that which conforms to its nature.

The matters reported from various authors may be resumed in lines from St. Thomas.[6] A being is good so far as it is; so far as it lacks its proper being, it lacks good and is evil. A blind man is good so far as he is, but it is an evil for him to lack sight. Now the principle and form of man is reason, and an action cannot be truly human if it falls short of this man-making principle. Hence we say that man's good is to be (*esse*) in accordance with reason, and that only an unruly will persistently opposes reason. Whatever in our actions is at war with right reason is moral evil. Actions such as inadvertently picking up a straw are outside the genus of moral; but if a man's action is reasonably directed toward bodily nourishment or rest, it "is also directed to the good of virtue."

The good of virtue is the good of our nature. The good of anything is that it should be, and fully be. Nature abhors destruction, and demands being; nature abhors a vacuum. So of human nature. But this has not its fulness and total complement of being at present, nor in any immortal life possible to it; and it can naturally go toward fulness only by action, yet not by in-

[5] See St. Thomas, *Summa theologica,* suppl. III, q.41, a.1.

[6] Ia IIae, qq.18, 19.

discriminate action, but by action fit for it, up to its dignity and worth, because up to its form.

So the Christian thinkers with remarkable consistency have said, and so Aristotle in his way said, and so the Stoics said. Hence the truth in saying that ethics is the science of what man ought to be by reason of what he is, and in saying that our duty consists in becoming what we are.

Objections will arise. First. "Well, of course, every man is a man and cannot help being a man in everything he does; so all action is good and right."

We reply that so far as man's action is truly human, it is good; but we hold that the action by which a man goes down the street chopping off neighbors' ears is ordinarily less than truly human and is therefore evil. So of asking us indiscriminately to hate Germans, Japanese, Russians, to hate that which is good, in war or peace.

Secondly. "Well, if the law is to follow our nature, and if, to use an ancient and medieval expression, the law is ingrained in our nature, why the Ten Commandments? Does God command what is already commanded in our nature? Does not the pragmatists' scolding of the 'supernal' have some justification?"

Experience stretched out through any year or two, and especially stretched out through history, gives the reply. It is difficult to know nature and more difficult to live up to it. Otherwise there would be no crime, no delinquency, no courts, and we would enjoy a minor paradise. Experience and observation make it clear that we have difficulty in living up to "human nature objectively and adequately considered." At times we would like to bypass our nature and set up new markers, as Adam and Eve did, and were scolded: "Ah, ha! you thought you'd be like God, knowing (deciding the bounds of) good and evil." If a man thinks he always lives up to human nature, he is ignorant or hopelessly conceited. It was the delusion of some recent romantic secularists that men were about to be as gods.

Over broad areas and long periods of time, we must tolerate

the semihuman, not that we approve of it, but it is then the best we can do. We have the ideal of permanent peace that would be grand for human nature; but apparently for a long while we may lack the reality and have to endure wars. Evidently, it is a task to know and live up to human nature. At times, says Sturzo in the *Inner Laws of Society,* we achieve only the pseudo-human which he calls the pseudo-rational, the semirational, and the relatively rational. He says slavery never can reach the truly human level, and that the working-class wage system does not reach it, whether in the laissez faire type, without protection, or the organized type of today, with legal safeguards but without economic defense against crises, or the collectivist type, as had in Russia.[7]

Third objection. "Why not let everybody decide good and evil for himself?"

Probably the greatest attempt to approach this ultraindividualism in standards has been made in modern times in the Occident. The result has been in some ways unsatisfactory; it has led at times to excesses, everyone going his own way in religion as prompted by the now almost ingrained principle of private interpretation, his own laissez faire way in economics and, perhaps, in art and culture. By the pragmatic test, the individualistic way is not good, even looked at directly and not yet seen in the collectivistic reaction against it. The way is bad, but I believe we must, in order to use the pragmatic standard, wait to see how things come out in the long run, and even then we can know they have come out badly only if we have a prior understanding of what is "bad" for man; this is, pragmatic standards are secondary.

Fourth objection. "But surely the mores are a good and abiding standard. Everybody always follows them, anyway."

We do commonly follow them, and in that sense the mores theory has empiric backing. When people are in Rome, they

[7] Sturzo, *Inner Laws of Society* (New York: Benziger, 1944), pp. 18–19; cf. pp. 25, 58, 135.

do as the Romans do; and people are always in some Rome or other. We are born into a world that acts and judges in such and such ways, and we tend to conform; it is convenient to do so; not every four-year-old has to start anew and discover standards.

All the same, just as the civil law in America or Russia can command what would be immoral, so can the mores of Chicago, Timbuktu, Siberia, or England. Everyone knows this. Over a large area and for a long time people can be wrong in moral theory or conduct or both, and people have been wrong, relative to important moral matters, such as head-hunting, slavery, human sacrifice, wars, and labor conditions. The mores approve such procedures, and yet the procedures, judged by some test more radical than the mores, are seen to be bad. Thus the mores can be wrong. But the rock-bottom standard, since it is that by which right and wrong are judged, cannot be wrong; it must be right and a *ne plus ultra.* Aristotle remarked when we judge whether to do this rather than that, we "must measure by a single standard," and St. Thomas refined the idea to "one first standard." [8] The mores nevertheless simply must be correct as a standard if we consider them in general and if, as is our presumption throughout, "man" generally cannot be wrong. "You can fool some of the people all of the time and all of the people some of the time." But the social democrat Lincoln is right in saying that "man" or "the people" cannot be fooled. Hence if the life of mankind everywhere and always—*"semper, ab omnibus et ubique"*—is taken as synonymous with "the mores," the mores cannot be wrong.[9] All democrats say that "man" cannot be wrong. But particular men, and even a majority of men over a considerable time and region, can be.

As usually understood, the mores are too narrow and aristocratic to serve as standard to judge man and his conduct. On the

[8] Aristotle, *De Anima,* 434a, 5–10; see St. Thomas, *Contra Gentiles,* III, c.9: ". . . *unam mensuram primam.*"

[9] For a remarkable treatment of the mores standard, see Eliseo Vivas, *The Moral Life and the Ethical Life* (Chicago Univ. Press, 1950), pp. 81–89.

contrary, man is the radical human standard by which to judge the mores, these being seen to be now on the track, now off the track.

Fifth objection. "What of the Churches? Do they not give the law to their constitutents, and is not a Church certainly right in these matters?"

For people to follow the lead of their Churches is common historically, and there is nothing new about it. A Church could be correct in pronouncements on conduct, and perhaps some Church is correct, generally or within limits, when it says that actions X and Y are good and actions A and B are evil. A "Church," in this connection, is a body of people united precisely as believers and as worshipers of God. In this sense a Church brings us again, as regards moral standards, to the mores, or social will and public opinion, and it would ordinarily be correct, but could be incorrect, in its judgments on morals. A Church guided directly by God could not be incorrect. The existence and credentials of any such Church are not examined in this book.

Sixth objection. "The pragmatic standard, at least on an obvious view, says actions are good if they work, and sometimes it says they are good if they have good consequences."

This last statement is circular and useless, as is the whole pragmatic "consequences" test, if we have not a prior standard. When do actions "work"? The bomb can blow up a community or a mountain and in that sense "work," but the question remains whether its use is morally justified.

Seventh objection. "The Greeks among others elaborated the theory of the mean: let nothing be underdone or overdone; then all is good." One difficulty in practice is that the mean, usually just and applicable, is sometimes very hard to apply. If a person reads Aristotle's *Ethics* (Books II–V, inclusive), he sees the difficulties. First, the mean does not universally apply, and where it does not, what does? Secondly, man needs what Aristotle calls "moral sense" and sensitivity to apply it; if that is true, it is not useful to everyone; it is determined by a nicely developed intelligence and is relative to persons and circumstances. Thirdly, as Aristotle handles it, the mean (see beginning of Book VI) seemingly is subordinate to a more basic standard, the logos or rational principle. Nevertheless, it is a useful standard and is widely used, and on the whole perhaps correctly used, in present-day American society.

The expediency standard is that of the Machiavellian and opportunist. A person holds an action is good because it helps him to the ends he desires; groups such as nations or labor unions often do the same; see the article, "Priests, Workers, and Communists" (*Harper's,* November, 1948) for the expediency standard apparently used by Red Mike Quill in first promoting Communism and then fighting it. People of the amoral as well as of the immoral type use the principle. What will help me or my group is acclaimed as thereby good; e.g., Stern Brothers, Macy's, and other New York City department stores were charged in the late 1940's with making an agreement with Communist unionism. In international affairs and war propaganda, every nation tends to revert to this principle. It amounts to making the end, which may be either good or bad, justify the means. Of course, some things that promote my good are good. The danger lies in turning my advantage into a basic principle.

Eighth objection. If "man" is the standard, why such variety and relativity in ethical judgments and practices? Human nature is basically what it is. Why then such a spread in the mores?

All are basically one: all are men. But from the first moment of his existence, every man is an individual: he is just this man, who has come to be in just these circumstances. He is unique, perfectly repeats no one and will never be repeated; the space-time dimensions and conditions of his body at the moment he comes to be settle this matter. In the same manner his environment, as he grows, is in the strictest sense, *his* environment, and is unique. Multiply his initial unique being by his unique environment, over five or ten or forty years, and the result can only be unique. Given his being and background, the totality of his ethical judgments, though most of them agree with those of others, is inevitably *sui generis.* His judgments on what may be done, on what ought or ought not to be done, are his, and when he faces particular issues and must act, he must use such equipment as he has. He could be "wrong," that is, his judgment "X is to be done" may not conform to what "man" is. *Subjectively* he may be justified; he has followed "conscience," which is a person's practical reason judging on what is here and now to be done, a practical judgment made according to some standard. *Objectively* his judgment may be more or less valid.

We can try to teach a man and help him be realistic and objective, but we cannot make his judgments for him. This is not merely because he is free, but because he has his own original being and also an environment that cannot be completely duplicated. As a result, he has his own lights. On this question, the existentialists are correct. The point they make is one always made by Thomists, namely, the man who must act must decide, and this he does from his unique "existentialist" position. But Thomists are more adequate, adding that a man need not act as devoid of all common principles, and he seldom if ever could do so. Besides, he has a past, which to some extent he has responsibly made and which to some extent determines his conduct, and his conduct in the present act, for which he is responsible, will have a future, since to some degree it determines his fate.

Man should learn to act habitually in the best light that history, sciences, and philosophy can give him, combining this light with any light given directly by God. He thus learns how to act as man, that is, he learns how to exercise his freedoms so as to go toward the end of human life. This virtue of knowing how is called *prudentia,* and judgment on such a basis, a judgment remaining to some degree unique, is called the prudential judgment. If it were totally unique, we would be reduced to individualistic atomism, and moral science would be impossible. We could only say with Sartre's last-gasp solipsism *"Unique, unique, unique."*

With ends and standards covered, we can complete the definition of moral order, given earlier in tentative form. Moral order is the interrelationship of before and after, among the acts of our freedom and the resulting habits and dispositions in persons and societies, according to human nature adequately and objectively considered, that is, in its essential make-up and its essential relations. This designation could be enlarged to include agent and end.

Ethics is the philosophical study of the moral order. As an earlier chapter supposes, "philosophical" here means in terms of causes, the matter-form causes and the end-agent causes. In this manner we grasp the being of the moral order.

## CHAPTER 7

# ST. THOMAS'S BELIEF IN MAN

THIS chapter expresses our position on good and evil, in the context of St. Thomas's hopeful view of man.

The great believers in man are great believers in man's spirit. They belong to what Urban in *The Intelligible World* (1929) called the great tradition in philosophy which Urban said affirms God, human spirit, and immortality.

Every great Western philosopher has belonged to this tradition. They do not all see God or human spirit in exactly the same light and some disbelieve in the reality of nonspirit, but they agree in the basic affirmations. Not one philosopher of major importance in the Occident has denied God or human spirit. We must search for an outstanding philosopher who is an atheist or a consistent materialist, and we would have to argue, in order to find such a philosopher, that Democritus or Lucretius or Hobbes or Marx is outstanding. Urban said with Berkeley that "the minute philosophers" have always had three main points: the denial of God, spirit, and immortality.

Such philosophical acceptance of God and the human spirit is an interesting historical fact as well as remarkable ground for optimism. It is difficult, so we may believe on the word of so many philosophers, to disbelieve in man. Here Plato and Aristotle, so often divided, are one, and with them are St. Augustine and St. Thomas, Plotinus, St. Bonaventure, Duns Scotus, Descartes, Spinoza, Leibniz, Pascal, Locke, Berkeley, Kant, Hegel, and Bergson.

Backed by such men, one could logically have strong faith

in man and maintain the optimism needed for a balanced life. Against this position would stand only men of smaller philosophical stature who have remained without faith in man or an abiding strong faith in God: such misery-preachers as Hobbes, who makes man's life in the original condition, presumed by Hobbes, antisocial and what he calls nasty, brutish, and short; and such "blues" philosophers as Schopenhauer and Bertrand Russell. Logically with these men are the totalitarians, represented by Nero, Hitler, and Stalin, who have little faith in man and little reverence for him.

Optimism is about good; about the possibilities and the existence of good. The optimist holds that good is being realized or will be realized; and even in difficult times, epidemics, and general catastrophes, he holds that good can be realized. For him this is not a bad world, after all. The pessimist balks on some or all of these points. He believes that good does not exist, or is not being worked out, will not be worked out at all or in the given case, and possibly he believes that it cannot be worked out. In his view any other thinking is as gushy and sentimental as Rousseau.

To say why particular persons are optimists or pessimists is not within our scope. Some are pessimists on more or less conscious grounds, because of frustration, as in a love affair, and because of hardships, such as loss of health, honors, fortune, or religious faith. Often the causes are more subtle and seem to be intimately connected in some instances with the organism, especially in persons who get fits of pessimism; with the original "complexion" of the body, and with one's early childhood experiences, as when one has had a "missed" youth so that the victim, suffering from a "father complex," wants to get even. In some the grounds may be logical; the person is pessimistic because, given his view of reality, he has reason to be pessimistic. Consider Bertrand Russell with his hopeless outlook; logically, Russell would be pessimistic; but we cannot say for sure that logic prompts his pessimism.

So for the grounds of optimism. The bouyant person full of health and vitality is not likely to be a pessimist, nor the person who from youth never knew heavy crosses. Temperament as well as experiences may sweeten or sour a person's world. But one may have logical grounds for optimism and, in spite of all that the pessimists allege, he remains an optimist. It is both these logical grounds for optimism and the fact of his optimism that we wish to review in St. Thomas' philosophy of man.

Perhaps the most basic point is the doctrine that nature is good. This is pervasive with him; he is always teaching it and applies it to God and man and things. Any positive thing is good so far as it is. St. Augustine put this truth in terms of man, using a personal language: "So far as we are, we are good." St. Thomas subscribes, since his own teaching is that being is universally good, and so far as we have it, our being in body and mind and their powers is good. It may be that (as Gilson, always wishing to minimize both nature and the Greeks, says) St. Thomas has this universalized doctrine first by faith, in the words that God saw that each type of being was good; but he could also have it from more plebeian sources.

That being is good—all and every being, and each so far as it is—this is plank number one in St. Thomas' optimism, and seemingly the most basic possible plank in any one's optimism.

Besides our bare being, there is the tendency and the totality of all tendencies in being. Kant said he did not care about such a body of fact; but the open-minded philosopher must consider it. Tendency may go by various names: "inclination," "nature" or "natural tendency," "direction" (as in Spinoza), by the word "law" (as in modern physics and biology), and "set," "preset," and "drive" (as in psychology). We may use the word "orientation," so long as we mean what is natural and not imposed; and from within the tendency, even such words as "demand," "urge," "libido," "struggle," "conation" and "hormé" make sense. Here we offer no proof of such inclination in nature, except to remark that living things have a natural demand to stay alive, and living and non-living have a similar demand to be.

St. Thomas' position is that the tendency of nature is to the good. He means nothing abstruse, since "the good," if we do not wish to locate it as "that toward which things tend," is, in equally denotative terms, the being and fulness of being in anything. On this view, it is good to be; a thing, so far as it is, desires to be; and so far as it is not, but is naturally and from within itself orientated to be, it "wants to" be and naturally demands to be in its fulness. This only says that plants and animals naturally tend to grow; they get food if any is within reach and try to survive and develop. Some things are destroyed in this process; but preservation with fulness of growth, rather than destruction, is in the line of nature.

So far we have said that everything wishes to be and fully to be, and also that being, in fact desired, is good, and fulness of being, also desired, is good. To say so much is to say "Yea" in the style of Genesis: "Let things be," and in the simple grand style of the universe; and to say so much is evidently to be an optimist.

The next step is this. Man is to go with nature. This is expressed in scores of Thomistic contexts. The doctrine is certainly that of Aristotle, and the Stoics, too, of Marcus Aurelius, for example; though we said Christians must supplement Aristotle's philosophy of essence with the more complete philosophy of existence, advising us that to live up to our nature, we need grace and need to know in a prudential way many vital details on humility, poverty, self-sacrifice and group-sacrifice that a pagan civilization hardly knows. We are to live up to our nature, and this mandate, for persons and groups and cultures, is immense and may be called "ideal" in the sense that we never once for all attain it, though it is at every moment our goal.

Look at the following strong statement: [1] "Man is directed by a natural tendency to an end connatural to him, which direction

[1] *Summa theologica,* Ia IIae, q.62, a.3.

proceeds along two lines. First, along the line of reason, inasmuch as this has in it the first universal principles, known to us by the natural light of intellect" [such principles as those of identity and contradiction]; "from which principles reason progresses in both the speculative and the practical order. Second, along the line of the will's rightness, tending by its nature to the good as defined by reason. . . . For the appetite of anything tends and is moved of its nature toward an end connatural to it," and this natural movement is due to "a certain proportion of the thing to its end." The intellect must equip itself with ideas if it is to understand, "but the very nature of the will," that is, its innate movement or tendency, "suffices for its natural movement toward the end, suffices (a) for its tending toward the end and (b) for its proportion to the end."

With Aristotle we say that men are born for virtues. Still St. Thomas holds [2] that in a sort of inchoate way virtue is born with us, because (a) it is natural for the reason of every man as man to get the basic principles of knowledge and action: *a thing is what it is,* and *good is to be done* (which principles are the seedlings for all intellectual and moral virtues); and (b) in the will is a natural appetite for good as known by reason.

Reason presides over appetite and is like a ruler over the thing ruled; the virtues of intellect perfect reason, and those of the will perfect the powers of appetite, so that they obey reason. It goes with our nature to have virtues; it is human, it is fundamentally the way with us as men. What being under the sun does not naturally desire to go along with its form, to act in line with its being, at every moment to be itself, and to come if possible into the fulness of its being? Fire burns. What else would we expect it to do, if burning expresses its inner, formal being? The form in man is his rational soul, so that there is in every man a natural tendency to act in agreement with reason.[3] St. Thomas is willing to take another step and say, with Aris-

[2] *Ibid.,* q.63, a.1.
[3] *Ibid.,* q.94, a.3.

totle, that when anything comes to the peak of its goodness, that is, arrives at excellence and perfection, "it is then if ever that we have the thing in its natural state."[4] Virtue which is a good habit and is a main road to good, implies a suitability to the nature of the thing.[5]

Intellect also has a natural tendency toward a good called "truth." The check against the intellect's action is reality: it ought to square with this, and then it achieves truth or "rightness," and, according to St. Thomas' optimistic view, it tends naturally to reality, having an *affinitas ad rem*. The check against the will's action is human nature: it ought to square with this, and then it achieves "rightness." Hence there is a "truth of the will," and medieval men often used the word *rectitudo*—like the straightness of valid logic—for the truth-goodness or goodness-truth of either intellect or will.

This philosophy holds that intellect tends naturally to truth, and the inner desire and demand of nature, a desire and demand enlightened in man's case by intellect, tend naturally to preserve and fulfill being, so that at this point we may use St. Thomas' formula: "The good, that is to say the end, is the proper object of the will." In short, man is made for good; made for the good of truth, and for the good simply, or the end.

What about evil and sin? Where does this leave St. Thomas' theory on man's goodness? Facing evil, does he still say that the will of fallen man, and the will of the repeatedly fallen man, of its nature tends to good?

Even before Protestant times, churchmen were perhaps not fond of saying that nature is good and tends to good, and in our day everyone has heard preachers, including Catholics, declare that nature is full of evil tendencies, and on occasion slice man in two and pronounce his body burdensome and full of "corruption." Should not St. Thomas as monk, medieval man, and saint have taught that man's most basic inclinations are toward evil?

[4] *Ibid.*, q.49, a.2, quoting Aristotle's *Physics*, 246a.
[5] *Ibid.*, a.3.

If they have Protestant background, philosophers sniff heresy in any thought that human nature is good, that it tends to good and all good. Reinhold Niebuhr, for instance, prefers a dour view of human nature.

For St. Thomas, that question is closed on the positive side. Nature is good and tends naturally to good, but St. Thomas allows for a doctrine of evil within the positive framework of his doctrine on nature and tendency. When we do evil, we go against nature. This is the only way we can sin. Evil is not natural. It is outside the original, natural tendency of man's being; it is even against nature. Moral evil is in an act of the will, and neither it nor error is embedded in the nature of things. It is in an act of a person's freedom, and since God does not perform any evil act, sin is in the act of men or of angels. In doing evil we take the world, at this point, into our hands, and the sinner, not assisted by God in the act of evil-doing, is as a first cause. If this doctrine, on which St. Thomas and Kant (I believe) agree, is true, it may yet leave man and his nature good, but declares that man, left to himself, is remarkably insufficient.

Words employed by St. Thomas to express the effects of original sin make him appear for a moment like a thirteenth-century Protestant. He says that now, after the sin, there is an *infectio* of nature that goes along with our nature. It is not merely that Adam is affected by sin, but each man at the moment he is begotten is man indeed, but man with sin integrated with his first being. "*Traducitur humana natura a parente in prolem, et simul cum natura infectio.*" [6] It is said that as a result of Adam's sin, all of us are "*proclives ad peccandum*" and that we have a "*pronitas ad malum.*" At first look, St. Thomas appears to be Protestant, since he literally uses the terrible word "corruptio." [7] If he merely used the word, it might not seem so awful, but he uses it in a vigorous context. He says a man's own sins as

[6] *Ibid.*, q. 81, a. 1.

[7] Treatise on vices and sins, *Summa theol.*, 1–2, qq. 71–90; and on original sin, qq. 82 ff.

he commits them do not "corrupt" nature; they affect the sinner as a personal agent and as a human character; but "do not corrupt nature precisely as nature." Evidently, it is suggested that original sin "corrupts nature precisely as nature."

In its widest sense, sin is a defect in some natural principle. A man limps, and that condition is a sin of nature, in his body rather than in his will. A man errs, and that is a sin of his intellect. The leg is supposed to go along in the normal way of nature and let a man walk, the intellect to go straight for things as they are. The will of man too has its nature: to go "straight," and achieve will-rightness and concomitantly the good of man. The will does not always do this. Sometimes man in his freedom is perverse, and then he lands in defect and disorder.

The order of reason, that is, things as seen by man's intellect, is the order for the will in its freedom to follow. The will does not always do this. The result is disorder, not in the intellect, but in the will, a defect-disorder usually called "sin."

Even then we seek good, though not the good as outlined for us by the intellect. What we seek is something such as pleasure or riches, which truly is good or perfective of man and proper to him, but a good which in the circumstances—and we always act in circumstances—is seen to be something here and now to be bypassed by us. In acting deliberately, we proceed on the grounds of a presumed syllogism: Good and only good is to be done. But this act is good. Hence it may be done. In an immoral act, however, the minor premise, as Aristotle remarked, is broken into conflicting minors. "Good and only good is to be done." We all approve so far. "But this act is good." We know that, and theoretically approve it. We say, "However, not to do it," or "To do the very contrary" is good in some way: it is pleasant, it gives me prestige, it gets me out of difficulty; and any of these ends is a possible good. Therefore we pass up what reason says we are here and now to do, and we do what reason says, in the circumstances, is not to be done by us.

We have acted against reason, against our nature, against

"the light" and "the candle of the Lord." This is the Christian meaning of "sin" which is at once against nature, reason, God, and our own good.[8]

There are other ways to express it. The object is called "an apparent good," not because the object, such as pleasure, is itself evil, but because in these circumstances to act for it is something seen by our reason as not good. The act, precisely as an act, is good, but so far as willed contrary to the light, it is not good. In any sin the will holds to a mutable good, whereas it ought—reason tells it so—to hold, directly or indirectly, to the immutable good. Again, we are to love ourselves; each thing is to cherish itself, and if anyone says this is a doctrine of selfishness and individualism, we reply that it is not love or self-love that makes actions good or evil, but the quality of our love and self-love. In any good act, there is a properly ordered self-love, and in sin there still is self-love, but it is disordered and "inordinate."

If that is its nature, then "sin" is the other side of what we have seen about "good." Still, the problem of original sin and its effects remains. The language used, we said, is strong. "The first sin infects human nature with a corruption belonging to nature." What are we to say for the alleged optimism of a theologian-philosopher who thus seemingly takes man to be evil in root and branch?

There are at least three parts to the reply. First, original justice, which is the positive state contrasted with the act of original sin, is seen as an original harmony, a balance and equilibrium, a proper relation of the will to God. This state is original order, so that original sin is a disordering of man in relation to God and of man's several powers among themselves and perhaps toward their proper goods. The positive word used is *harmonia,* with the suggestion that we might speak of an *ordinatio*. Secondly, original sin, therefore, is not a total privation or destruction of man's nature or his will, or even of his

[8] *Contra Gentiles,* III, c.122.

relationship to God and of his powers to each other and to their goods. Rather, in its effects it means "the inordinate disposition of the soul's parts" or powers, and it may even be called "an inordinate disposition of nature." Briefly, it is *inordinatio*. Thirdly, how literally are we then to take the saying that original sin—unlike our actual sins which leave us with "a proneness to sin"—"corrupts nature precisely inasmuch as it is nature"?

Aquinas replies that in human nature are three goods. There is the good of its own principles, namely body and soul and the powers flowing from them. Next, "since man has from nature an inclination to virtue, this inclination to virtue is a good of nature." Lastly, there is the gift of original justice. That first good is neither diminished nor destroyed by sin. The third was deleted by original sin. What about the second good—really our problem in this chapter? "The second good of nature, namely, the natural inclination to virtue, is diminished by sin." Sin is an inordinateness, and in this way a diminution of the good of nature. The aforesaid inclination to good is rooted in rational nature and tends to the good of virtue as its term and end. Now (according to St. Thomas) sin does not diminish that root or rational nature in us. But the inclination is lessened in its effectiveness in going toward its term and end. Without original justice, the powers of the soul are left "destitute of their proper order," a condition which we may call a wounding of nature, a torpid condition called by St. Augustine and St. Thomas "*languor naturae*." There is the wound of ignorance or an ineptitude in going to truth and fact; the wound of "malice" or a not-too-effective will in going to the good of virtue; a kind of general weakness in facing and in overcoming difficulty; and the wound of concupiscence, immoderation in striving for the goods of pleasure. "These are the four wounds inflicted on the whole of human nature as the result of our first parents' sin." By our actual sins the wounds are increased, so that "reason is obscured, especially in practical matters, the will is made obdurate to evil, good actions become more difficult and concupiscence more impetuous."

Are we therefore to say that "nature" becomes totally bad, that it is wiped out, that for man evil has become his good? Not any of this has occurred, or is possible. Nature remains, and is good. There plainly is a loss to nature, but not a destruction of nature. The privation [9] resulting from the totality of sins, though serious, is the loss of "the due commensuration of reason, but is not such as to destroy the order of reason altogether; an evil that were simply evil would destroy itself, since in that case neither the substance of the act nor the affection of the agent would remain"—that is, there would be no act or agent—"if there did not remain something of reason's order." In sum: 1. Nature is disordered, nature is weakened. 2. Translated, "*corruptio*" means weakened or diminished. 3. Nature is not destroyed.

The author for one is glad to see so great a theologian and philosopher as Aquinas with an absolutely fundamental respect for human nature. "I believe in God the Father Almighty." St. Thomas might perhaps have been expected with this faith in God to have little faith in man. Whatever the expectancy, such is not the fact. Man is good. Each of his powers, such as body, intellect, or will, is by nature good. The fallen man is good, and after a thousand falls a John Dillinger remains radically good. No sin makes man evil in nature. Nature remains; since "only He who makes nature can take nature away," and God does not take it away.

The treatise on law [10] in a sort of incidental way tells the same story. In its more theoretic or static concept, law is a plan and formal cause of order; and in the practical sphere, it is a plan for action, as a traffic law, or the federal Constitution.

[9] *Summa theol.*, Ia IIae, q.73, a.2.
[10] *Ibid.*, qq.90 ff.

What the law must do is conform to human nature. This the "natural law" does: it is the way of nature and of good for man; and any civil law to qualify as law must also conform to human nature. Of course, the law of things, precisely as things—that found, say, in inorganic chemistry—automatically squares with the natures in question.

Suppose a law made in Indiana or New Guatemala does not square with human nature. Then it is not properly a law. Our nature is the rational nature, and a law that bucks our nature does not qualify. The totalitarian law of some Nero or other is "a bond of iniquity." Law to be law must mesh with our nature, and not our nature with law. *Caveat legislator!*

Another dictum often cited from St. Thomas, favoring human nature and making it the fulcrum, reads: "Man is not subordinate in all that he is and all that he has to the political community."[11]

Important texts suggest that if St. Thomas is an optimist he is far from an intemperate one. He says, for instance, that because people's senses develop before their intellects, more people follow the lead of sense than the order of reason. He says that without grace man cannot avoid mortal sin. Young people above all are inclined to undue pleasures, and discipline is needed. We cannot start off, as Rousseau supposed, doing things "in line with virtue"; we come to this, but nature does not at first without inquiry and a social tutoring come to it. Not by nature's first promptings, but by investigation we find things helpful to living well.[12]

To learn how to live and how to live as a Christian is not a knowledge that comes to us ready-made; we must acquire this virtue of *prudentia*. Living as men is absolutely required if we are to learn how to live. Good living builds up the habit; evil living destroys it in persons and societies. Delicacy of conscience

[11] *Ibid.,* q.21, a.4 ad3.
[12] *Ibid.,* q.94, a.3.

embraces the attitude that helps to foster the learning how to live as men and as Christians, and this delicacy [13] is destroyed in one who lives a passionate and evil life. The evil-living person at last does not really care. So we may say in line with cases and also with Aristotle, St. Thomas, and Spinoza. Yet, if Aristotle and Spinoza perhaps hold that the evil-doing man is on the road to becoming simply a bad man, St. Thomas holds only that the man's radically good nature becomes possessed by evil habits.

The darkest text says that more will be damned than saved.[14] St. Thomas says that only God knows how many are destined for heaven, but gives his opinion that more will be lost because, granting that most go with the common state of nature, eternal bliss is beyond nature, above all a nature lacking its original integrity.

Two texts relative to man's goodness summarize what has been said: 1. Granting that a good or a bad habit gives a new tendency to man's actions and is like second nature, still "in no one does the prudence of the flesh so dominate that the whole good of nature is destroyed (*corrumpatur*), and in the man there remains the tendency to do those actions that are of the eternal law—for it was established above that sin does not take away the whole good of nature." [15] 2. "Since the will is directed by nature to what is truly good, when through an evil act or habit or disposition a man is turned from what is truly good he acts as a slave, if we consider the natural order itself of the will." [16]

[13] *Contra Gentiles,* III, c. 122, "Aestimatio prudentiae."
[14] *Summa theol.,* Ia, q. 23, a. 7.
[15] *Ibid.,* Ia IIae, q. 93, a. 6 ad 2; cf. q. 85, a. 2.
[16] *Contra Gentiles,* IV, c. 22.

CHAPTER 8

# MARITAIN ON "MAN" AS STANDARD

THE present chapter tries to go down the center of Jacques Maritain's humanism, which he describes as Christian, personalistic, and democratic. His humanism may be justly put in the one word "man." Maritain's is a theocentric and Christocentric humanism, since he takes man to be dependent on God and especially related to God through Christ. He nowhere relinquishes theocentrism and Christocentrism. But in the first years after his conversion to Catholicism (1906) he was, for all his love and sympathy, a bit intolerant in expressing his philosophy, and tended, for instance, in *Art and Scholasticism* (which appeared in 1920), to work in a theological way from God to things and their limited, relative values.

The doctrine does not change, but the direction and method do. Waldemar Gurian has shown (*Thomist,* January, 1943; reprinted in the Maritain volume) that Maritain's more liberal, fully democratic social, political philosophy, within which his standard of values appears, is first clearly evident in 1927. From that time there is progress till, with the appearance of *True Humanism* in 1936, Maritain says that man's vocation is great enough, man in his nature and destiny is great enough and sacred enough to serve as the end and as the standard by which to measure all the goods of this world. We review his teaching on man as standard of moral and all human values as it has developed in works published between 1927 and 1951.[1]

[1] *The Things That Are Not Caesar's* (1927; tr. 1930). *Freedom and the Modern World* (1933; tr. 1936). *True Humanism* (1936; tr. 1938). *Ran-*

*True Humanism* is the most comprehensive of these works, and doctrines on values and standards expressed in other works are here put better into focus. This work is a set of lectures delivered in Spanish, and the Spanish title, "Spiritual and Temporal Problems of a New Christendom," suggests their breadth. Since it is within his doctrines on humanism, freedom, human rights, education, and the limits of political jurisdiction that Maritain expresses his theory of values and standards, we must include his statement of an intelligible if tentative pattern for a new Christendom.

Here and there we have bits of a living Christian humanism, but we wish those brought to life, integrated, and completed. Lingering medievalists, clinging to what is dead in the temporal ideal of medieval Christendom, cannot build a new vital Christian world. The past, with its goods and evils, is interred, and is no longer serviceable. We need a new temporal Christian order, and for three reasons the medieval order does not meet requirements. First, the past, however good or bad, cannot be repeated. Secondly, it is impossible for a vital thinker to suppose that the sufferings, sacrifices, and aspirations of modern man mean nothing and point in no constructive direction. Thirdly, granting that God has a plan in history, it would be to go against that plan and against God to allow to the temporal Christian order only a once-for-all univocal form and to suppose that some dead order out of the past represents the only possible good society for men. This would make static our arts and sciences, our economic, political, and social forms, and society itself.

The Church does not pass away, but civilizations do; and God does not give us or expect us to work out a universal and unchangeable social, temporal pattern, a *ne plus ultra* ideal and model. We face an earthly task, since civilization is subordinated to a temporal end; but the task is a Christian earthly one, the

---

*soming the Time* (tr. 1941). *The Rights of Man and the Natural Law* (1942; tr. 1943). *Education at the Crossroads* (1943). *Christianity and Democracy* (1943; tr. 1944). *The Person and the Common Good* (1947). *Man and the State* (1951).

civilization in question being by hypothesis Christian. The task is to work out in social and temporal terms the truth of the Gospel. And if the Gospel is primarily concerned with matters beyond sociology and philosophy, still it gives rules for conduct on which any truly Christian civilization keeps its eye. But a Christian civilization does this according to the diverse and dynamic conditions of history.

A new and vital social, temporal order is the purpose and task. To work out a basic philosophy of modern history is the philosopher's work which is of primary importance, at least in the line of intelligibility.

The end of the theoretic and also the practical task is a veritable social, temporal realization of the evangelical concern for humanity. This is the goal of the order demanded. The standard is man and the Gospel concern for man.

Surely everyone is for such a standard and end. Maritain says this is not evident. Nostalgic medievalists oppose this standard and end in any livable modern terms. So does the bourgeois mind, too easy-going to have a theory, but in practice tending to paralyze personal and social life according to the Gospel. So does a type of liberalism, in the name either of the autonomous Kantian individual or of the autonomous, immanent, self-sufficient social body. Neither autonomous individualism nor autonomous Socialism allows intervention from the outside, from revelation and grace, the tradition of human wisdom, or "the authority of a law of which man is not the author, or of a sovereign good which solicits his will, or finally of an objective reality which would measure and regulate his intelligence." Of course, each of the groups named affirms "man," but a more or less maimed and mutilated man: the mere individual, the mere collective man, the man of time only, the now impossible man out of a dead past, the bourgeois half man. The bourgeois model, for example, takes man as an economic animal and so far is one with Communism; it believes only halfheartedly and by lip service in spirit, accepts the values of science as its due; and on its ideal horizon are only the goods of time and comfort: hygiene, sanitation, vitamins, dogs and other pets, external conveniences, planes, bombs, movies, and general mechanization. The bourgeois mind desires peace without conflict, tries to replace the principle of asceticism with a technological principle, and desires an easy road to the highest goods, including social order and progress. This mind accepts the inhuman position imposed by uncontrolled capitalism on the proletariat; is well content with itself, its religion at best being a "materialized spirituality." If "man" is here the standard, it is, Maritain thinks, a somewhat truncated man.

Against such a philosophy, the dynamic forces of atheism and Communism have the game in their hands. Consider, next, the case of Communism and its affirmation of man. On the positive side, Maritain says, there is a lightning flash of truth in Marx's work. Marx saw the heteronomy and loss of freedom produced in the capitalist world by wage slavery, and the dehumanization of both the possessing class and the proletariat. "Heteronomy" is the word to cover the fact that men hired in industry have almost no say; all is arranged for them, run by someone else, and thus in the work and its products the men are run by someone else and do not operate fully as human persons. This dehumanizing heteronomy is what Marx saw. But he immediately conceptualized it into an exclusively anthropocentric and monist metaphysic, and said that the economic and material cause is the whole cause, and that this dehumanization must cease in the name, not of human personality, but of the collective man.

The trouble with each type of modern humanism is not that it is, at least to some degree, truly a humanism, but that it is partial and, therefore, in a measure an untrue, because incomplete, theory of man. At the center of a genuine and integral humanism must be "man," not the fake man of materialized bourgeois spirituality, nor the maimed man in the all-collective robot of Communism cut off from human freedom and from man's roots in God.

As a rapid historical summary, Maritain names three moments of modern humanism. The first was in the sixteenth and seventeenth century, when human reason thought it could set up by its own force a truly human order, to be conceived nevertheless in the earlier pattern. This was the *classical* moment of modern culture, the time of Christian naturalism, and one may suppose that typical of its assumptions was Descartes, who meant to operate in *puris naturalibus* and at the same time to be a philosopher and a Christian, but not a Christian philosopher. The next moment, roughly of course, was in the two following centuries, when it was seen that a culture apart from the supreme supernatural dimensions must take up arms against these. Civilization was asked to free man from revealed religion and let him feel his natural goodness, understood in a Rousseauistic sense, and at the same time open up vistas of perfect security to this all-sufficient rational animal. This is the moment of rationalistic *optimism,* the bourgeois hour of modern culture, into which we have been born, rather than into the classical or the hour after the bourgeois. To this moment belong Voltaire and the rationalists, Hume and the sensists, Rousseau and his sentimental humanism, the utilitarians, secularistic pragmatists and all the half-Christians. The third, into which we have entered in various degrees, is the moment of *revolution.* Socialism stands between the humanitarian-bourgeois hour and this last; on its right it is bourgeois and looks for some sort of minor heaven on easy terms, and on its left it yields to progress and perfection by revolution. In this third moment, man sets his last end in himself, and because he will not bear the injustices of the world he makes a desperate effort, out of a radical atheism, to achieve a new humanity.

Let us see what, in terms of human being and human good, in terms of "man," these moments become. The first is a reversal in the order of ends; the proper good of culture, which is earthly happiness, is not directed toward eternal life. On the contrary, culture seeks its supreme good in itself and in the domination of matter, God not being simply ruled out, but allowed as witness and guarantor of this domination. The second is like "a demiurgic imperialism" relative to the forces of matter, and instead of man's prime endeavor being to perfect his nature by a process in line with the deepest demands of his being and by the inner development of a wisdom penetrating action and knowledge, he sets out to subordinate all to a mastery of outer nature by technological processes.

The third is of interest on both its positive and negative sides. It protests with vigor against the bourgeois mind and is more aware than is this of what it does. The third is terribly destructive of man, nevertheless, because on principle as well as in fact it is "the progressive forcing back of the human by the material." Why cannot this moment be taken apart from its atheism? Simply because "as it exists" in Communism, it is at its core atheist: it is a system of doctrine and of life; it claims to reveal the meaning of existence and answer the fundamental questions; it manifests an unequalled power of totalitarianism. It is not the sickly thing that the bourgeois mind is, from which however Maritain says it is sprung (it would "out-bourgeois" the bourgeois, to cite Berdyaev,[2] of whose thought Maritain makes much use). But it is radically destructive of man.

To scold these types of humanism is not enough. Our task is to determine the lineaments, not of the Church or of Christianity, but of a new social, temporal Christian order.

Why not a theocracy something like that of ancient Israel or of the Middle Ages? A consecrational concept of our world is now out of the question. Maritain says that with St. Augustine's help the Middle Ages boldly laid down a solution of our doing evil, of God's permitting evil, and the value of man's temporal and secular work; but did not advance far into those obscure problems, and St. Thomas's handling of them came centuries too late. The result was, and to a degree remains, a pessimistic

[2] N. Berdyaev, *The Russian Revolution:* Its implications in Religion and Psychology (New York: Sheed and Ward, 1931).

imagery, too simple a dramatization of fallen human nature, of the divine election and our destiny, and "a certain theological inhumanity," ideas of which Calvin and Molina were to make the most.

What we need is to go with and to exploit in man's favor the main positive demand of our time. Above all, this demand is for freedom, but the end is at once something more inclusive and more circumspect than the word "freedom," often uncritically used, suggests. Man fundamentally wants God, and under errant and perverse forms man still acts for this end. More intimately within himself the end man wishes and desires is to be. He desires to be man, and fully to be man. Now man by nature is a person, and by nature he demands to be fully and thoroughly a human person. Never have conditions allowed every man, especially the poor and common man, the chance to be all that his nature desires him to be. Fortunately, in modern times he has progressively become conscious of, though vaguely and ineffectively conscious of, this implacable gnawing desire. Man desires to be what by nature he is supposed to be. Modern Western man, more than man of other times and places, is conscious of this natural desire.

In Maritain's statement: "A certain divine exigence torments the modern world." This comes to an awareness, a certain practical discovery of man's proper dignity, hidden in the depths of his being. Much progress has been made toward the realization of the demand, as expressed in various human-rights programs, a progress especially in the world of reflexion and of self-consciousness, and the result has been to renew to some degree through art, science, and even the vices and passions, the proper spirituality of man. The drawback is that this progress has often been prompted by a spirit of exclusive anthropocentrism, by a naturalistic concept of man, and has been accomplished not under unity, but under all kinds of division.

In positive terms, what the new order would be may be put into the phrase, "a Christian personalism." This means that from the outset the new order would respect above all the human person in his nature and his liberties. It would be a communal order, in the sense of having as rightful and specifying end (of its myriad activities) the common good, with its social policy essentially directed to such conditions as would allow men generally the chance to reach a level of material, moral, and intellectual life in accord with the good and peace of all, and positively assist each in the conquest of a full personal life and spiritual liberty. But the common good itself must respect the supratemporal ends of the human person. It is true that each person is to the community as a part to the whole and is in some ways subordinate to it, and yet, despite the collectivistic rampage in our time, man is not subordinate, in all that he is and all that he has, to the political community.[8]

Communal, as serving the common good, personalist, as respecting the rights of the human person and putting some of these above the state, Christian, as seeing the human person not as absolute either in his individual or his social capacity: such is the story so far; but this is not the whole story of a modern social, temporal Christian order. As personalist, it must look more effectively, if perhaps not more consciously, to the liberties of the person than do many contemporary attempts at order. It must see his liberties as sacred by nature, and also afford him, precisely for his development as a person, access to economic goods. "Primarily by reason of the needs of human personality considered as working in and elaborating matter in subjecting it to the forms of reason," the appropriation of such goods should be private, even though the primal destination of material goods is the benefit of the human species. This aspect of a truly human order, namely, the common good of all, was lost in the era of liberal individualism, and we need not be surprised by the century-old drift toward Socialism.

The reaction toward collectivisms is abnormal, and disastrous. People who give personality the value it deserves and understand

[8] *Summa theol.,* Ia IIae, q.21, a.4 ad 3.

how precarious is its condition and how constantly it is menaced by environment, will see that the law of personal appropriation, in a strictly individual or a social form, is no less imperious than that of common use. The remedy for the abuses of individualism in the use of ownership must be sought, not in its abolition but in the diffusion, the popularization of the defenses which it builds around the person. The point is to give each person the concrete possibility of achieving the advantages of private ownership, in ways which can remain very diverse, but do not exclude necessary collectivizations; the evil is to reserve these advantages to a small number of privileged individuals.

For persons to own is the personalistic redemption of economic goods. To democratize the good of ownership and to obtain the human values possible in and through it, we need not run into any form of state ownership or Communism, but what is needed is "a form (as I think) of *association* that ownership should take in the sphere of industrial economy." In his great essay on "Human Equality" (chapter 1 of *Ransoming the Time*), Maritain says he is far from arguing for a sentimental and impossible absolute egalitarianism, but does argue for a realist social equality, including universal rights in the political and economic orders as something to be developed on the basis of man's "unity and equality in nature." In the industrial sphere the result would be copartnership instead of the payroll.

Of course, we would like to have this freer situation arise from generosity and joy in work, but for fallen humanity such a result is never easy. It would have to proceed also from self-interest, not in an egotistic and grasping sense, but self-interest taught to look to the common good and transformed by a sense of human communion. What is radically wanted is to emancipate and deproletarianize man. Perhaps we can achieve this end only gradually and in a relative and a permanently precarious sense. But as stewards and pedagogues of the human person we may not aim lower.

Our temporal community must live in terms of the common

good. But service of this good should not be forced; it should be based on brotherly love and look to the realization of a fraternal life. Where would it get its dynamism? From love, and from the idea of man's dignity as a person; from the person's spiritual vocation and the love due to it. The task of the state would be to work out a temporal order conforming to that dignity, that vocation, and that love; a task "arduous, paradoxical, heroic: it claims no tepid humanism." And though we may not ask the state to make all men good and full of love for one another, we demand that its social structures, laws, and institutions be in line with such an amity.

With many ideologies among men and nations, many theologies and religions, and many political and economic systems, how can Maritain think it possible to achieve, let us not say amity and brotherhood, but so much as the turning of our main social energies toward the common good?

His reply is a main feature of his social philosophy. Neither now nor in the near future can we reach the unity of the thirteenth century. In reasonableness we may aim only at minimal, not maximal unity. By no means will we in a good modern society have merely individualistic ownership, for example, or merely collective ownership. Economic evolution and technical developments allow and call for much corporate as well as much individual ownership, but also for a family economy, and again for a cooperative economy, and a trade-union style of organization to help control work, industry, and ownership, and also for some general collectivization. This is a mixed and "pluralist" economy. We must accept "pluralism" in many fields, such as politics, education, and religion; within the social and political body, groups should be encouraged to exist and operate in freedom, for their own good and the good of the whole. We may not think of shutting unbelievers or Christians or Jews outside the freedoms of the city. All are to live and share together in the same temporal commonwealth. For peace and liberty of conscience, the state should tolerate, though it need not approve, ways of worship that do not conform on all points to the truth, and ways of conceiving the meaning of life and modes of behavior. Of course, it must oppose errors threatening its life and the common good. We would get a "pluriform juridical structure," and though the whole would point toward integral Christianity and be vitally Christian, non-Christian groups within it would enjoy liberty. In the concrete, the Irish Free State has tried to carry out a pluralism, and Maritain says in his work on the rights of man that the Declaration of Independence keeps close to "the originally Christian character of human rights."

The new vital Christian order would be "peregrinal." Man has here only an equilibrium of tension and movement, and his social, temporal life demands genuine heroism. Yet temporal civilization, not a mere means to eternal life, has a being, a good, an autonomy, and an end of its own. This autonomy is not absolute, but its end enjoys the dignity of a high secondary "infra-valent" place.

In sum, the Christian social, temporal order would be communal, peregrinal, pluralist, and personalist. Its purpose would be the development of the person in and with the society created by him and his fellows for their common good. The claims of persons are first, and some of these claims are supreme and may not be touched by any political community. Persons are free to hold any nonsubversive ideologies and faiths; persons and groups belong together and have liberties and responsibilities in the temporal *convivium*. Life in this type of society would have an end not totally autonomous, and would be communal because aimed primarily at the common good of all.

This, Maritain says, is tentative, an effort to determine the main features of a society adequate at once to the exigencies of man and the exigencies of our era.

What would be its standard of human values? Maritain says "Man." Let us see how he elaborates this reply.

Maritain speaks "in the interests of the person" and "the supratemporal interests of the person," and for that reason "personalism" better describes his position than does "humanism," to say nothing of moribund "individualism." Man, or the human person, is to be the measure of things, and not vice versa. "Thus a St. Francis understood that, before being exploited by our industry to our use, material nature demands in some way to be itself familiarized by our love: I mean that in loving things and the being in them man should rather draw things up to the human level than reduce humanity to their measure."

Politics in its theoretic and practical aspects exists for the good of man, and "this good is essentially human, and thus is measured above all by reference to the ends of the human being." That end is not, as with Croce, a bundle of utilities, but is an end, namely, the good and worthy social life, and to achieve this is "a good and worthy common task for men to accomplish."

Not to man, however, do we tend to refer things in our time, when everything "is referred to standards which are not human but external to man: to the laws of material production, to a technical domination of nature, to the utilization of all the resources of the world for the fecundity of money. In a truly humanist condition of culture, it would be to man and his standard that the things of the world would be referred."

We must make machines serve men, and choose between an essentially industrial-financial civilization and an essentially human one for which industry and its triumphs would have the function of means only.

In this light, the aim of planning would be a political and economic wisdom subordinated to "a science of freedom . . . and in continuity with the nature of human beings." Given a Christian philosophy of man, of work, and ownership, our whole outlook on basic social problems is changed.

In the concrete, the doctrine on standards comes to the following. Modern civilization would hardly stand a patching up. What is needed is "a total and substantial reformation, a transvaluation of its cultural principles." With "man" as standard, here is part of the order suggested by Maritain:

the primacy of quality over quantity
the primacy of work, i.e. workmanship, over money
the primacy of the human over technological means
the primacy of wisdom over science
the primacy of the common service of man over unlimited riches
the primacy of that same service over the state's unlimited power.

Man is great enough. Man in his nature as a person with a demand to give and to receive personal love and to achieve wisdom and to order his universe: this man is great enough. Man as thus like God is great enough so that all the goods of this world are to be measured in terms of him, and not man in terms of them. Man in his calling or vocation is great enough, in his calling to work out a humanized and Christianized world of wisdom and love and in his freedom to direct all the goods of time to an end and good beyond time. In these senses man is great enough, and is the measure.

Maritain is not a secularist, because the man of rationalism and secularism is an unrealistic and even an unreal man and because, though man is a person and controls and orders things, man remains a limited person, able to know God and direct himself toward God, but unable to be God. Really to know, really to make technological developments serve man and to build economic and political systems fit to serve the higher good of the person: such is the work of man, who is truly the measure, the orderer, and the end for all the goods of this world.

We close with a summary [4] of Maritain on the rights of man:

A. The Rights of the *Human Person*
    1. The right to existence
    2. The right to personal liberty

[4] Two undergraduates did this summary, and found the standard used, as a term paper. Source: Maritain's *The Rights of Man and Natural Law* (Tr., Scribners, 1943; the quotation, from page 81, is inexact).

3. The right to pursuit of perfection
4. The right to the pursuit of eternal life
5. The right of the Church to free exercise of spiritual activity
6. The right to pursue a religious vocation
7. The right to marry
8. The right of the human family to receive respect for its constitution
9. The right to keep one's body whole
10. The right to property
11. The right of human persons to be treated as persons, not things

B. The Rights of the *Civic Person*

1. The right of all citizens to participate in political life
2. The right of the people to establish a constitution and choose a government
3. The right of association
4. The right of free investigation
5. The right of political equality
6. The right to an independent judiciary power
7. The right to equal possibility of admission to public employment

C. The Rights of the *Working Person*

1. The right to choose one's own work
2. The right to form trade unions
3. The right to be considered an adult
4. The right of economic groups to freedom and autonomy
5. The right to a just wage
6. The right to work
7. The right to relief
8. The right to a participation in the elementary goods, material and spiritual, of civilization

D. *The Standard of the Human Person*

"The consciousness of the rights of the person (and of the Civic and working person as well) has its origin in the conception of man and the Natural Law established by centuries of Christian Philosophy."

## CHAPTER 9

# KANT ON STANDARD AND END

THE standard, or formal principle, and again the materials, and the agent: all these lead to, make way for, and really are subordinated to, the end; but none of them is the end.

It is convenient that Kant handles together problems of the standard and of the end, or highest good, and that the materials are assembled by Abbott in *Fundamental Principles of the Metaphysic of Ethics*.[1] Kant is formalistic and legalistic. He seeks a kind of disembodied form in a vacuum and has little interest in any possible content. He falls into a rigid formalism, an extreme which neither Greek morals nor Greek art suffered, but which late medieval morals did suffer. If Kant mishandles problems of ends and standards, it is all the more lamentable, since in important senses he is the greatest of modern moral philosophers. In his upbringing Kant is a Pietist, and he retains a Calvinist mind, somewhat severe toward human nature. He has slight regard for the data relevant to human nature; as he says, he does not care about any tendency or the totality of tendencies in our nature. Nor, he says, does he care what the sciences of man, then called by the literal word "anthropology," may have to say about man.

Thus Kant is particularly antimodern, as we notice when we recall that even the great deductionists, Descartes, Hobbes, and Spinoza, made notable overtures toward observation and induction, that Bacon's name in this new lead is immortal, that Locke

[1] "Extracted from *Kant's Critique of Practical Reason,* and other works on the theory of ethics." Tenth edition; new impression. Longmans, 1926.

meant what he said when he used the word "historical" and factual—"in matter of fact"—of his method, and that many recent philosophers, such as Meyerson in epistemology, Durkheim in philosophy of religion, Pareto in social philosophy, Dawson and Luigi Sturzo in social philosophy, in great part rest their several cases on a wealth of observed fact. No such method for Kant.

Our own position, as expressed in the chapters on Aristotle, on the completion of Aristotle, on the standard, and Maritain on "man" as standard, is that man's fundamental tendencies, as individual and as social, give us the best light on what man is, what the form and rule of conduct is, and what, from a sociotemporal point of view, is the end for man. Form and end in nature can never be known and studied at firsthand, and can be discovered only by scrutiny of man's activities and his fundamental tendencies. In all cases, tendencies tell about nature, and tendencies and nature tell about the end; and form must be such as to lead to the end. In nature as in art, "form follows function"; because the end is such and such, so too, and in line with it, must be the form.

Kant does not believe in the law of finding ends and forms from natures; and he begins his study of conduct by shelving a method so native to man's mind.

Look at these remarkable statements. Everyone, he says, must admit that "the basis of obligation must not be sought in the nature of man, or in the circumstances in the world in which he is placed, but a priori simply in the conceptions of pure reason; and although any other precept that is founded on principles of mere experience may be in certain respects universal, yet, in as far as it rests even in the least degree on an empirical basis, perhaps only as to a motive, such a precept, while it may be a practical rule, can never be called a moral law." "For, in order that an action should be morally good, it is not enough that it should *conform* to the moral law, but it must also be done *for the sake of the law,* otherwise that conformity is only very contingent and uncertain." "I limit the question suggested to this: Whether it is not of the utmost necessity to construct a pure moral philosophy, perfectly cleared of everything which is only empirical, and which belongs to anthropology?"

The empirical, the experiential is irrelevant to Kant's study of ethics. Kant desires an ethics foreign to this world. This is, partly at least, because of his rather severe and forced religious background. But it is rooted also in an error about "will" in relation to "nature." When Kant sees that will with its "ought" is not duplicated in the subvolitional, he concludes that will does not belong to nature at all. As pointed out by St. Thomas, the will, though radically different in kind from lower natures, is a particular nature. Why should we not study it as we study other natures, beginning with experience and observing its activities and tendencies? A priori study of the will seems no more justified than a priori studies in physics or biology.

On the standard of conduct Kant is famous, and even his phrase for it, the "Categorical Imperative," as well as two of its three interrelated expressions, has made history. One of these formulations of the standard Kant has stated in this way: Always treat human nature, whether in thyself or another, as an end, and never as a means.

This seems tremendous, and not merely attractive. It makes an appeal to "all that is best in us," and those concerned with the spiritual bases of the universe have commonly liked it. Some Catholic philosophers, for example the late John A. Ryan, use the principle with effectiveness. Treat man never as a means, but simply and totally as an end.

It is proper to be impressed with the categorical imperative in this form, but not to accept it. It tells us what to do and what not to do, even if, as Kant intends, only in the most general terms; it appears to urge and boost man, to compliment and eulogize him. But taken universally it is not sound and its hortatory tone and the sense of human dignity suggested by it are misleading. The trouble is that we cannot obey the command.

Every day and every hour we use human nature, in ourselves and others, just as Kant, at least if understood literally, told us not to use it. We do this and must do it. We use our intellects as means, though intellect is integral and specific to us. We use our wills as means, and our bodily powers, though will and bodily powers are integral to human nature. Let Kant or any one try for one waking hour not to use body and will and intellect as means!

Besides, we use others. We use their strength, time, and labor to get lunch for us, to drive buses for us, and run engines, to grow potatoes, to serve as catcher when we pitch and as pitcher when we catch. We use their wills and, of course, their good will, their intellects, and their bodily powers. Not that we exploit people; not that we may misuse the person either in ourselves or others; but that is a second question. The truth is that we use and must use people. That is the way of the real human world, and we have no acquaintance with a world where Kant's categorical imperative would fit.

In the light of practice, Kant's principle, which sounds so well, does not make sense. Any principle that tells us "categorically" to do what we cannot do, must be at best legalistic and formalistic, a mere form, empty and unreal, incapable of content. At bottom, it is meaningless. It may suffice in paradise, but not in the world of human relationships, the world of "anthropology" discarded at the outset by Kant. The result would be different if Kant were to make distinctions. If Kant were to say that in certain aspects, such as some of its freedoms, human nature is sacrosanct and not to be invaded and used as a means, we could agree. Our strictures on so great a thinker as Kant are bold; but when one reads Kant with ordinary care, he sees that Kant himself comes to doubt the possibility of the categorical imperative in this first form.

Kant soon begins to back away from his unrestricted statement and to use the modifier "merely." Rational beings, he says, are called persons, "because their very nature points them out as ends in themselves, that is as something which must not be used merely as means . . . not merely subjective ends whose existence has a worth *for us* . . . but *objective ends* . . . : an end moreover for which no other can be substituted, which they should subserve merely as means . . . that the subject of all ends, i.e., the rational being himself, be never employed merely as means, but as the supreme condition restricting the use of all means, that is in every case as an end likewise."

In his first sweeping statement of the form for conduct Kant is unreal and is outside the human world. One wonders whether the doctrine of end-in-itself is dictated by the individualism flourishing in Kant's and Adam Smith's day.

His second statement of the categorical imperative reads as follows: Act in such a way that thy action may serve as a universal law for mankind. What he means is not only that "thou" shouldst be willing that the act would be taken as form and law for anyone acting in such a situation, but that such a rule must be possible as a universal principle and that the world of human relations could operate on such a principle. Kant says: Let us suppose that a man does not use his talents. Such a person, of course, might be willing that no one should use talents, but the human world could not operate on this principle, once it were universalized as law. So, too, a person might wish to dodge debts or even be tempted to commit suicide in the face of difficulties. But our world could not operate on a universalized principle of dodging debts or of committing suicide, and thus an act of this type cannot be the form and rule of morality.

Kant is here much closer to reality. The only question is whether, supposing the present statement of his principle to be valid, either for all actions or for certain ones, this condition obtains because Kant's law possesses an a priori and self-evident character, or because man possesses a certain kind of being.

We come now to Kant's doctrine on "the good without qualification." As a rule, Kant is a difficult and forbidding author, both in the style and the content of his philosophy. But he says in a rousing statement that on earth and in heaven just one thing is good without qualification. Just one thing can be. This one thing is a good will. Gifts of mind are certainly good and gifts of character, and virtue, health and wealth, fame and position, and wit and genius. But any of them can on occasion be exceedingly mischievous and bad. It can be and it is, if there is lacking the circumstance and complement of a good will. Intellect's good is allowed by Kant to be good; and moderation and coolness and poise, lauded so much (Kant notes) by the ancients, are good, too, but, in a gangster, any of these can be bad. Health is a great and intimate good, but can be used to wreck the person and others; as can fortune and friends. Not so with a good will.

Not a good intellect, then, or any of its products is the good without qualification, says Kant, and the sole good that always and everywhere unqualifiedly is worthy of this unique position is a good will.

But why is a good will good? He says it is good not because of something effected or to be effected by it, and Kant shies away not only from any approach to pragmatism (suggested in the second statement of the categorical imperative), but from the faintest breath of teleology, the doctrine of end seeking in nature. Kant says the will is good not because any end is fulfilled or to be fulfilled and not because this will goes with the tendency or the totality of tendencies in human nature. He says the will is good by itself, in itself, by the merit of its own volition. It is not good for, and not good of, but simply good.

This is Kant in his most formal dress. What are we to think of his pronouncements? What of his bypassing history, anthropology, and psychology to get to the will good in itself?

What, if anything, is good in itself, and for that reason is not a means at all, but the end and supreme good? What would "a good will" itself be? Why does Kant remain aloof from the problem of defining or delimiting what he takes as the unqualified good? It is true that he does suggest a reason, even while he says so vigorously that there is no reason. The good will is not *good because,* but is simply good. That is his constant teaching. He does nevertheless say that other goods, such as health, wealth, and knowledge, can be misused and are therefore not good without qualification, and he implies that the good will is good without qualification, because it cannot be misused. Here again Kant raises several questions. First, what is a good will, and is it good solely in itself and without a why or wherefore? Is there some good that is unqualified, and if so, is a good will in every instance such a good? If the human will turns out to be this good, and thus to be the end, has Kant identified it with God?

As for the will's act, we must say that, in spite of Kant, its being good depends on circumstances. There is no human will that in its acts is good in a void. Man's will in its acts is good or bad in a particular case, and it is good *if* and *when* and *because.* It is good because it lines up with the standard and end. It is good when it does so, and so far as it does so. If it so lines up, it is good; if, and only if. To bring out the point, we shall review St. Thomas' doctrine on the will and its object, and see what, in his view, makes the will's act good. The negative side is first stated.

Evil in the will's act "is preceded by lack of subordination to reason, and to the proper end of the will: to reason, for instance when the will, on the sudden apprehension of one of the senses, tends to a good that is pleasant to the sense," but is not then in line with reason; "to the due end of the will," for example, when intellect considers and sees that a good is, after all, not good now or in some particular way, "and yet the will tends to that good as though it were its proper good." This voluntary lack of order is the evil in the present act of the will.[2] For the will [3] is the desire of a previously known good. Accordingly, good in the will is the will's squaring in its action with "man,"

[2] *Contra Gentiles,* III, c. 10.
[3] *Ibid.,* c. 16.

with the rational, which is the specifying factor in man, or with the end. But what is this "due end of will"?

For reply we take a statement of St. Thomas [4] where he outdoes the Kantian tautology. "Man is good by the fact that he has a good will, by which he actualizes whatever of good there is in him. And the will is good by the fact that it wills good, and most of all the highest good, which is the end. The more then his will wills a good of this kind, the more is the man good." The end completely fulfilling the will and standing as end is God, the end fulfillment and love fulfillment of nature and of human nature. For though in its subpersonal way the rest of nature compulsorily seeks this end, man's will is said [5] not to be right or "good" until, guided by intelligence, it freely and personally seeks God as end. Thus to seek and love the end which is God, is the rightness and goodness par excellence of man's will.

St. Thomas is committing himself on several points. First the human will's goodness is a "because-goodness," an "if-and-when goodness," and not an unrelated goodness. Next, an attempt is made to circumscribe the good of man's will. This will may have other tests of its goodness, but is certainly good when and if and because it wills good, and most of all the highest good. Contrary at every turn to Kant's doctrine of unrelated good will is this Thomistic position. It is the will as related, and as related in such and such a way, that is good; no other human will can be good in its act. Above all, the end, or object willed, makes the will's act good.

No doubt it is this question, of related or unrelated, that Kant has in mind. But the form of his reply, in terms of "the unqualified good," at least seems to raise another question. How good is a good will?

It is one of the unavoidable facts of our being and living that we must evaluate goods up and down on a scale. We must make or "take" a hierarchy of them, and waiving now how far

[4] *Ibid.*, c. 116.
[5] *De veritate,* 22, a. 2.

we make the gradation of goods and how far we "take" it as given in nature, we cannot see all goods as on a level. Perpetually we find or make a value order, and therefore use some formal cause, and since ours is a complicated world where most people see only secondary and tertiary causes, we use a plurality of formal causes for the value order. At present we shirk the task of looking for the formal cause of the total value order, and confine our attention to St. Thomas' statement on the outline of this order in terms of the end. What is the truly unqualified good, and how does a good will rank among the goods commonly accessible to man?

The end is the highest and chief good. It is automatically in a class by itself, and any other good is a means, and while it may be of extraordinary excellence it is good as rightly related to the end. But the end is, strictly speaking, the good, which is to say only that whereas other goods, such as a house, an education, a friend, obviously and rightly on a hundred occasions are ends, still in the justest description they can be only means, and therefore are always of secondary goodness. None of them can be "simply good," and any of them has to be a good with qualification: good indeed, but good because and if and when; good with a grain of salt.

Where does the goodness of a good will land in this shuffle? If the end is God, in terms of us the end is God-to-be-enjoyed; it is blessedness or felicity, which is our enjoyment of God in an immediate knowledge-and-love association with Him. Other things are good at the time we are in transit toward that end if they help us toward that end, and just so far as they help us toward it. In the passage we are using (*Contra Gentiles,* III, c. 141), St. Thomas is in disagreement with Aristotle, who had said that intellectual good is better for man than the good of the will. Aristotle said this on the seemingly irrefutable ground that reason causes us to be what we specifically are, and the will's goodness, at least in one of its tests, consists in its living up to the light of reason. St. Thomas says "Amen," but goes on to say—and Kant would be committed to saying with him—that it all depends on "when" and "where." In itself, St. Thomas says that the intellect's life is better: this is to speak absolutely; and also when we see God face to face, intellectual life is better. But relatively speaking, or in relation to the circumstances of our life while we are in transit to the end, intellectual goodness does not so surely lead to the end as does the will's goodness. Here we meet the old paradox that a man of good intellect, such as artist, mathematician, or historian, can be a bad man, and fail to be on the road to the end. On the other hand, a good will, which must conform to the light of intellect, is indefectibly making progress toward the end. This is all it can do, and if the will fails in this, it is certainly not a good will; and it does not matter, on either the positive, creative side or the negative, destructive side, whether we refer to the good disposition of the will, to some or all of its good habits or only to one good act. In each case the man by having a good will, goes surely toward the end. Whether the man having a good intellect does or does not go toward the end, we cannot say in advance.

The sum of the argument so far is that, with the end as the supreme good, a good will is the best means, because the only indefectible means. A good intellect with all its proper achievements is next. After these goods is the good of a strong and healthy body, which not only is the best servant of intellect and will, but is itself an inner and proper good of man, and falls into third place among all good means. Least and last of goods are external goods, which are goods precisely because we are able to use them as auxiliaries to inner goods such as health and virtue.

This ranking of human values may be charted summarily:

I. The sovereign good of man: his peak blessedness.
II. a) Nearest to this is moral virtue and whatever helps to-

ward the good operation of man whereby he comes to blessedness.

b) The due disposition of reason and of the powers subordinated to it.

c) Bodily health.

d) Exterior goods.

On this view, how good is goodness of the will? It is the unqualifiedly good means, but it is only a means and is not to be mistaken for the end. Means as such is a qualified good. A good will is the best means, the one indefectible means; as Kant says, unlike gifts of intellect and of the body, the will can never be misused; but any virtue of intellect or of will can be made an object of evil, for example, a person can hate science or justice or be proud of them; but no one can "make a bad use of a virtue as a principle of action, in such a way that an act of virtue would be evil." [6] As means, a good will is automatically qualified: means is not the end, the unqualified. Besides, it is only the unqualifiedly good human means. This modifier "human" again qualifies its goodness, because man who is qualified, relative, dependent in being, cannot be unqualified and absolute in goodness, and thus what is the unqualifiedly good means for him is a doubly qualified good.

It is qualified a) as means, and b) as of man, in man, by and for man. Nothing in man, or by man, for or of man, can be greater than man, and man is qualified in his being and consequently in his goodness.

In sum, it seems just to say that Kant's initial mistake in the matter of the end and the standard lies in his refusal to bring his philosophy of man out of the a priori and unreal mould he has given it, and in his refusal to submit it to the light of what we know of man from observing the tendencies, demands, and direction naturally in man, and what we can know of man's

[6] *Summa theol.*, Ia IIae, q. 55, a. 4 ad 5.

nature from such sciences as history, anthropology, and psychology. We may say in passing that, not for arts and sciences, but for the good use of arts or sciences—products of intellectual virtues—man must have a good will, and this is a will directed and subordinated to the end.[7]

[7] *Ibid.*, q.57, a.3; a.4.

# PART II

# THE STANDARD OF MORALITY APPLIED TO CASES

## CHAPTER 10

# ETHICS AND NATURAL RESOURCES

THE good life, because it includes man's total innate and acquired disposition toward good, has many beauties, many aspects, many virtues. Though only the acts of our freedom with their habits and dispositions come directly into the moral world, indirectly any act or object on which our freedom can operate is matter for the moral order. Included are such objects as science, philosophy, art, God, pleasures, friends, economic goods; anything precisely as an object of freedom.

We wish to consider particular objects, so as to see how the standard already affirmed is applicable. Morality is order, immorality is disorder, and the business of ethics as a science is to see how human life in its freedom naturally makes a fundamental sense and has a good direction. In Santayana's words, ethics is the science of all good and of how it can be accomplished.

How does the standard apply to various fields: to the life of ownership, the life of worship, the life of learning, the life of play and work, the life of love, friendship, and family, the political life, the life of pleasures and of pains? [1] This chapter considers population and natural resources.

Two features have been outstanding in regard to natural resources in the United States. The first is incredibly rapid development; the second is waste. A third that becomes more conspicuous with each census is imbalance in control over re-

[1] See the remarkable work, *The Good Life,* by E. Jordan (Chicago University Press, 1949).

sources: the very rich against the very poor; richer and richer against poorer and poorer.

At least to some degree, man is obliged to develop resources: those of nature and those in himself.[2] He has not a title to either in fee simple; he has not a right to be profligate with his health, his eyes, or bodily powers, his mind or will. All these are given to him by nature and God, by his family and society. He is a kind of god and exists, relatively, to himself. But at every turn he is subject to God, is a child of God, accountable for the talents he has as this child. Within this duty to serve God according to his powers and opportunities is the duty to serve society; and in later chapters we shall see details of his duty to society.

Even in a primitive status men are bound to develop natural resources. These are given in a raw condition, and often it takes energy, ingenuity, and sacrifice to convert them into food and better food, into shelter and clothes. Even to secure these most needed external goods, men must have already converted nature's raw goods into tools, boats, wagons.

Primitive man needs instruments to secure and condition basic necessities. We may not say that man as such is morally bound to do more than be a good man, which is possible with little of this world's goods. However, he does at last go from savagery to barbarism and then to a semicivilized state, whether or not he is bound to do so.

Is the savage morally obligated to use his intelligence, his will, his powers, and the resources of the earth in such a way that in his progeny he will become at least a barbarian? If we say "yes," on what reasoning do we base our reply? And then are barbarians bound to try to become semicivilized? What are the radical obligations of the semicivilized with regard to natu-

[2] Though man, as everything else, belongs to "nature" and has "a nature," he is unique and justifies the modern terms "nature" and "man," the ancient terms "nature" and "art," the medieval terms "nature" and "will."

ral resources? What persons are bound to try to secure and develop these?

Anyone who needs natural resources in such a way that he cannot live without them must try, within the limits of human nature, to secure them. This fact includes everyone in the normal democratic society, where few are economic aristocrats. It requires no formal or deep reasoning to show men that they need things that they may live.

Things are given in nature. Regarding the use of them by man, things can be made better or worse by man. In the process of control and use, man can husband them, or can make them practically useless. Since man cannot live without them, the way they are preserved is a question of ethics and not merely of pressure cookers. Man lives in part by bread, and to turn wheat into whitened soggy bread, de-enriched and re-enriched, is to act against the good of man. The good wheat given by God and nature and man, is more or less ruined. So of other foods: notably sugar.

But sugar and wheat are secondary and processed. Much more serious is the fact that Americans have destroyed primary natural resources. Over the last two hundred years, our fathers and grandfathers have washed more good soil into the Gulf of Mexico than any other nation ever possessed. In the present state of science, little of this can be fished out or in any way recovered. We still plunder the earth as vandals, as if it were not God's earth that we husband and use, but ours to destroy.

This conduct is contrary to any standards we have reason to approve: to the standard of man or human nature, to God's will, to the pragmatic standard. This conduct will not, even in the medium long run, work. It is as clearly as anything against God's will, if we are in any important matter God's stewards. It will not aid men to develop and grow strong in strong societies. Yet nature demands such growth.

Consider what we do in many states. In Illinois we allow strip mining. This means that the soil, which otherwise might be used for the next hundred years and the next hundred thousand years, is permanently destroyed in order to get quick profits. The standard used is easily seen, and also the immorality. Iowa, Kentucky, Minnesota, Ohio, Indiana,[3] and, without a doubt, other states have allowed the same antihuman action. Some of the topsoil destroyed is only three or four inches deep; nevertheless, it belongs to man, and no king or pope or profitseeker has the right to destroy it. Much of the topsoil destroyed in northern Illinois coal mining is more than twenty inches deep, some of the best soil on earth. Its destruction has already, following War II, meant suffering for thousands, and it will always continue to result in human hunger.

Farming in the United States has, like strip mining, meant the destruction of soil. Most of us still have the impression that American resources, in soil, water, coal, timber, iron, and oil, are inexhaustible. One of the best timber areas we then had, that in upper Michigan and Wisconsin and northeastern Minnesota, was turned into quick profits following World War I, and the same quick-profit destruction probably occurred during and after World War II in the timber of Oregon and Washington. In 1620 virgin forests covered roughly fifty per cent of what is now United States territory; by 1850 nearly half of them were gone; by 1940 not ten per cent remained.[4]

The dangerous line of thought is that which is based on the wrong standard: the quicker and bigger the profits, the better; let society's future look out for itself!

We cannot build and maintain a strong nation in that way; we cannot live normally without adequate resources; we cannot do our material part for international good unless we have resources. A washed-out soil lacks mineral content and cannot put mineral content into food raised on it. Lack of fluorine or of

[3] Some allow strip mining only if topsoil is saved and replaced.

[4] U.S. Forestry Service. Cf. Ollie E. Fink, *Conservation for Tomorrow's America* (Columbus, Ohio: Ohio Div. of Conservation and Natural Resources, 2nd printing, April 1943), p. 57.

iodine in soil or water, or the presence of either, makes the point evident. In some regions of Florida, soil is devoid of iron and sixty-eight to ninety per cent of the children are suffering from anemia.[5]

Without iron: anemia

Without flourine: early tooth decay

Without iodine: goitre and cretinism.

The list could be multiplied. A soil cannot give what it has not. The conclusion is evident. Destruction of soil, oil, coal, timber, uranium, and iron is a sin against generations of people, and, therefore, against God. Preservation of man depends on the preservation of nature, and this is, accordingly, a natural law binding on man.

Favoring this destruction is the argument that a) we must leave man totally free in everything, and b) it is this freedom that has enabled us to develop resources to such a peak.

The reply is that a freedom exercised at the cost of people's good and at the cost of national and international good is a freedom that man may not exercise and yet remain within the bounds of morality. Such freedom of action may be tolerated only in an emergency. I may not do in the name of freedom, enterprise, and profit the type of act that is sure ultimately to weaken my nation and make it extremely difficult, if not impossible, for people to live. God has not given me any such freedom.

[5] *Ibid.*, p. 19. See Frank A. Gilbert, *Mineral Nutrition of Plants and Animals* (Oklahoma Univ. Press, 1948), p. 95: "Mineral deficiencies in human beings result from the consumption of inadequately fortified food—vegetable, animal, or both. The animal cannot be healthy without receiving nutritious forage; and the forage, to have the proper quality, must come from productive soil containing the needed mineral constituents . . . the nutritive value to us is the final consideration. There is also another phase of the problem . . . creating a public demand for a superior quality of food. This may be the most difficult phase." Page 97: Where Florida soil had a rock phosphate subsoil, only 3 per cent of the children had anemia; but where nearby soil had not this subsoil, 96 per cent of the children had anemia.

A second issue raised is neo-Malthusianism, or the popular resources-against-population question. Science has helped profit enterprise to exploit nature. Unfortunately, most USA scientists in our time lack a general and integrated Christian education and lack a grasp of social problems, conditions, and possibilities. Consider the two following cases. 1. Scientists hardly finished finding ways for persons with predatory drives to exploit resources, when some scientists and journalists began to blurt out that we have too many people, our planet is plundered, and there is no road to survival. They do not mention that science and profit, working hand in glove, have helped to bring on the present situation. It would, therefore, seem that scientists and profitseekers, working hand in glove, have the first responsibility to correct matters. 2. Agricultural schools, making it possible to produce vastly more on farms, have not worked on the problew of how people can live happy, free, and contented lives on farms. Far from it!

Even if all the persons in any way responsible were doing all they could on the problem, it would not be solved, especially in the face of the problem of resources vs. population as posed by India, China, and Japan. People born on farms cannot all stay on farms, since reproduction rates in rural areas are high. Migration is expected and it always occurs. But it can be vastly overdone, and it is encouraged in the United States by ads, by the specious glamor of cities for rural youth, and it is encouraged positively and negatively by persons in responsible positions. Among these persons are urban and rural teachers, not all, of course, but very many, including some nuns, pastors in country towns who in many instances appreciate little of rural life, its problems and values, and heads of seminaries who, cases seem to suggest, fail to train prospective clergymen for the rural apostolate, and the operators of the aforesaid agricultural colleges.

What could be done? First, people must know how they can

live in the country, a complicated know-how that includes a score of problems in financing a farm, in operating machinery, in animal husbandry, in soil conservation, in crop rotation, and so on. Secondly, young people could be advised in matters now neglected. For instance, from every country community scores of girls have gone during recent generations to help carry on the increasing bureaucracy problem of industry and government. Few of these girls ever come back except to visit. One result is that they cannot marry, since there are not enough boys in the cities to marry them, and they learn too late that the city is mankind's graveyard. But in advance they could be coached to see that if they must for two or three years go to a mecca like Chicago or Washington, D.C., they should, from the outset, consider saving money so that they could return and marry. Perhaps mothers should be matchmakers as well as job getters. Before the girl goes, it would be excellent if she were attached to the boy back home. Of course, it will be said that the girl in the city cannot save. If she wishes to save in order to marry, she can, and this is truest when she is new in the big city and has not yet learnt to pour out her income for bare survival. She still has rural pecuniary habits and thinks that fifteen hundred dollars a year is a fortune. A type of school new to us might at least be experimented with, a school perhaps to be developed on lines somewhat like the Danish folk schools, the Nova Scotia and the Ohio cooperative study clubs, or the British Labor schools.

Thirdly, we must spend ourselves also on the "why." The Catholic Worker farms, as farms so wretched, have the merit of helping a small but increasing number to be Christians and farmers, persons who otherwise would not have been either. So too of the Catholic rural life conference, which has inspired many, even if it has been hesitant about seeing farm life on a fully American plan. Also, the Rural Life Association which is officially Quaker, but like the Catholic conference, works with persons of many faiths and helps young couples to see rural life in the family and the community as an apostolate.[6]

Fourthly, the government of each State and of the nation must make perpetual studies of difficulties and possibilities. Each has long done this through the agricultural colleges and the Department of Agriculture, but we have the problem of breaking down the results of the studies, most of them still buried, and of getting them to the people. The government must be ready to make long-term, low-interest loans to young farm families, since few if any can, as people could in an earlier day, start from nothing on an American farm with the staggering cost of land, buildings, cows, equipment, and taxes.

More families on farms would indicate more people with freedoms, and more food for a hungry world, since statistics show that big commercial farming, which produces more per man, produces much less per county. In terms of national production something may still be said for the man with the hoe. Mennonites and Amish persistently demonstrate this point. The Farm Security Administration showed that thousands, if furnished supervision and self-liquidating loans, are more prosperous, as regards themselves and the nation, on farms than in industrial work.

With respect to available land, we have land that should, at least pro tempore, be taken out of cultivation and used at most for pasture or timber. But it is said by soil scientists [7] that we have additional usable land "here in the United States—at least to a net of 450 million acres, possibly to 500 million." Charles E. Kellogg says that, besides, north of the temperate zone in the Podzol region only about one per cent of the soil is cultivated.

[6] Catholic Worker, New York; Catholic Rural Life, Des Moines, Iowa; Rural Life Association, Richmond, Ind.

[7] See Charles E. Kellogg, "The Earth can feed the People," *The Christian Farmer,* April, 1949. See also the competent "Population and Food Supply; the Current Scare," by M. K. Bennett, *Scientific Monthly,* January 1949 (XLVI), 17–26.

Consider (he says) the Podzol areas in the northern hemisphere, in North Europe and Asia and North America. "Suppose these lands were handled as the folks of Scandanavia are handling theirs. If only 10 percent of these lands were brought into cultivation, we would add over 300 million acres of new farm land. Experience has shown that they can be developed for dairying and for potatoes and other vegetables." The case is yet more promising in the tropics, a fact depreciated by scaremongers such as Vogt. Says Kellogg, "The great resources of the tropical soils have been hardly more than scratched." If only one-fifth of the unused soils in Central and South America alone were brought into cultivation probably 900 million more acres of farm land could be added.

Kellogg's conclusion on the problem of available land is that we have enough land on the earth, if rightly handled, to feed many more people.

He mentions other great food sources. He says that careful estimates by the U.S. Department of Agriculture and the agricultural colleges show that we could increase most farm products by a fifth without adding new lands, though the retiring of submarginal lands would tend to offset this gain. Kellogg's summary so far, on availablt land and increased productivity, takes no account of new discoveries in farming techniques, another source of immense gain. "As far as the resources and technical knowledge is concerned the upward limit is somewhere above the present food needs of the world—probably a long way above. . . . There is great need in the tropics now for fundamental research."

A merit of Kellogg's observations is his frankness and insistence on the fact that to make land—in the realistic phrase used by the pioneers—is not easy from any point of view; it requires a pioneering and self-sacrificial spirit. The making of land has cost man time, energy, and suffering in Scandinavia, to mention one place, but has given compensation in a rich culture. Hardly a generation ago a small group of families left

Denmark and pioneered in a somewhat barren section of northwestern New Brunswick where the settlement now contains very attractive homes.

Regarding the problem of resources vs. population, we are justified in raising questions. Why is it assumed that on this problem science is bankrupt? Why is it assumed that the pioneer who makes land and homes and helps to build communities is out of date? Do we assume that in industrialized society the pioneering spirit is dead and expect everything to be put into collectivist, ready order for us? Why assume that the only remedy for population problems is artificial birth control? Has man defaulted, and the Christian abnegated, when we assume that human controls are impossible?

In short, why assume that we may destroy nature, both in man and in "nature," but may not be expected to work with nature?

On land conservation, we have persons and groups who try to carry out another line of conduct. They see that man was destroying nature in ignorance or greed and now must learn to conserve land as our basic natural resource. In the present state of soil science and control, some loss of soil by runoff is inevitable, but much of the loss in the last century was preventable.

Since 1935 the national Soil Conservation Service is a permanent agency within the Department of Agriculture. The service already is incredible. In the Southeast, where the need is so great because cotton, with little rootage to hold soil, has destroyed land, the treated acres, cumulative to June 30, 1947, were roughly two and one-third million in Alabama, three and three-quarters in Georgia, and two million in Mississippi, and the active conservation plans were to treat about another eight million acres in those three states. In Iowa nearly 900,000 acres had been treated, and plans called for treating twice as many; figures were roughly the same for Illinois.

Treatment and active plans came too late, but better late than never; in every state we have millions of acres that need treatment and that can be saved for production. By June, 1947, we had 1,889 soil conservation districts. These are local and largely spontaneous with the farmers concerned, and their effectiveness depends on local spirit and leadership. What tells the story is the productiveness of farms treated; for instance, terraced or contoured. On a southwestern Michigan farm in the Spring of 1949, specialists on conservation from the state college collaborated with farm owners, the press, implement dealers, and high school students in a one-day, face-lifting job on a dilapidated farm. The farm was contoured to make the water "walk," and not "run," down the hills; and was planted with pines and cherry trees, with a scheme to plant sudan grass and soybeans—the latter, left to themselves are a great cause of runoff—between the contour rows of cherries. This ordinary case indicates the fact of collaboration for the common good in conservation practices.

In every American community, people are obliged to know about the problem of conservation. If the red soil is washed away in the region of Oklahoma City, business must suffer, employment and labor must suffer, the quality and quantity of food must decline, the health of the people must decline, and perhaps morals will be weakened. So of the people in Chicago if Illinois and Midwest soil suffers. The problem is ethical and religious as well as scientific, and the work of such men as David Lindstrom of Illinois University, Monsignor Ligutti of Catholic Rural Life, Stanley Hamilton of the Rural Life Association, and Eugene Smathers in his parish in Tennessee is a religious work. These men see farmers and farm owners, not as miners, but as "stewards of the soil."

An independent group, the Friends of the Land, has done excellent work on the national level. Their members are farmers, bankers, doctors, priests, teachers, industrialists, who see the ethical injunction, made concrete in our time and place, to save soil and rebuild soil.[8]

Such scientists as biochemists and soil scientists must serve the public in this regard. Agricultural colleges must continue to work for conservation. Farmers must learn conservation practices. Courses in ethics may no longer neglect this basic ethical problem. Clergymen must learn to encourage farmers and include "conservation" within the seventh commandment, and rural pastors might consider setting up in front of the church, as one has done, model soil-conservation farms. We should use movies, ads, newspapers, television, and all propaganda sources to sell to the public what the public so badly needs. The city fathers, working with state officials, must learn how to use garbage and sewage to rebuild soils. Where the water level is falling, for example, in New York City and in much of Indiana, the state must proceed with appropriate studies and action.

Soil, air, and water are the number one trinity of resources. We are ethically obliged to learn about problems and methods of forest protection and of reforestation, how to conserve oil, coal, timber, and iron, and all the resources so lavishly given us.

A more difficult problem than the Neo-Malthusianism one of resources vs. population is at present not met or posed. What will technological progress finally do to resources? Can resources such as minerals and timber ultimately stand up under a vigorously prosecuted technological development? On the short view, it is clear that this development, the chief outward mark of Western nations for over a hundred years, has made vastly more goods available.

The problem nevertheless remains. "If timber goes, science will find substitutes, and so for coal and oil." This may be true. But we already suffer from lack of building and publishing ma-

[8] Address: Friends of the Land, 1368 N. High St., Columbus, Ohio. These people engage in lectures and discussions on conservation from coast to coast, and especially for business men, and publish an excellent quarterly, *The Land* (Bel Air, Md.).

teiials, and substitutes eat into the total amount of raw goods at man's disposal. The problem arises from the fact that in processing goods, technology does not produce or reproduce goods; it puts them on the road to unavailibility; technological equipment is not productive property, and the technologist is not a primary producer. Animals, land, and sea reproduce, but technology functions only by lowering the availability of material goods. Much of the iron used in war—the trainloads of it shipped during War II from the Iron Range in Minnesota—is now irrecoverable, not to mention reproducible. The level has gone down; the level of substitutes, once processed and used, also will go down. The same is true of all industrial products, in peace and war.

What then are the ethical responsibilities of persons and various groups including the schools, the Church, labor, business organizations, the State, and international society to take into account the fact that a technological civilization, in making many goods of many kinds available, also makes goods to some degree forever unavailable and in that way reduces the potential of natural resources? Are business groups culpable in neglecting this question? Do nature and the seventh commandment require us to consider the welfare of man in the future? Is justice a law of nature only with regard to our contemporaries?

*The Failure of Technology* by Juenger is a brilliant little book on this subject and on the main points is sound. Juenger says: [9]

> In every healthy economy, the substance with which it works is preserved and used sparingly, so that consumption and destruction do not overstep the limit beyond which the substance itself would be endangered or destroyed. Since technology presupposes destruction, since its development depends upon destruction, it cannot be fitted into any healthy economic system; one cannot look at it from an economic point of view. The radical consumption of oil, coal, and ore cannot be called an economy.

[9] Friedrich Georg Juenger, *The Failure of Technology* (written in 1939; first published in 1946 as *Die Perfektion der Technik;* in translation, 1949, by Henry Regnery Co., Chicago).

CHAPTER 11

# ETHICS AND SOCIALIZED MEDICINE

HAVE people a right to health? Have they a right to dental, medical, and surgical care? Has a person a duty to look after his health? Has anyone a duty to look after another's health? Has the nation a duty to look after the health of any persons, even to look after all persons' health? Has Arkansas or Missouri a duty to see to the condition of children's teeth, their eyes, ears, and tonsils, to see to children's diet or to anyone's diet?

These questions are in some cases current, in others permanent issues. A person would have to have good reason for sacrificing his life, and yet one may give up this good for his country or friends; for their sake, he may take chances of an extraordinary kind.

To kill oneself would be another matter. To deny life's basic demand and to do this because one suffers and fears pain, or is a nuisance because of disease or age, is directly against nature. People suffering hopelessly are still subject to God and nature and, difficult as their lot is, they may not take or be given the quitter's way of "mercy release."

Where one and not two can escape alive from a plane, one may let the other live. We may not kill one to save the other, but may let one die precisely in order to save the other. This is what two priests did when, in 1912, the *Titanic* was sinking; they gave their path to life to others. That is what Father Damien did when he went to serve the lepers of Molokai at the cost of exile, leprosy, and death. No greater love has any man.

The suicide bomber, whether volunteer or not, does not commit suicide, any more than did the heroes of the *Titanic* or of Molokai. He lets himself be killed to save others. Others besides soldiers may have to die in the attempt to perform functions: priest, doctor, nurse, lawyer, scientist, teacher, editor. Possibly the merchant as well as anyone else ought to have a "due occasion" of death.

The principle used is the double effect, one good and intended, such as saving one's friends, one's country, the health and life of people, to seek or teach the truth, to defend freedoms, justice, or virtue; the other effect, such as likely or certain death of oneself or another, likely or certain imprisonment, exile, torture, madness at Dachau or in Siberia, is not intended and not desired or desirable, though foreseen. In November, 1948 a Colorado girl of eighteen was killed defending her purity and after tremendous struggle; the surrender of her purity to save her life would have been immoral.

A person not otherwise bound, as the father of a family, may take chances for the good of others, but he is not obliged to. In order to avoid the almost certain killing of others, the driver of a truck may risk going at sixty onto soft shoulders; or at the risk of their lives, he may keep to his lane.

Most of the things we do have complex social results; if we were to wait till sure of no foreseen, but unintended, evil results, we would seldom act.

Surgeons continually use the double-effect principle; they remove a leg or an eye to save a life, remove ovaries or castrate if the sacrifice is necessary and if the patient consents. The action is not evil, and the good saved is so great that a person will give up hand or eye or potency to achieve it. Surgeons have yet more difficult cases. Sometimes they remove the Fallopian tube with the living foetus in it, knowing that as a result the foetus will die; they do not kill it or wish it to die; they work to save the mother's life and, if she is willing that her life be saved though as a result the foetus will die, it seems that even in so difficult a case surgeons may proceed.[1] Of course it is for the best medical advice to decide what must be done to save life.

Ordinarily we are bound to look after our life and health, our children's, our patients' and those affected by our action, and the community's. The initial human entity that each of us is includes at least a modicum of health, and we have not a right to go against nature and waste, destroy, or needlessly endanger this good. American sports raise ethical questions, notably pugilism, in which fighters seem not adequately protected, and also football, which leaves boys crippled for life. I have not a right to become a dope fiend, wrecking my will, or to sell dope, except so far as allowed by well advised law. I have the right, if conditions demand it, to let myself starve to death, since sometimes such drastic action is the only way I can wage effective war against intolerable tyranny. On this ground the death by starvation of Mayor McSweeney of Cork (1921) was justified, and if Gandhi had died of starvation his action would have been justified.

I have not a right to become an alcoholic, and if I see myself starting down that road I and those close to me must, for my health, my happiness, my family and community life as well as my freedoms, see whether I cannot turn back. I must seek the aids of nature and grace, including the method worked out by Alcoholics Anonymous.[2] Temperance in regard to liquors is a good rule. Some, however, cannot follow it, and among the failures the college graduates, men and women, have their full quota. In no decent company is total abstinence a disgrace, though in any decent company drunkenness is a disgrace, and never does it conform to the rational nature of man.

In this matter, a secondary standard such as the mean or the mores will prove sufficient for most. But for some the mean

[1] This is the position and argument of T. L. Bouscaren, S.J., in a closely written work, *Ethics of Ectopic Operations* (Chicago: Loyola University Press, 1933).

[2] Well expressed in "A.A. Tradition." Works Publishing, P.O. box 459 (Grand Central Annex) New York, N.Y.

is far from the middle; as Aristotle remarks, it is on the side of what for others is an extreme. Certain social or occupational groups, certain families, certain nationalities are especially subject to the drink habit; but we may not say that any are simply immune.

Spreading bad habits, by example or teaching, is a great sin, and no one is more criminal than he who deliberately teaches evil. Jail sentence for the perversion of minors is just.

To spread disease is an evil to body or mind, and knowingly to spread it is a moral evil, serious or slight, depending chiefly on the disease spread. To spit on the sidewalk "may spread disease," and if I do it, I am willing to spread a cold or virus pneumonia or tuberculosis. Every child half way through high school should know better. To spread social diseases is an evil to minds and bodies, and I am obliged to help the community extirpate such evils. Not that physical and mental evils are the sole evils or that to avoid them is to avoid all evil; certain uses of sex are sins against nature, whether or not diseases are spread, but knowingly to spread these is still another sin.

Two correlative considerations on the question of health and medicine are being brought more and more into the light. In late years *The Peckham Experiment* was carried on in a poor district of London for several years,[3] and the findings may be of lasting importance. It was found that health service is best afforded on a family basis. Membership in the experiment is by families, and when a man says he can come for his "check up" ("overhaul") he is asked whether his wife and children can also come that day. "Check up" is made of man or wife in the presence of the other, and the report is in the presence of the other; the children one by one get their overhaul in the presence of the parents, and the report is given to the parents. A medical "check-up" is a family medical "check up."

[3] Pearse and Crocker, *The Peckham Experiment* (New Haven: Yale Univ. Press, 1945). This is a great work in the sociology of health, though it makes a few freakish theological and philosophical assertions.

Next, among interesting findings is that the best place, normally, for a child to be born is at home. Birth belongs in a basic way to family and home, and not, unless conditions make this imperative, to the hospital. Unless conditions of home, house, or occupation make it necessary, father, mother, and child should not be separated on this day, psychologically the greatest in the parents' lives and biologically, and perhaps psychologically, a great day in the child's life. (A native case of this good sense is reported in the unpublished diary of an Iowa woman of the 1880's who notes that she and her husband took care of each child the first night after its birth, and birth occurred at home.)

The second consideration is that soil is decisive in health, a claim backed by experiment. The Cheshire Panel was a group of six hundred English medical men who set out to see what they could do to cure and prevent disease. They found they were far more effective in curing and that like other medical men they were trying to cure or palliate cases many of which should not have arisen; preventive medicine is neglected, with great loss of time, money, health, and life. In *Medical Testament,* Dr. L. J. Picton reported for the Panel in language the layman can understand. The six hundred doctors, probably not an unfair sample, were little devoted to positive programs of health. But health, he said, would depend on food and diet, and this, as he says in his larger and delightful *Nutrition and the Soil,* would depend not merely on soil, but on qualified soil. The current practices of treating disease and of vaccinating are needful, but he says such practices might have been forestalled by nothing more remote than feeding, and the idea of his larger volume and its title in Great Britain is "thoughts on feeding." But if feeding is so basic and the quality of food is primary among requisites for health, who then, asks Dr. Picton, is to blame? The doctors do not grow the food, nor do they process or distribute it. He asks how far thoughts on feeding influence the teaching of medical students; he says these thoughts were nearly inoperative in his student days.

At last, so he judges, he found out what, above all, counts. It is diet, food, soil. His work forced the conclusion on him; all the cases a busy practitioner encounters, his reading in the history of medicine, and his experiences with the Cheshire Panel pointed in the same direction. He found that the identification of vitamins and experiments with animals seemed to tell the same story. Also, Sir Robert McCarrison had apparently come to the same result by comparative studies in health. Sir Robert had seen that in parts of India people were strong and relatively disease-free, but elsewhere open to diseases hardly known to others whose ethics, hygiene, and religion fairly well matched those of the sickly groups; his conclusion was that the radical difference was diet.

It was observed that the Hunza usually reached fifty years of age before they suffered the common ills of humanity, and though many factors may contribute to make a people hardy, it did seem that food, diet, soil were here the chief factors.

Then Dr. Picton learned that Sir Albert Howard had made prolonged comparative studies in soils in India and had learnt (so Sir Albert and Dr. Picton thought) the kind of soil required for growing health foods.

On this view the basic question is not medicine, surgery, or dentistry, but a soil fed by natural manures, animal and plant refuse. Here we come to the edge of technical matters not directly relevant to ethical problems.[4] What the authors say in effect is

[4] On the food and diet problem, see L. J. Picton, *Nutrition and the Soil* (where "Medical Testament" is included in its entirety) (New York: Devin-Adair, 1949). On food, diet and soil consult *The Friends of the Land,* 1368 N. High St., Columbus, Ohio; and ask *The Interpreter* (Brookville, Ohio) for a sample copy of this semimonthly always friendly to questions raised in the preceding paragraphs. Sir Albert Howard's famous work is *Agricultural Testament* (London and New York: Oxford Univ. Press, 1940; 1943). See also his *Soil and Health* (New York: Devin-Adair, 1947). A magazine, *Biodynamic Gardening,* is published monthly at Emmaus, Pa., to promote the care of soil by composting. An issue is raised between the evident acreage and volume of what we may call "big-time"

that we may in time be forced to rediscover nature and return more and more to nature. Highly artificialized foods and somewhat artificialized treatment of soils and the neglect of the "natural and normal" turn out to be bad for health. So claim the people mentioned.

The community may not let disease impair its strength and welfare; it must try to forestall epidemics and to get rid of them, and on occasion take positive steps to maintain health and promote health. It must—if we may believe Dr. Picton, the Cheshire Panel, Sir Robert McCarrison, and Sir Albert Howard—find out the diets good for us, "good for" meaning that we may be able to preserve our being and likewise to build up our being.

People were shocked to see a large percentage of youths declared unfit in the early 1940's for general military service. The figures were high, but for three reasons we need not be shocked. First, to some degree we have false ideas and bad habits in relation to soil, food, diet. Secondly, it is conceivable that, as Dr. Picton, Dr. Jonathan Forman, and others hold, we disjoint our digestive and assimilative system by forgetting our ancestry and the kind of animal we are. Thirdly, to judge our national health we must consider the standards in the light of which so many were rejectees.

Still, the actual percentage and numbers were high. Some percentages were as follows.[5]

---

farming, where commercial fertilizers are likely to be used; and the, to date, smaller acreage and volume of biodynamic and compost people who, however, claim quality in their product.

[5] See R. H. Britten and Geo. St. J. Perrott, "Causes of Physical Disqualification under the Selective Service Law. Early Indications," *Public Health Reports,* LVI, part 1 (May 9, 1941), pp. 1017 ff. Later summaries do not greatly vary these. See *Science News Letter,* June 26, 1943, p. 409; October 2, 1943: in December, 1942 and February, 1943, 23.8 per cent of whites and 45.5 per cent of Negroes were rejected by local boards; January 1, 1944: 3.2 per cent of registrants had "specific nutritional defects," and fourteen times as many had other defects which may have come in part from nutritional deficiency.

| Rejected for: | not qualified for gen'l military service: | not qualified for any service: | qualified only for limited service: |
|---|---|---|---|
| All causes | 42.68 per cent | 27.92 per cent | 14.76 per cent |
| Defective or deficient teeth | 8.32 per cent | 4.33 per cent | 3.99 per cent |
| Eye diseases | 5.03 " " | 2.51 " " | 2.53 " " |
| Cardio-vascular diseases | 3.69 " " | 3.02 " " | .67 " " |
| Muscular-skeleton diseases | 3.17 " " | 2.11 " " | 1.07 " " |
| Nervous and mental diseases | 2.95 " " | 2.54 " " | .41 " " |

It seems remarkable that, even with severe standards, over forty per cent should be unfit for general military service and over twenty-seven per cent unfit for any military service. Many rejectees could have missed that classification by preventive and remediable care in their childhood, a fact brought out by a special study,[6] reporting that "the childhood state of nutrition was definitely associated with the development that 15 years later disqualified the adult"; most disturbing was the fact that though it was known which children in a community would grow up physically handicapped, the health professions and society as a whole apparently had not used the knowledge.

Popular statements based on studies were brought out by Public Affairs pamphlets. One of them [7] used the report of the National Health Survey (with grants from the WPA) which between October 1, 1935 and March 3, 1936 canvassed 740,000 urban families in 19 states and 36,000 rural families in three states. The finding was that 4.5 per cent of the 2⅓ millions covered were disabled on the day investigated. This would mean that each winter day about six millions in the United States are unable to work, go to school, or otherwise perform usual activities. The "average" citizen was disabled about ten days a year; to the nation, the disablement means about a billion and

[6] See Ciocco, Klein, and Palmer, "Child Health and the Selective Service Physical Standards," *Public Health Reports,* LVI, part 2, December 12, 1941, pp. 2365 ff.

[7] "Who can afford health?" Public Affairs Pamphlets, no. 27 (1939).

a quarter days annually lost from school, work at home, or as wage earner. The Committee on Medical Costs estimated that our national sickness bill plus lost wages was ten billion a year, or 12 per cent of the 1929 income.

Poorer families suffer more. The National Health Survey said we had 57 per cent more illnesses of a week or longer among families on relief than among families with current incomes of $3,000 or over; 47 per cent more acute illnesses and 87 per cent more chronic illnesses. The poor family (with a 1936 income of $850) cannot cover its tracks by budgeting ahead; the individual cannot do it alone, the individual family cannot do it alone. "The cost of illness, like the cost of death, can be budgeted only by a large group." Costs must be spread among many and over periods of time.

In 1938 representatives of labor unions, farm organizations, and women's clubs met with leading physicians, social workers, and health experts, and a five-point program was proposed, as follows:

1. Expand maternal and child health services, with emphasis on prevention of sickness.
2. Extend hospital facilities, chiefly in small towns and rural areas.
3. Provide care at public expense for those at the lowest one-third income level.
4. Spread the cost of care either by state medical insurance or federal subsidies.
5. Furnish disability insurance on a federal-state basis.

Another pamphlet [8] reports that the poor family cannot have clinical or hospital services, that not one person in ten has an annual "check-up" or one in four the needed dental care, that the service from physicians has been "only 43 per cent of that considered essential for adequate care," that doctors, in charity or perforce, do about twenty per cent of their work gratis, that

[8] "Doctors, Dollars, and Diseases," Public Affairs pamphlet, No. 10 (reprinted), 1941.

half the sick in crowded centers receive no medical care, that we spend twenty-nine dollars to treat disease as against one dollar to prevent it, that the condition is accountable for needless suffering, deaths, and economic waste. What can be done to right matters?

Without group financing, the needed care will continue 30 to 50 per cent short. Adequate care for all would cost more though not vastly more than the three billion a year we now spend on inadequate care. Today medicine has a considerably mixed economy: private, governmental, and the group kind provided by labor unions and by cooperative ventures for example in Rochester, N.Y., in the Ross-Loos group of Los Angeles, in the three-cents-a-day plan of NYC with a million beneficiaries, and in D.C. Group Health.

The outstanding instance, not mentioned by the pamphlet, is that of the Elk County, Oklahoma, group organized by Dr. Michael Shadid.[9] This group has provided dental, medical, surgical, and hospital care of a quality never before known in that area, and during the depression did it at the rate of $25.00 a year per family, with extra yet correspondingly low charges for stipulated services and supplies. The Shadid plan has spread to other centers in Oklahoma, Texas, and the Northwest.

Group hospitalization has grown and is an unquestionable success, whereas group medicine on a voluntary basis has lagged, in spite of the need and of Dr. Shadid's fight and triumph and of the decision of the Supreme Court in favor of group health in the D.C. case.

In 1948 *The Nation's Health*[10] was published by the government, after a presumably careful study. Its important points may be stated under the following few heads.

We are seriously short on medical manpower and need by

[9] See Michael Shadid, *A Doctor for the People* (New York: Vanguard Press, 1939).

[10] Oscar R. Ewing, *The Nation's Health.* A report to the President (Superintendent of Documents, U.S. Printing Office, Washington, D.C., 1948).

1960 to increase it 40 to 50 per cent; physicians by 20 per cent, psychiatrists and pediatricians by 300 per cent; public health workers by 75 per cent; the output of dental schools by at least 20 per cent, and of nursing schools by 50 per cent.

The present supply depends on per capita income. In 1946, New York had one physician to 500 persons, Mississippi one to 1,500; California had one dentist to 1,300, South Carolina one to 5,000; Connecticut one nurse to 200 persons, Arkansas one to 2,100. In New York there were 4.8 general hospital beds per 1,000; in Mississippi only 1.9; New York people received an average of 1.42 days of hospital care each. Mississippi people 0.44 days of care each.

Millions do not have a chance for health, and the chance in any case is unequal; it depends on income. New York's per capita income in 1946 was $1,633; Mississippi's $555. "For the most part, the well-to-do States have relatively abundant hospital facilities, a higher amount of hospital care per person, larger numbers of medical manpower in proportion to population, a higher percentage of births occurring in hospitals, a lower maternal and infant mortality rate."

Negroes are 10 per cent of the population, but produce only 2 per cent of the physicians; the Negro student, physician, and patient suffer discrimination. Many counties have no acceptable hospitals; color, racial, and national minorities often are excluded.

Many lack adequate care, for three reasons: the cost of modern scientific care; the irregular, unpredictable occurrence of sickness and of accompanying costs; the low income levels of some persons and communities.

Poor families cannot meet the costs. Figures for 1946 showed that 12.8 per cent of families had less than $1,000 gross cash income; 15.4 per cent had $1,000 to 2,000; 19.5 per cent had $2,000 to 3,000; 31.4 per cent had $3,000 to 5,000; 20.9 had over $5,000. Nearly 50 per cent had less than $3,000 per family, and these seventy million find it hard, if not impossible, to provide "adequate minimal care." As we know, they usually do not do it. Hospital bills and doctor bills frighten them, because they lack income and reserves or liquid assets; the Federal Reserve Board in 1947 found that 24 per cent of consumer units had no liquid assets, another 26 per cent had less than $500. "Various studies of small loan business show that payment of doctor and hospital bills is the chief reason why people take out these high interest loans."

Look at the alternatives: 1. Exhaustion of savings. 2. Heavy debts. 3. Some form of charity care (from doctors or others). 4. A gamble with health; delay, and hope for the best.

Meeting with the author of *The Nation's Health* was the National Health Assembly whose planning committee reached these conclusions: adequate medical service should be available to all, regardless of race, creed, color, residence, or economic status; prepayment health insurance should be the basic method to meet the costs for the large majority; voluntary prepayment group health plans offer the best of medical care, are the best available means to improve medical distribution especially in rural areas and should be encouraged "by every means"; the people have the right—as contrasted with restrictions in some States as of 1948—to establish voluntary medical insurance plans on a cooperative basis; medical care programs must be coordinated with efforts to provide adequate housing, a living wage, continuous employment under safe conditions.

The Planning Committee differed on the best type of prepayment, some holding for voluntary plans only, others for a national health insurance plan.

The author of the report stood for the latter. On the one hand, he said, were the inadequacy of benefits offered, the number of people covered, and the distribution of coverage; on the other, the nation's good, its present great losses, running to 27 billion in 1947, through sickness, incapacitation, and partial disability, to which he said we might add 11 billion through premature deaths and the loss of life-years; on this side also the insufficiency of voluntary plans. His conclusion was that the nation has the responsibility to take feasible steps to improve the national health as far as possible.

All in all, then—and political ammunition aside—the case for somehow getting medical and dental care to the people in the wealthy United States is strong. First, diet is bad. Secondly, the health of young men in the prime of life is far from being as good as we might reasonably expect and as we need it to be. Thirdly, all studies report, and we believe with objectivity, that medical care is far from adequate. Fourthly, the present system, excellent in many ways, is far from being satisfactory and shows no promise of taking up the slack. Fifthly, voluntary plans such as Group Health in D.C. have, to date, reached relatively few: voluntary group hospitalization grows fast enough to let us hope it might relieve inadequacy, at least in cities, but group medicine and dentistry do not show anything like the required speed. Sixthly, preventive medicine hardly exists.

What therefore are people to do: let the situation stand? Wait for group practice, which in a hundred years might meet the need? Wait for the American Medical Association, which especially under the influence of Dr. Fishbein has propagandized notoriously for the present unsatisfactory system?

Or are we ethically obliged to fight for government provision of care? Are the doctors and the A.M.A. leadership immoral in fighting against all government plans while promising little if anything better than conventional inadequate services?

The work is to be done; it can probably be done; we can afford it. The doctors and the A.M.A. have not done it and are unlikely to do it.

We who with Pius XI accept socialization when we have to and who believe it best for the State to assume only what persons and voluntary groups fail to do and what, nevertheless, must be done, are sorry that the doctors and the A.M.A. have stood in their own way and in the way of the public good. If socialization is a last resort, last because it limits freedoms and is subject to inefficiency, waste, corruption, and ill service, why does an honorable profession force it on us? If socialization is the only way we can have adequate service, we are for it. But is it the only way? The reply cannot be given by ethics. But it is our right and duty as ethicists and as responsible citizens to continue saying that the problem is serious, is not being solved, and demands an adequate solution.

Not to take this position is to assume that the submerged one-third must always, even in matters of health, remain submerged. We are not morally allowed to provide adequate care only for those who have money. We have the means, including the intelligence and freedom, to see that the submerged one-third has a chance for normal health. The least we can do is to provide State medical care for the medically submerged one-third, the government working in copartnership with doctors, a rejuvenated A.M.A., with hospitals, with the CIO and AFL, with the farm organizations, and with many voluntary health groups.[11] If all this fails, we are morally obliged to take additional steps.

[11] In 1949 the A.M.A. finally discussed the problem with the Farm Bureau, the Grange, the CIO, AFL, and the Cooperative Health Federation. The representatives said: ". . . We are in substantial agreement that voluntary prepayment medical care plans should be developed." The nonmedical representatives wished to say: "consumer-sponsored plans."

## Chapter 12

# OWNERSHIP AND THE HUMAN PERSON

Many ethical problems are tied to ownership and property. What kind of human good is an economic good? What has ownership to do with the person and his freedoms? How do contemporary times reply in the concrete to that question? Is it immoral to be a monopolist? Has the State any right to regulate economic activities? Has the State a right to perform such activities and enter into competition with private enterprise? As nations become industrialized, are they fatally bound for some form of socialism? Is the road to socialism the road to serfdom? Must America follow Europe down the well-trodden path?

What is the status of ownership in the United States? Have we really achieved a satisfactory system? Is a mixed economy a bad one; or is it best to try for a simple economy, all-State, all-corporation, all-personal, all-familial, all-cooperative? If diffusion of ownership is desirable, what steps would help to effect diffusion? To make a living a man need not own and operate a business with a turn-over of many millions. Is he immoral if he does operate a "big business"?

It is obvious that economic goods raise ethical problems. For one thing, everybody says so, with the exception of the economic imperialist, who desires no hand of nature or society to restrain him. Men exercise their freedom in acquiring, possessing, and using economic goods, and any act of freedom so exercised is likely to be morally either good or evil.

Because economic goods can help man to be, they are good for him, a perfect instance of instrumental good. To seek them as ends, a phenomenon occurring in all societies, is a kind of craziness and despair. They are a necessary instrumental good because without them man's being ceases. So far as they help us to be, they are good for us. Exactly how far a particular economic good, such as a loaf of bread or a pile of stocks and bonds, can help a man to be is a problem that neither economics nor ethics can solve.

An economic good is purely an instrument, as Aristotle says; like a musical instrument or any instrument; potentially a good servant, but first and last a bad master.

Those who think they are big because they are in the moneyed class, are dehumanized to some extent, and at best confused. Extreme cases of these people are old, starving, freezing misers, wretches not essentially different from the man who desires a hundred thousand dollars, then half a million, then a million. He thinks that being a millionaire has something inherently to do with being, just as the old man and woman thought that a grip on every penny has something inherently to do with being.

Everything wants being, says St. Thomas in a wonderful formula: everything wants being *suo modo;* as is borne out by observation, each thing wants being according to its type or "mode" of being: the elephant wants to be in his type, the tiger in his type, the elm in its type, and man in his type. This is the fundamental expression and drive of nature in God, man, demon, and the stone.

If this is true, it would be a perversion for a man to desire, not being, but money. Gold naturally seeks to be gold, but man ought to go with his nature and thus not seek gold, but his own being as end. Obviously money cannot qualify as this end.

Where do people get the notion that money can so qualify? We mention three sources. 1. People cannot survive without economic goods. Most people are hard-pressed for such goods and must work and save in order to have anything resembling an assured income. Always lacking these goods, they envy those who have them, exaggerate the importance of them, and turn them from means into ends. Such hard-pressed people live for them, they work, not merely to have them as needed, but as somehow the end-all and be-all. 2. In any society it is most difficult for the majority of people to get and keep money, with the result that this majority tends to admire and respect those who can and do possess these economic goods. Rich men are "well off," are "doing well," are "well-to-do;" Jones is "worth" so much. Money becomes the standard of excellence, and the propertied man becomes the good man. These falsifications dominate the United States, but it is easy to see them operative in other countries, such as France and Ireland. 3. Historians of economics and of religion say that Luther and Calvin in effect cooperated to give us the money-making qualities such as industry, sobriety, and thrift as the highest Christian virtues. In *Religion and the Rise of Capitalism,* Tawney says that on matters economic Luther was more medieval than the medievalist; the latter said economic drives are dangerous and must be sanctified; Luther, holding that only faith in God's word is holy, considered such drives the works of the devil and incapable of being sanctified; and the logic of his position had its effect in spite of his good intentions. The effect was to saddle onto the Western world an unhappy dualism of

<table>
<tr><td>Religion, which is faith in the word of God</td><td>vs.</td><td>social realities, such as:<br>the law, industry, work,<br>economic life and goods,<br>the State.</td></tr>
</table>

As this dualism developed, religion was emptied of its social content and society was robbed of its soul. Calvinism made the money-making man the respectable and good man.

In America, where no official social classes exist, money goes farther than anything else to stratify society and furnish social levels. This fact does not indicate merely the emergence of snobs and social climbers, inevitable in any society, but constitutes another question and concerns degrees of excellence.

So far we have dealt with two ethical principles arising out of economic life. First, it is unethical to make property and economic goods the end. Secondly, it is an oddity unworthy of free, intelligent, and Christian people to make income or possessions the proof of goodness and to make the degree of a man's goodness depend on his pocketbook.

Virgil Michel's last will and testament was his realistic article on ownership and the human person.[1] Ownership, he says, must take its cues from the human person and not vice versa. Our times have tried to change that law of nature, and individualism, with its emphasis on what this or that man likes and desires, and, in economics, on what the man of power wishes and can do, has effectively turned many a man, first, from a person into a hand, and then with the help of the machine has turned him into a robot. Man as hand-robot, says Virgil Michel, exists to increase the income and property of "the operators," and the idea of property as a quasi extension of the person, as really personal property, something which his labor and freedom have produced and into which something of his personal self has gone, is lost. A few men plan and order and exercise a person's prerogatives; others do less and less a person's work and more and more approach the machine status. Voting also is to some degree mechanical, and political rule is the function of power and not merely of authority; here again the average person is a kind of robot.

Finally, economic power is to all intents and purposes at war with political power: lord against lord. In this warfare, allegations are made; in its early stages the economic lords appear not to be bound by truth; later the politicos reciprocate.

The State, attempting to control monopolies, gets into business; it assumes business functions gradually, because it has failed to control and regulate. In time it is difficult to discern business from politics. Economic lords effectively rule the na-

[1] Virgil Michel, O.S.B., "Ownership and the Human Person," *Review of Politics,* I (1939), 155–77.

tion, or political powers dominate business, crush it, make it feel hesitant about any big job, any throwing of itself into new ventures. Its enterprise is chilled and not much better than dead. When the State goes collectivistic, business makes terms and exists at the mercy of the State, and people, in or out of business, suffer under Communism, Fascism, or some less drastic socialistic form, with most freedoms gone, freedom of speech and worship, freedom to help run the State, freedom of education, freedom of economic enterprise.

The human person, says Virgil Michel, suffers in this exchange of civilities. The "favored few have become superpersons, quasi omnipotent, in both the economic and the political fields." In that way modern civilization has dehumanized the person "into an atomistic and mechanistic individual" and has "apotheosized private property." This last is held to be sacred and inviolable, characters which attach only to the person.

The person requires property for security, for freedom, and the developments possible to relatively secure and free persons and groups. We have next to note that many persons and families, even in the United States, have little effective control over property. Because they do not own, they are neither free nor secure. The question of who ought to own, in the interests of freedoms, security, and the possible consequent developments, is an ethical question.

By nature, man has the right to growth, to exercise some control over his economic destiny and his religious, political, and educational destiny. Unless he is a criminal he and his family have such rights—taking right as a moral claim based either on the political decree or, in the case of the rights in question, on man's nature and consequent needs.

But man cannot meet such needs and fulfill his destiny, a destiny not given him by Stalin, Franco, Hitler, or by the democratic state, unless he has effective control over property.

In that sense, private ownership is natural. How, in fact, the goods of the earth, which by nature belong to mankind, are divided up is due to historical circumstances and not directly to nature. The diffusion of ownership is always a problem. When land and cattle were the types of property, a relatively few chiefs seized them. The same is true now, in various degrees, of ownership and control over real estate, factories, stocks, and bonds. Political democracy has come in many Western nations, but hardly anybody claims that economic democracy will soon come. People with the power tend to monopolize business and capital.

Perhaps the State is obliged to let them do it in the name of private property. Some would then think, however, that the concession occurred in the misuse of that name.

Do the masses of people in the United States have property? How much effective ownership have John Brown and his family on Main Street over property? Where is the land they own? The farm, the house, and garden? The car? The refrigerator, the television set? They own some clothes and usually own such furnishings as chairs, tables, beds, curtains; perhaps the stove, everything else has been purchased on the installment plan. Wages are likely gone before they come, to pay for food and clothes and to meet installments on the house (unless they pay rent), on the car, the television set. In good times people are everywhere offered goods on credit, that is on installment, and many never really own the house or other durable goods. They cannot catch up, or think they cannot. If they borrow from the legal small-loan companies, in Iowa, Illinois, and Indiana they pay more than 20 per cent interest as a minimum and may be required to pay as much as 42 per cent.[2]

That they could have managed and saved everywhere except in the deep South is the thesis of Father Edward Keller, whose public statements have aroused such adverse criticism because

[2] See Roy J. Bergengren, *Cuna Emerges* (4th ed., Madison, Wisconsin, 1939). "Cuna" means "credit union North America"; "that money is the servant of man, that the savings of the masses are organized for their direct benefit, proving in a modest way the brotherhood of man."

their philosophy is against the papal doctrines and is bad, as well as illiberal, ethics. His case is that people are paid enough if they would save their pennies and that people have themselves to blame, and that big business is automatically good.

Here is a mass of problems, economic, political, and ethical. The common man, above all in industrial areas, has little property. What he conceivably could have had pays no bills. He does not own the plant in which he works or any notable share of it; consequently he has no control over its policies and objectives. He has no say, owns none of its product, disposes of nothing made by it. Who is "he"? The thousand, the ten thousand, the hundred thousand working in the shoe factory, in General Motors, at Ford's, in General Electric, in American Telephone and Telegraph. Because men own and control nothing in the plant, it is not surprising that they do not love it, and are ready for strikes and sabotage.

But, it will be said, they are paid a just wage. What more do they have a just claim to? If the business can stand it, they must be paid a just wage; otherwise the operation is unethical. But besides a just wage, a man wishes something different in kind. Man is made by nature to exercise freedoms, to own, to control, to plan, to keep or dispose of what he plans and makes.

For society to ask man to submit to the proletarian condition where he is totally wage-dependent and, when employment lapses, totally State-dependent, is to ask much. Man desires to be, and in the proletarian condition this demand is terribly cramped. Not that he cannot at all worthily be in that condition, but we may not expect him to submit joyously to it.

In *The Proletariat,* Goetz Briefs [3] remarks that the basis of acquiring an independent income is property, "and property has in the course of a long historical development come to be the hereditary privilege of a certain fairly small social group." The workers once were slaves, but with the development of self-consciousness in modern times the workers, successors of literal

[3] Goetz Briefs, *The Proletariat* (New York: McGraw-Hill, 1937); chapters 1, 2, 3, 4, 14.

slaves, revolt against a status that deflates them. Over a long time Christianity has taught us that we are like God, that each of us is to be respected as a person. The notion was that the privileged man has responsibilities—noblesse oblige: one could be a nobleman, but that position gave him responsibilities. The present way is for group to oppose group: interests against interests, power against power. We now have "a whole stratum of human beings who have no property." That fact sets our most serious social problem. "A slave certainly is not a person; the individual in a merely mechanized social or political order is not a person. . . . Being a person means to be endowed with reason and free will, having inalienable value, to be vested with an untransferable responsibility." Property allows independence, growth, and responsibility, and this from generation to generation. History shows that propertylessness is bearable as an individual fate, but not as a social institution for a large sector of the people who otherwise enjoy full citizen rights. Social insurance gives labor a guaranteed security, but (a) man needs more than this, and (b) in cash terms, social insurance is a costly form of payment. Wage labor is without glory; in terms of meaning, it comes to the wage plus the profits which it cannot touch and the utilities produced; hence wage labor is no substitute for property in developing the person. The outcome is a "secularized collective impersonalism."

Here is Briefs' concluding sentence: "The challenge to Western civilization will be raised as long as the laboring man can safeguard his personality only by anchoring it in collective organizations and public institutions, without any relation to the truly communitarian orders of his life" [the family and the church] "to those which, after all, are the essential social forms in which man as a person grows and matures."

In their study of the corporation and private property Berle and Means[4] claimed that property was in transition, since

[4] A. A. Berle, and Gardiner C. Means, *The Modern Corporation and Private Property* (New York: Macmillan, 1933), Part I, chaps. 1–3; Part IV, chap. 3.

ownership, in the hands of stockholders, by no means insured control. Rockefeller interests in Standard Oil of Indiana were said to be only 14.5 per cent and yet they controlled the corporation; in American Telephone and Telegraph the largest stockholder was in no position to exercise control, which apparently went to the directors or titular managers, able, it was said, to manipulate matters so as to become a self-perpetuating body. Property had become impersonal. The American corporation, dating from about 1800, swung the railroads, banks, insurance companies, and mines, and later went into merchandizing and agriculture. Berle and Means said we may expect the day when practically all economic activity will be in the corporate form. The concentration by 1930 was immense. The two hundred nonbanking corporations—nearly all with assets of over one hundred million, and fifteen with over a billion dollars—amounted to nearly half the corporate wealth in the United States, and American Telephone and Telegraph controlled more wealth than was contained within the borders of twenty-one states.

The authors claimed that Adam Smith's picture of "private property, private enterprise, individual initiative, the profit motive, wealth, competition," though it has dominated the thinking of economists, lawyers, and businessmen, is out of date. In relation to the giant corporations, that thinking is obsolete. The quest for profits does not spur absentee owners to efficiency.

What is important for ethics is that ownership is no longer ownership by a person. With ten or a thousand shares in a monopoly corporation, John Brown does not own as a person.

Elaborate studies by the institute of economics in the Brookings Institution indicate the same conclusion regarding the concentration of wealth.[5]

We cite several studies on wages and the cost of living.

[5] For example, Spurgeon Bell, *Productivity, Wages, and National Income* (Washington, D.C.: The Brookings Institution, 1940) (Vol. VI in the series on distribution of wealth and income. . . .).

I. Studies made by the Bureau of Labor Statistics[6] for 1934–36, after the lowest levels of employment and wages, showed that the average family of wage earners and clerical workers in eight cities in the east North Central region had an income of $1,481; the white families $1,517, the Negro families (in Cincinnati and Indianapolis) $1,000. "The average family in this region spent a total of $1,502, practically all its income, for current family living." Food, clothing, and housing took about two-thirds; with about five hundred dollars left for household operation, furnishings and equipment, medical care, auto and other transportation, education, recreation, gifts, taxes, miscellaneous. This break-down shows how difficult it is for families to meet emergencies, or to buy commodities adding variety to urban life.

II. In New York City at the same time for the same groups, family income for whites averaged $1,745; for Negroes $1,446. Disbursements were relatively the same as in group I; in neither I, II, nor III is the report fully representative, since families on relief and families with income under $500 or with the chief wage earner in domestic service were not included (nor were consumer units of one person each).

III. At that time for the same groups, a study of 3,668 families in twelve cities from Houston, Texas, through Richmond, Virginia, showed an average family income of $1,369; for whites other than Mexican, $1,464; for Negroes, $875; for 100 Mexican families covered in Houston, $924. "The average family in this region spent practically all its income for current family living with a total of $1,353." Food, clothing and housing took more than 70 per cent, and for everything else the average family had about $400.

IV. Information by the Bureau of Labor Statistics in 1948 showed that in 1947, when much was spent for durable goods, the net family income (under $10,000) was $4,610 in Washington,

[6] Bureau of Labor Statistics, U.S. Dept. of Labor. For I, see bulletin 636; for II, bulletin 637; for III, bulletin 640.

D.C., $3,594 in Richmond, Va., and in Manchester, N.H. (under $7,500) $3,408; D.C. families studied had 1.7, Richmond families 1.6, and Manchester families 1.8 earners per family; the families in each city averaged 3.3 persons. In D.C. the annual savings or "net surpluses" were $36 per family, in Richmond $220 per family, but Manchester showed a deficit of $148 per family.[7]

V. A study by the New York State department of labor,[8] based on prices in eleven cities for September, 1948, reported that a working girl living with her family needed $40.13 a week to live in a parsimonious way. The girl wore her "old look" clothes, spent $12.01 for housing, food at home, and other household expense; $7.34 a week for clothes and clothing upkeep, $3.05 for lunches, $2.83 in leisure time. New York city was 3 per cent higher in costs than the average upstate city. One can imagine how poorly the out-of-town girl, often on a much lower salary, has to live, a matter reported in lively detail by Catherine de Hueck.[9]

These reports suggest that it is difficult for the family of the wage earner or of the clerical worker to support itself, much less save, through insurance or otherwise, and thus acquire property. The reason may be maldistribution of income or wealth, or a bad economic system or a good one functioning badly, or bad habits, or a combination of such causes. The fact is that the wage earner and clerical worker in industrial centers cannot have property.

In any society some persons are unwilling, or for some reason unable, to face the responsibilities incident to ownership, planning, and management: of a farm, a shop, a factory; a house and garden is the utmost they could manage. We suppose at least these persons would work for others. In our times with land,

[7] Helen M. Humes, "Family Income and Expenditures in 1947." *Monthly Labor Review,* LXVIII (April, 1949), 389–97; the single man or woman who composed a consumer unit was included.

[8] See *The Labor Leader,* April 11, 1949.

[9] Catherine de Hueck, *Dear Bishop* (New York: Sheed and Ward, 1947).

industrial, commercial and banking ownership tied up in relatively few corporations, and so much money in government bonds (the Corn Exchange Bank, New York City, reported in September, 1948, 60 per cent of savings invested in government bonds), many must work in others' industries or in government bureaucracy or the military. Few own and manage.

Deprived of ownership, they run into problems of doing a day's work, of workmanship, of fulfilling contracts, of honesty and justice, of nonsabotage, of "only just pressures."

The owners are usually absent, yet owners and managers also run into ethical problems. They have the general problem of treating workers as persons. It is difficult, in many instances, to allow and encourage workers to be fine workmen, respecting their materials, procedures, and products.

Nearly all gains made in the conditions of workingmen have been effected by workingmen. Firms seldom initiate better working conditions and higher wages. When may workers strike? For a long time, many thought that it is unethical to strike at all; some still hold this doctrine. When are workers ethically bound to strike? By way of financial or psychological occult compensation when, if ever, may workers steal materials and tools from the shop? It is claimed that workers in a Chicago plant by collusion carried off piecemeal every part of a Diesel engine and set it up for use or sale or fun. Could such action in some circumstances be ethically justified?

Some workmen take pride in their work, a pride which we think human and good. Many factory workers do not; probably most cannot. Is it right for men, supposing they could get other work, to stay where they cannot love their work? What, if anything, can be done in this situation where workers do not own or manage more than their gardens, a situation in which trouble, more or less serious, is always brewing?

Here are obvious and readily achievable procedures:

1. Some simple steps such as those mentioned by Elton Mayo; for example, rest periods, and these preferably arranged by the

workers; plus a readiness on the part of management to honor at any time a bill of complaints.[10]

2. Ownership in plants by workers in those plants. Conceivably this cannot always be worked out; but its possibilities are not exhausted.

3. Some word in management, the workers having some voice in what they do. This can be realized in small shops, and as labor matures and reaches a better balance it can be realized in larger groups. What we manage must be good; what we own we must make and keep good. Cases show that an approach to industrial democracy gets better human results.

4. Profit sharing is no longer in the purely experimental stage.[11] So many plants have tried it and found it less unsatisfactory than "wages against profits" that we may no longer pretend that it is impracticable.

5. Putting the cards on the table. This should progressively be done by labor and by owners and managers. Exactly what the profits are, exactly what managers and owners spend on advertising, what salary the managers draw, what pressures and racketeering labor uses through this or that affiliate, what pressures, such as bribery and propaganda, the management uses on the clergy, colleges, the press, the public, and on government. To confess such matters may be more effective than a cooling-off period.

6. Labor should learn step by step to give up bludgeon methods. So should management and operators. A good end will rarely justify intimidation and force.

Along with these steps to be taken, we as teachers, clergy, heads of families, management, labor, and government must encourage and develop labor unionism. Think how badly, in general, the Catholic, Protestant, and Jewish clergy of this

[10] Elton Mayo, *The Social Problems of an Industrial Civilization* (Boston: Harvard School of Business Administration, 1945): Pompous and pontifical at the start, but the case-studies tell the tale.

[11] A group known as the Council of Profit Sharing Industries, 1600 Roxbury Road, Columbus 12, Ohio, exists; but we do not know its value.

country have thus far failed the poor, the miners, the farmers, the workingmen. It is easy to name exceptions; but they are exceptions. Clergymen associate with industrialists and bankers, go to Rotarian dinners, visit wealthy doctors and lawyers. The clergymen should do this, but many stop there. Undoubtedly some are stopped by bribes such as vacations, country houses, cars, large stipends. As a rule they do not take part in the professional lives of farmers and laborers; in my own county and my city they scarcely know at all, sympathize with, and take part in the 4-H, the Farm Bureau, the AFL, and the CIO. In effect they say: "All right, come to church on Sunday; but your hopes and aspirations and work are secularized." To go with their hopes and their work is what is demanded in our time and place, if we are to honor man and God under present conditions.[12]

Farm organizations, labor unions, and credit unions give farmers and workers importance and standing, and the labor union gives labor a kind of parity with ownership and management. In the socioeconomic field it is difficult to name another development such as Socialism, cooperatives, or Rotary that has done as much for the masses as has unionism, though this good is marred by many evils. Somewhat on a level with it in America are the farm groups, the old and tried Grange, the newer Farmers Union and Farm Bureau; and the 4-H as the greatest American youth movement to date.

Other techniques to help siphon off economic aristocracy must be abetted and developed, even if they but slightly advance ownership. For example:

1. Encourage small and diffused ownership, by education especially in the colleges that now effectively promote the contrary effect; by the press, movies, radio, and television, which today hardly think of such a good work; by the clergy in and out of the pulpit; by legislation; by "a little businessman's RFC."

[12] Wonderful reports come from post-war France, in books by Clare Bishop, Abbé Michonneau, Henri Perrin, Maisie Sheed, and Jacques Loew.

2. Research, necessarily subsidized, to help small businessmen and the small farmer who with his family operates his own farm; and to aid and encourage quite small equipment such as the one-cow or the two- or three- or five-cow silo. This is the kind of job not yet commonly done, at least west of the Alleghenies, by the agricultural colleges, which have gone in for volume and, in effect, for fewer owners and fewer operators of farm land.[13] "As many family farms as possible" may involve penalizing supercommercial farmers, usually absentees, who plow up five or six thousand acres for wheat or run cattle and sheep over twenty thousand acres. We wish also as many small businessmen as economic pressures will allow, and since this is a question of diffused ownership and of freedom, law must stand on this, the people's side.

3. The census in 1940 for the first time took separate account of the rural nonfarm population, made up of people who live neither in cities (of 25,000 and up) nor on farms, but in small cities, towns, and villages, and on all sides of large cities. The 1950 census found these people to be the fastest growing segment of the population. Nearly their whole cash income comes from employment in cities; each family has half an acre or two or three acres, and produces part of its food, and usually has a garden and sometimes a cow, poultry, and berries. The cost of commuting is more and that of getting children to school possibly more than in the city; but the family annually saves about one month's salary; it has more independence and it owns and plans and works together.[14]

By state figures the average dairy cow in a good Wisconsin county in the 1940's annually grossed $340. Little of this would be cash for a family with one cow, but the family would have plenty of dairy products. One estimate is that we have five mil-

[13] *Postwar Agricultural Policy* (1944). Available from any land-grant college. The favored policy is fewer farmers and bigger farms. See pp. 11, 35–36.

[14] Independence and family life are stressed by Willis Nutting in *Reclamation of Independence* (Nevada City, Cal.: Berliner, 1947).

lion family cows in the United States. We could readily double the number, and if the net in food were $200 a year, the additional value in the best food would run annually to a billion.

Around most cities in the United States, we have possibilities for this type of growth. It profits most when young couples plan and build their own houses as some do. Some groups are buying and building in view of family and community life, on a cooperative basis, and a Catholic Action or other religious basis.

4. Cooperatives help families to own, and to build communities. By purchasing groceries for eleven years at the cooperative an Englishwoman in an industrial center saved a nest egg that she would not otherwise have had; by building cooperatives a Cape Breton village lifted itself out of relief into relative security and independence; a community of Minnesota farmers put itself on the way to ownership and freedom instead of tenancy and slavery; and people have learnt that they can own factories at no cost.[15]

5. By education, preaching, time, and sacrifice it is conceivable that we could re-create a property ideal and abandon the present debt system. This would require effort, readjustment in ideas and practices; on the current view it would mean thrift, retreat from our high standard of spending. We must learn moderation; people cannot perpetually spend all current income and expect to have family and community security.

Many think saving is narrow, old-fashioned, a return to peasantry. For one thing, if we do not save—and we will not!—the government will save for us and compel us to be secure. The effect will be forced on us, and one way or another we the people will then have saved. We cannot save freely, we can under compulsion: are we really on the road to freedom?

The author lived a year in Belgium, where poor people save

[15] For the English case see S. R. Eliott, *The English Cooperatives* (Yale Univ. Press, 1937); for the Cape Breton village, see Leo R. Ward, *Nova Scotia, Land of Cooperators* (Sheed and Ward, 1942), chap. 6; for the Minnesota community, see Leo R. Ward, *Ourselves, Inc.* (Harpers, 1945), chap. 6; and for free factories, *ibid.*, chap. 12.

a dowry for girls. Social custom requires this, and it is done without state subvention, without low standards or niggardliness.

6. What is immoral about the ideal of holy poverty? Has it evaporated? Why do colleges not teach it as integral to a Christian economics? In these schools one hardly hears that ownership is stewardship, and never effectively hears about Gospel poverty.

7. Ruskin asks in *Unto This Last* a question that remains relevant. He remarks that the soldier has a social work and is a traitor if he does not do it, the clergyman has a social mission and is guilty of simony if he sells out, the physician, too, or he is a quack, and the lawyer or he is a shyster. Each ought on due occasion to face death in order to do his duty. What is the merchant's social function and what is his "due occasion" of death? What social work has the merchant to do and be ready to die rather than fail to do? Is he to seek profit and, at best, incidentally to serve society? Has society for a long time wished a false, unworthy end on the merchant class?

To find out what, in the name of God and society, the businessman is to do is a perpetual problem. To ask the questions is better than to bypass them. Is it immoral to engage in an occupation only because the acts done are immoral, for example, to run a house of prostitution; or because the acts evidently lead to immorality, for example, to operate a saloon, a hotel, an apartment house, a dance hall, or any business or factory in such a way as to promote drunkenness or adultery or birth control or abortion or bad living conditions? Is it immoral and against our nature to run a business primarily to make unneeded money?

May we through advertising and pressure "sell" the public? Is it a sin a) immediately against the persons "sold," and b) against the national good, to unload on people things they cannot afford? May I do it nevertheless for profit? Are Dale Carnegie's "principles" to any degree a code of immorality?

If a man or a corporation processing foods or producing clothing or household appliances or cars or cameras or chemicals or oil or colas can, with safety to the business and therefore to the service presumably done for the community, manage on a net profit, after taxes, reserves, allowances for expansion, and so forth, of ten million dollars a year, what is the morality of extracting ten times that sum? May businessmen take all they can get? [16]

Are builders immoral when they provide a bottleneck to control materials? Why was the cost of building houses after World War II prohibitive for people of ordinary means? Were labor groups immoral in this regard; real estate contractor groups, and groups controlling materials?

Problems on the ethics of economics thus arising may be brought under two large questions:

First, on the level of society, we ask whether the progressive impoverishment of the masses endangers the being along with the well-being of society. (And this in spite of the possible palliatives mentioned.)

Secondly, on the levels of person, family, and society, we ask whether freedom is generally possible without access to ownership; by what means such access can be general in urban and highly industrialized centers; whether urban life nevertheless has an inevitable trend toward loss of freedom; whether, again, creativity is a common urge and need of man; and if so, whether creativity generally has a chance in industrialized society; whether human life generally can be full and deep and rich without a developed family life: whether, in other words, ownership is especially desirable and creativity generally possible except in and by and for the family; whether family life can be de-

[16] National City Bank of NYC said in April, 1949, that 2,100 leading American corporations made 20 per cent more profit in '48 than in '47; that 3,262 leading corporations had in 1948 a net income after taxes of over eleven billion dollars, which was an increase of 22.4 per cent over the net income of 1947; and a net return on investment of 14 per cent which was an increase of 1.7 per cent. The May statement of the Bank was that "leading corporations" had, in the first quarter of 1949, 6.5 per cent more net income than in the first quarter of 1948, but 18.2 per cent less than in the fourth quarter of 1948.

veloped, can itself be rich and deep and full in vast cities.[17]

Two things are required in order to make use of even the palliatives. One is constant vigilance. The other is constant education and, above all, adult education: a few persons working together to find out their condition and what techniques have proved helpful to do anything toward ownership. The pattern of small adult educational groups has, to some extent, been worked out in the Danish folk schools, the British Labor schools, the Antigonish and the Ohio cooperative study groups, and the Catholic Action cells of Europe and America. If such as these were worked hard, ownership and freedoms might be saved; they cannot be saved by the supercorporation or by the collectivism to which it leads.

[17] See Vincent McNabb, O.P., *Old Principles and the New Order* (New York: Sheed & Ward, 1942), pp. 111–22; Elmer T. Peterson, *Cities Are Abnormal* (Oklahoma Univ. Press, 1946).

CHAPTER 13

# ETHICS OF SEX AND THE FAMILY

TO SANCTION conduct in the use of the sex organs, people appeal to a variety of standards, singly or in combinations. At times a person defends his action in the light of the mores: everybody is doing these things; why shouldn't I? Some clamor for expediency: I desire this pleasure and this conquest; it is good because I desire it; we desire comfort, health, child spacing, and a college education.

Hedonism remains a favorite in this field.

The primary doctrine of Christianity on the use of sex is that the sex organs have a function. To honor this function is to honor man and woman and to honor God. Honor, respect, not of a mere animal function, but of a human animal function: this is normal, necessary, natural, and good. Disrespect for this natural function is, in various degrees, unnatural, perversion.

Nature is good, sex goes with nature, and its use is good. It is not easy to name other matters on which the ethical teaching of Christianity is so unambiguous and so directly patterned on nature.

In normal, healthy persons the sex drive is strong and sometimes urgent. This is normal, to be expected, and, on the part of society, to be desired; a nation that cannot or will not reproduce is inferior; a long and rather consistent decline in population is a bad sign. The situation will be rationalized; it will be said that the nation produces quality, that its people are leaders, and the nation, resenting the vigor and growth of neighboring nations, will say that the neighbors are barbarous war makers.

We cannot say that there is any special merit in lacking sex drive, or that persons who are quasi-asexual are therefore good persons or specially blest.

If that is so, the sex problem is to have and to control sex desire. The problem of having desire is automatically solved, though we may not ask all peoples of all climates, times, nations, races, and creeds to have a standard uniform sex desire, since nothing of the kind exists; nor all persons within any climate, any nation, any race, any family: a standard of morals is not true if it does not allow wide variation in many matters.

The second problem gives trouble. Some sort of control is necessary for ordinary young persons in the late teens, for some in the early teens, and possibly for most persons till well into the forties: this time, from the teens through the forties, is "their generation." People can hardly marry in their teens; people in married life also need control of sex impulse, and are not obliged to produce as many children as they can or to reproduce as fast as they can.

Control of man by himself must see man as a being with intelligence, freedoms, and responsibilities. "Birth control" and "planned parenthood" propagandists take another view. They suppose that man is a frenetic and can be controlled only as a frenetic: by mechanical means, by tying him up.

Human controls are never subhuman, and among the normal, socially and personally healthful controls are the following.

1. A vigorous tradition of control. This will never be 100 per cent effective, in or out of marriage; no nation, no religious group is untouched by sex sins. But a good tradition is important in the community, in the Church, and the national life, and thus in the person's life. Industrial life, the car, the wars, movies, television, a somewhat irresponsible journalism, the weakening of religious faith, and the spread of contraceptives have made the tradition of control less effective.

2. A vital religious creed and practice, including sacramental protection for the family.[1] For the good of virtue, people need

[1] See Emerson Hynes, "Sacramental Protection for the Family," 3801 Grand Ave., Des Moines, Iowa; also his "Seven Keys to a Christian

the fear and love of God, and to be brought up in these, as Plato would say, from their youth. If they realize that the body is the temple of God, they are more likely to be chaste, and to value the virtue of chastity.

3. A normal home life, ordinarily including father and mother and boys and girls. This is life together; work, play, worship together. Entertainment exclusively away from home and work exclusively away from home split life along unnatural lines. If a healthy, sane, balanced life is lived, persons are much less likely to go astray on matters of sex. It is tremendous what the Christian groups are doing, family helping family to understand their common problems, to see opportunities, face difficulties, and to work out the apostolate of young married people in America. One thing we may say for certain: they find out that the apostolate begins close to home.

Persons in these groups, and persons out of them and yet in fairly normal homes, do not cease to have bodies and sex demands. But they learn in theory and practice what, in our time and place granting the conditions and the mores, are the problems, the aids, and what are the bounds of nature and of Christian life.

4. Social conditions. The housing problem makes marriage difficult and sex controls inside or outside marriage difficult. So about employment problems, factory work which does not do justice to man's or woman's freedoms and makes reaction toward drink and sex more difficult to control. People require the wherewithal to live, they need personal and productive property; they need security; they need light and space and air; they need privacy. They need their own home, they need an economic cushion, they need the prestige which comes only with private ownership. Those working in any prudent way for "the welfare community" and for wider distribution of ownership, are working for the good of society.

5. Close contact with nature. The "natural" and "normal"

---

Home." (Each pamphlet, 20 cents.); also "For Happier Families," Christian Family Action, Room no. 1808, 100 W. Monroe, Chicago (35 cents).

imply contact with nature, with growing things, with plants and animals, and this includes ordinary observation of breeding, as well as feeding and gambolling. Touch with vital realities helps people from the time before their teens to take sex in a sane, almost routine manner, and to get beyond the smirk of walled-in people who never see nature operate as it spontaneously does operate.

6. A normal sane marriage. This aid to sex control overlaps the other aids. Even in nature and without reference to a divine life in man, a sane marriage is a help to control, as St. Paul assumes it to be.[2] We refer, among other qualities, to a marriage within the two families—not that boy or girl marries the in-laws; but that the parents of each are in a real sense parties to the marriage: they know of it, would ordinarily desire it, and bless it. It is a home-and-home event, uniting the families and forming a new family. Besides, in the Christian world we do not have a merely natural marriage, but the marriage of person to person much as Christ is married to the Church.[3] Marriage in the Church gives higher graces, not simply for the wedding day, but throughout life.

Before we enumerate the great values of marriage, going in the main with St. Augustine, we name some virtues without which marriage is a farce and the values of marriage an impossibility. One of these is fidelity, fidelity in a strict and fundamental sense. If the man will suit his own pleasure and individualistic standards, or if the woman will do this, marriage as a happy, permanent state is at best difficult. Fecundity is a physical-psychological good rather than a virtue. A second virtue is chastity within marriage. The unmarried person is asked by nature to live a life of continence; that is, he is not to practice abuse, sodomy, fornication, or adultery. For many, this is a heavy assignment, and the person requires every natural aid as well as a sacramental life. In the married life, persons need

[2] I Cor. 7.
[3] Ephes. 5:21 ff.

natural and supernatural aids for a life of wedded chastity—to use their sex powers to reproduce or in such a way that they never freely block reproduction. Our statement implies that it is best not to use the rhythm period, and yet implies that if there is good reason to use it—if it would be hazardous for the woman to bear another child or to bear one at an early time, or difficult for one or both persons to restrain sex desire—the couple seems not to act against nature in the use of the so-called safe period. It is most normal if the couple never even thinks of this period, and it would be best—we may not lay down as general law the "best"—if the couple would have relations only when reproduction is most likely to occur. This would be going most completely with nature and therefore with the law of God. One does not see why the doctrine of the most likely period should not also be propounded; above all when so many men and women wish to be complete and consecrated Christians within the married state.

The practice of continence, chastity, and fidelity best gives to married persons and their families and thus to society the tremendous values of the married life. These values are summarized by St. Augustine as *prolis, fides,* and *sacramentum.*

The first is the good of offspring, and is intimately joined, in both natural and sacramental marriage, with the second good. This first good is the essential purpose of the reproductive organs. Nature heads in that direction, *is* in that direction. Husband and wife desire offspring; and nature, as the basic matrix of this desire, demands offspring. It is wrong to thwart nature, to balk and stall nature; in any matter, such action goes against the grain of our being and hence against any good in our being; and the use of the sex organs is something fundamental and essential to the human race. We are allowed to use these organs within the order set by nature.

Fortunately, no ordinary sane person, on the barbarous, savage, or semicivilized level, has failed to see offspring as a major good. If we say, with St. Thomas, that to pervert the order of man's entering into life is evil, we must say with the voice of humanity and of nature that it is good to reproduce and that the fear of having children, no matter what the mores, comes from inhibitions having little to do with the direction of the human species to good.

"Ah, yes, but in our circumstances, with the cost of living already high, with our dubious, minimum security, it is exceedingly difficult to raise children!"

No one would deny that to have children has always been hard, even if greatly rewarding. To work out a fully human life, to create employment and a "living," to plan and build the family house and family home, is difficult. It is much easier to practice contraception, and to have the State look after housing, employment, and health: a kind of mechanistic and bourgeois paradise. We must, however, ask about nature's and God's purposes in the human world. Is the direction of nature primarily toward the indulgence of sex pleasure? Or is it primarily toward reproduction through the use of sex? Is the good in the use of sex primarily the good of offspring, with pleasure as a normal attendant on that use? Or is it primarily the good of pleasure, with offspring a burden that on occasion must be suffered?

In the use of sex or any power, is pleasure justified as a supreme and final end or is pleasure properly a means which has its last-word justification not in itself? What is subordinated to what? And by whose fiat, the mores fiat, the individualistic fiat, the hedonistic fiat, or the fiat of nature?

"Yes, but everything is nature, if not in one way, then in another." This is probably true. It is difficult to see how we could operate, unless on the level of the supernatural, and not to a degree go with nature. John Dillinger perhaps went with nature in many senses and in varying degrees, and so did Hitler. Yet each did some distinguished evils; and these are evils, not as judged by hedonistic, by the mores, or by individualistic standards, but in the light of man's nature and being. If what

Hitler did went with our nature and being, Hitler was an excellent man, and I could only be a madman in not being with him. What Hitler did was wrong because it was against the direction of our nature. Sodomy takes the same "against," wrong direction, and so does abuse and the kind of control that supposes man a frenetic.

We see people go silly over their children. This may be extreme and sentimental, but a liberal dose of it is natural. Children are a considerable good; they are a basic physical good, if the survival of the human race is good; they are also an intimate psychological good. They are our children, and we can scarcely see faults in them. They are ours, they are of us, they are ourselves over again. To say this is to be no more sentimental than to say that the earth goes around the sun. Ours, something intimately close to us, something outside ourselves, almost and yet not quite ourselves, to which we can and to which we like to, and ought to, give ourselves: this is what our children are.

We need something outside our own hides to which we can give time and energy, something to which we can pay the burnt offering of ourselves, yet something very near to us. Answering to the description are the family members, husband, wife, children, parents, grandparents, and grandchildren. We came out of a family, and in the general human economy, our work is to found a family.

That life should try to preserve itself is a law attested by the reactions of plant, brute, and man. But this law cannot be fulfilled by a man unless he learns to give his life for others. Unless the grain of wheat falling into the ground die, itself remaineth alone. If a man will keep his life, he will lose it, but if he gives it for My sake and the Gospel's, he will find it. Science, history, and ordinary current observation, for instance, of a good mother's life, attest it as the Gospel does.

We need to love and be loved, but may not expect this reciprocal love in a continuous, sacrificial way except from our spouse, parents, children. We need this in order to be and to grow as persons, and in the family alone, in the everyday case, we get and give this love. Hence the sacredness of the hearth, the unsentimental loveliness of home life, and the wrongness of everything that upsets the home: nagging, neglect, discourtesies, infidelity, stepping on tender toes, unwillingness to forbear and forgive, divorce, multiple marriage, publicity that makes the most of infidelity and broken homes.

That we in our kind should be: this is a law of nature. That we in our own blood and in our families should be, seems also a law of nature. We like to be, things desire to be; this is a law applicable to God, man, thing.

That is the purpose of sex life, the *to be* of mankind. Hence the fundamental and existential character of the law. "To be or not to be" is not the question. "To be" is the law.

That is the sense and direction of life, which cannot be without the reproductive act and without this used, and this used in its natural sense and direction. "But," people complain, "nature wastes semen at a great rate, in plant and animal. It cannot be wrong for us to do what nature does." This is like saying that, though the law of nature is for us to honor and protect people, if we did now and then kill a hundred million, our action could be good since the human race would still exist; and, besides, does not nature kill people by a thousand accidents, and are not all killed off ultimately? Why not smash heads, whenever it suits our pleasure and convenience?

The family cherishes us even in our prenatal days, and the whole life of the parents-to-be is enriched and made more intimate in the thought of the new life that is so close to them. The warmth and grandeur do not die when the baby is born and when his brothers and sisters are born. Not merely to be, but to be together is now the proper goal and good. Hence we have the family in some form at all cultural levels.

Despite divorce and sex action with sex frustration, the

direction described is so natural that most people still know that the family is the primary institution in society, and it is difficult for people not to perceive, as soon as they have children, that the primary good of the family and of sex is offspring. Of course, young couples are swayed by passion and love of pleasure when they copulate. This circumstance is to be expected and need not approach sin. Thomas Aquinas was a celibate and a monk, and yet he says: [4] "Even in the just"—by which he means very good people—"in the act of generation, there is actual libido while the power of desire tends immoderately toward the pleasure of flesh, and [so does] the will, and if the desire does and wishes nothing against reason, nevertheless on account of the vehemence of passion it does not at present attend to the order of reason." That is, in the act of intercourse, the good person does not advert consciously to the order of reason and yet this person does and wishes nothing contrary to reason. He is a good man in fact, does nothing wrong, and though to do nothing against reason is obviously a minimum, we may not always exact a maximum. Constant attention to standards would probably do little to build up human good.

Pleasure, says Aristotle, is the kind of good people would wish if it led no farther; it can lead farther and is a quasi end through essentially a means. The pleasure of sex should be used within a standard that is not pleasure or the hedonistic standard itself. This standard should be subordinated to something more independent and basically truthworthy than sex pleasure, and this something is our total human nature and human good. Sex pleasure with responsibility: that is nature's law. But nature is best seen by the ends toward which the working of the power in question properly tends. Sex let loose can wreck persons and is not good for societies; it must be subordinated and sublimated to something more human. This higher good is the good of the race, which it reaches by way

[4] *De malo,* q.4, a.6 ad 18.

of offspring. In short, sex is not autonomous, and a standard that is a hybrid between the hedonistic, the mores, and the individualistic, cannot make it autonomous.

Democracy, stretched out full length, keeps saying this: it keeps saying that the end of sex life is offspring. People say they do not know until they have their first child how immense is this good. "We were considering at breakfast this morning, Virginia's first birthday, the nature of life before we had her. We remember things we did, but what was life like, what could it have been like!" The child is mainly a problem till it comes or is about to come. Each child is an immeasurable good.

Of course, offspring is possible without marriage, but a world of human good is lost, a fact put positively when we say that the second good of marriage is *fides,* a good of such magnitude that, so long as we respect the first good, we can hardly over-accentuate the second.

This second good means that this man becomes more physically, psychologically, and spiritually one with this woman, and she with him, than either ever was with any other unless he with his mother and she with hers. The new life together is planned; it is hoped for, normally in all decently prepared marriages, by the two together; talked about to just each other. Until now nothing like this togetherness has been within their orbits. They shall be one flesh, and also, as is wondrously evident to them, they *are* one altogether.

*Fides* is usually translated "mutual trust." It is this, at least. It means and demands marriage fidelity, and also means, fortunately in most instances, that each person studies to be "one in heart and mind and will" with the other. It means a giving of self. It means surrender, in order to learn and to do, and for many it always keeps meaning sacrifice. The persons learn by doing, by meeting problems largely as they arise, problems of finance, of who is boss in this or that, problems of keeping mum on what hurts the other, of learning and doing what makes life together truly a life together. The persons need not be one in taste, and it is evident that in part they cannot be; but each learns to allow for likes, dislikes, fears, hopes, weak points, and strong points. Each remains properly and totally himself, a fact that must be respected.

It is far more in accordance with nature and God's law if man and wife learn to respect and reverence each other, and a man should be advised not to marry a woman unless he profoundly respects her. How can he love her if he does not respect her?

The two are building a home, and the presumption is that if they do not love, they at least respect each other and have sympathy and understanding. Most youths in our society, in spite of the divorce mills, have a normal home life, and after life and the sacraments, this is the greatest blessing they have. Their business now is to build a home, in love and mutual faith. It is best for them really to have this faith, to hide nothing from each other. With the child or children, the love circle and the mutual-faith circle widens. Loving and trusting the child, their mutual love and faith deepens. Each thinks all day, and not necessarily sentimentally, of the child and the love circle; this last goes with each wherever he goes. Soon it is not merely the love of man and woman, but of the child for them, and of child for child, and, as everybody knows, of grandparents for the grandchildren: how often are troubles with in-laws bypassed when the child appears!

In a year of life in Belgium I saw things I did not like. But the family unity is impressive; so good and united that possibly on some points it is overdone. A person's friends and associates are the members of his family. Godparents are selected with a view to what they can do financially for children, but there is a strong tie between godparents and godchild. Feast days, birthdays, holidays, father's and mother's days, the days of the Communion Solennelle are great days in the family; members for three generations flock together, gifts are handed round, best clothes worn, best wines drunk, and everyone, little and big, is off for a walk in the park: the whole event, in preparation, in celebration and in retrospect, is a kind of hand-in-hand party. So too of the Jewish people, on feasts and all the time; possibly this love of family is one reason why the Jews cannot be destroyed.

With mutual faith all around, the family builds a new cosmos. A person requires self-discipline and self-schooling, and here is his chance. We love ourselves, and, with Aristotle and St. Thomas, this book holds that every act of God, angel, man, animal, plant and the inorganic, is to some degree self-seeking: it is, and it must be. But self-seeking has ruined our world, especially during the four or five centuries in which we so seriously suffered from rugged individualism. In the home, we have a natural set-up demanding self-sacrifice for the general good; family life, the school of mankind, is a constant schooling in altruism.

The third good named by St. Augustine is the sacrament of marriage, a supernatural good to help man and wife live a life which, if beautiful and attractive, is really difficult. As married people they will encounter great problems. The two become one. This is their new good, and their new and perpetual problem. As Christ is united with and one with the Church, man is one with woman. If so much is asked, divine help is needed.

In the Christian the other goods, which can be only natural in the non-Christian, have a new richness and a new possibility of attainment. People who receive the sacrament understand better than others that marriage is not a plaything, not a romantic holiday that may be terminated when people please; problems are sure to come and must be faced.

Where does woman's "career" land in such a doctrine? Has she not a right to a career if she desires one? That all depends. Normally her career is at home. Her first care, as her first and last love is at home; if she has intermittently to work outside, she is properly a home-maker. If careering forces women to neglect home and family and in that way to do what, deep in them, they do not desire to do, it is against basic human need and human good. So far as movies point in an antihome direction, they are a menace, and so of other forces such as schools, including many colleges for women. If a man can give his life or a woman give her life directly to the service of God, they may do this, and thus not marry, but they may do it only for this more direct love of God, which is a greater good. Some few, Christ says, can, and He says, Let them do it. Marriage remains the ordinary and common means to great goods for person and society.

We must return as many marriages as possible to the Church and even to the Sacrament; prepare for marriage, as Quakers do, and as girls do at Grailville school at Loveland, Ohio, by prayer, meditation, and study; we must see the home again as fortress and sanctuary; help young couples to work on their common problems as they do in Cana and pre-Cana groups and in the Christian family movement; encourage people to save in view of marriage and after marriage, so as to own homes; encourage them to live outside cities and acquire productive property such as land and a cow—a cow can do wonders for a family!—to raise and process food, to make things at home and in general to work together in the family, to play together, and to pray together. The family on its knees together every night in the home is a fairly well-redeemed family. The family that prays together stays together, is Father Peyton's formula. The family that prays together, plays together and works together and, at least to some extent, owns together, is a family with more stability, more ballast, more happiness.

With tremendous pressures—of nature, of heavy populations in India, e.g., of economics, of propaganda, of naturalistic secularism—against the family, against purity and fidelity, it will take all that nature and grace can do to promote personal and social continence and family unity. What God and nature command, can be done, though in this matter and against natural and artificial odds, we need a certain heroism.

CHAPTER 14

# EDUCATION: RIGHT AND RESPONSIBILITY

HAVE Communists a right to teach in American schools? Did the Supreme Court violate anyone's rights in the McCollum decision, or in the school-bus decision? Is a person bound by nature to develop his intelligence, or is he bound by the State only "to go to school"? Are persons and groups morally bound to promote science? What right has the State to make children attend schools until they are sixteen? Why does not the federal government make everyone "go through" high school? Are we morally bound to maintain excellent Christian and Jewish schools? Who, if anyone, has a right to go to college? What is the parents' obligation to oversee schooling? Who, if anyone, is immoral when many are religiously illiterate? The draft for War II showed that the greatest cause for rejection of Negro draftees, ages 18 and 19, was educational deficiency. Who is to blame for that condition: Jim Crow, the politicos, the "owners and operators," Southern prejudice, or the Negro's mental incapacity?

What are we to think of the snobs from the colleges? What of the social responsibilities of colleges and their graduates? What of the impact of 60,000,000 comic books a month: what do these do to minds, virtue, culture? Are movies a blessing or a menace? The radio? Television? The press? Have people a duty to decree, by law, or by pressure, that certain things shall not be shown, or be told in the press? Has anyone a right to unlimited freedom of speech: in peace? in war? This chapter considers some of these questions.

In 1948–49 avowed Communists were denied the right to teach in the State University of Washington. Had the University the right and duty to dismiss them? Our reply is that any school has the duty to dismiss Communists found on its faculty. Among the reasons are these. If we have a duty to try to preserve our nation's life and freedoms, and if Communists are sworn to destroy these, we are bound not to hire them and bound to dismiss them as soon as found. Secondly, it cannot be shown that we must allow anyone freedom to teach anything to anyone in any way he pleases; it is romantic and paradoxical to hold that we must allow a freedom that destroys. Thirdly, this is no longer a theoretic nineteenth-century question. The Communist is sworn to promote Communism, and our trying to make him free could not succeed. He is a party liner, not free to seek or teach the truth.[1]

In the 1940's two decisions on school questions by the federal Supreme Court raised great ructions. In the Everson case the decision was that the First Amendment does not prohibit a state "from spending tax-raised funds to pay the bus fares of parochial school pupils as a part of a general program under which it pays the fares of pupils attending public and other schools."[2] The decision was based on nondiscrimination: if buses for some, why not for all? It raised in an engaging context the issue of discrimination.

In the second, the McCollum case (1948), the question was whether a state may allow public school buildings to be used for the "released-time" teaching of denominational religions. The decision was against this use, on the ground that it would result in too close a connection between tax-supported property and the promotion of particular religions; ". . . the close cooperation between the school authorities and the religious council in promoting religious education . . . : This is beyond all question

[1] See Sidney Hook, "Should Communists be permitted to teach?" *N.Y. Times,* Magazine Sect., Febr. 27, 1949.

[2] Everson vs. Bd. of Ed. (1947), 330 U.S.

a utilization of the tax-established and tax-supported public-school system to aid religious groups to spread their faith," and is banned by the First and Fourteenth Amendments.[3]

The decision was difficult: Justices gave a supporting opinion, a concurring (but not fully supporting) opinion, and a dissenting opinion. About the decision many are unhappy, convinced that, so long as it remains law, the public schools are officially made secularistic, and secularism is declared the official religion of America.

Whatever their faith, millions do not perceive how we as a nation can afford to have the courts banish religion. These millions feel that the decision is bad for future citizens, bad for homes, for Labor, professions and future farmers, since children are taught, by silence and exclusion, that religious doctrines and practices have nothing to do with life, with the nation's welfare or with truths learned in literature, history, and social science. Localities and persons will continue to teach religion as a part of the child's total formation; but the decision tends to put a quietus on teaching religion in public schools. A question decided by the Court can be reconsidered and re-adjudicated, though this is not likely to be done and cannot easily be done.

The official position in the United States now has two parts: a) we must have schools, with the majority in the grades and in high schools being required to attend public schools; and b) these schools must teach no religion except secularism.

A special feature of the McCollum decision was cited by Justice Reed in dissent. If it is unconstitutional to have religion —Catholic, Jewish, and Protestant religions—taught in public school buildings outside of school hours, and if the reason is that to allow the teaching would be against "separation" of Church and State, consistency would suggest that we cancel all services of chaplains to the military. These chaplains and services are "tax-supported."

The legal question is whether the Court overworked the

[3] People vs. Bd. of Ed. (1948), 333 U.S. 203.

principle of "separation" of Church and State, and some of the Justices raised this question. What is needed is integration, not separation.

Before we raise particular problems we underline some points with regard to learning. First, learning is an immense human good. A man can be a good man without great stores of speculative knowledge; he must know only what it is, in his case, to be a good man. But most must have much more knowledge, such persons as parents, pastors, teachers, doctors, lawyers, and citizens of a democracy; each must understand his station and its duties and use the relevant knowledge; otherwise he is, so far, a bad man. In addition, knowledge is a good, whether useful or not; it is a terminal good; only extreme pragmatic obscurantists fight against such knowledge. Secondly, contrary to what Socrates held, knowledge is not the only good, since intellect is not the whole of man; neither body nor will can be reduced to intellect. Some human goods are specifically the good of will, some of intellect, some of body. "A healthy mind in a healthy body" implies two irreducible kinds of goods. "I know, but do not do" implies distinct powers in man, each with its irreducible type of good.

Hence the error of extreme intellectuals, rare indeed, who tend to delete moral good, and the opposite error of puritanic, pragmatic moralizers who would make all virtue practical and moral.

Thirdly, we mention the question whether moral virtue can be taught. We know for sure that it can be learned, if the child is at first totally nude of intellectual and moral virtue. When people say that moral virtue cannot be taught they mean that, though it is acquired, it is not acquired as speculative intellectual virtue is: "mainly by teaching," as Aristotle holds.[4] Persons become moral: they acquire moral virtue by practice; by habituation, by going through the paces. This is the way we learn arts and skills; we practice typing or the ABC's or golfing, and if

[4] *Ethics,* II, c. 1.

teachers help us much, properly it is we who learn. So too teachers and schools help us to become good, but finally it is we who, somewhat because of them, become good or who, because of them or in spite of them, become evil.

The person is ethically obliged, if he can do it, to learn enough so that he knows how to be a good man. This modicum is more than the aristocratic temper might allow the commoner, as it includes knowledge of the basic practical principle that good is to be done and evil avoided, knowledge therefore of "good" and "evil" and the demarcation between them, and some rudimentary knowledge of which lines of conduct are good and which are evil. The man knowing these things is not a simpleton, and the primitive roughly knows them, even if he does not know that he knows them; and we may not say that great advance in metaphysics, arts, and sciences will make a man morally better.

There is no inherent connection between being moral and having theoretic, speculative knowledge. On the other hand, a man cannot understand moral goodness unless he is a good man. If a man lives an evil life he will tend to rationalize his position, defend it and eventually hold that his way is good. In other words, the man of evil life is blinded so that he cannot grasp truths regarding the good life.[5] So of groups, religious, national, or other.

The basic responsibility is that each is obliged to learn enough so that he will not be an evil man, thus destroying his own chance to develop character and concurrently turning more or less into a social menace. But he begins as a foetus, an infant, a child, and his parents and school, Church and State direct him toward virtue or vice. With the help of society, nature, and grace it is his duty to become good, and the duty of society to help him along that road.

Society does this in many ways. The State puts up "no left turn" signs, each of which looks negative but is a double-negative

[5] On these matters, see Aristotle's *Ethics,* Book II.

positive: Do not hurt your neighbor in his life, his freedom, his rights, his goods. The Church says: Honor and love God, honor and love thy neighbor as thyself, commandments implying that each loves himself, but he can so love as to destroy himself unless this natural and indestructible self-love is complemented and sublimated in the love of God and neighbor.

Great and pervasive as State or Church is, the child learns the good life most effectively at home; like charity, the normal person's learning goodness and rightness of love begins at home. If the home is weak on unity and stability because of ubiquitous divorce or on love of the quiet life and prayer and worship, or if parents are scarcely at all in the home because of drink and night clubs or of work far from home, it has not sufficient character to do its work of showing the children the glory and grandeur of virtue and of saying to them, "Right turns only."

Then people come to a desperate conclusion: the school must teach goodness; the school must make children good. Where the school is a State school, the State enters the sanctuary of freedom and of character.

In the circumstances this conclusion makes a sort of sense. Home and Church, the first and greatest teachers relative to goodness, have defaulted. Then we say, The school must make the child good. If the home is more or less non-existent, we wish a considerable task on the school in asking it to mend matters. Our high schools by no means make it evident that they are able and willing to do the task. To expect it of them is unreasonable.

What the schools on all levels can do is to try to carry on good traditions and habits already learned by children. Teachers can help students to begin to understand the splendor and survival value of virtue. Perhaps teachers in towns and small cities are put unreasonably in a difficult position and are expected to be puritanic, but people may not tolerate evil living in the teacher who on every level can help the student see in literature and history the wonders and glamor of goodness, and let him see the horror in Shakespeare's villains, in Dante's Inferno, in Faust, in Dr. Jekyll and Mr. Hyde.[6]

The school should do what it can to protect youth from evil, but should not try to track and hound children at every turn and, least of all, those getting up to legal age, when we may suppose them capable of discretion and responsibility. Children learn better if allowed some freedom and leisure.

Example is the primary teacher, at home, in the school, in religious bodies, in the street, in movies and television, on the air, and in general society. The mores are an efficient teacher. Children are likely to do what adults do. "Like father, like son." This is most true where parent, teacher, churchman, rich man, movie star, or athlete is the child's hero. If children know what Bing Crosby does off stage and when he's not singing those everlasting, sad, quavering songs on the air, his conduct must influence them considerably; and when young and old hear the "stars" saying the rosary on the air, they are ready to say it with their heroes.

We have the problem of the movies which, built on profits and dime-novel sentiment, have inevitably been teachers. How much have they built up cultural and moral life? Have people any right to censor the movies? Have Catholics any right to an operative Legion of Decency? Has any person or group the right to bring the pressure of public opinion, of a deflated box office, or of politics to bear on the question of what will or will not be shown in the movies?

It is not merely Catholics who have the right and not merely Christian bodies. It is people. We the people have the right and duty to know what kind of food we are being sold, what kind of medical treatment we get, what kind of schools we have, what kind of stage shows and movies, what kind of televised programs. We have responsibilities toward ourselves, our

[6] See Maritain, *Education at the Crossroads,* pp. 93–97; and Sir Richard Livingstone, *On Education* (New York: Macmillan), part 2, chap. 4.

children, our children's children, and all society. We may not let people teach that white is black, that dirty is clean.

What we may and must do regarding movies we may and must do regarding comic books, the press, publishing houses, radio, television, and recreation centers.

Each of these is a teacher, telling the truth and telling lies, glamorizing good and glamorizing evil. To invoke freedom and say that anybody may teach anything is unrealistic. Those who censor groups for censoring movies claim thereby for themselves the right to censorship which they deny to others. Whether censorship is well-exercised in a particular case is, of course, an open question; even so wise a man as Plato would have been an unsatisfactory censor.

People have the duty to find out what the schools do, and what, at least in some approximate terms, they might ideally do, a duty devolving on parents, on superintendents, teachers, school boards, the Parent Teachers Association and, at times, on government. We cannot afford to pour money into a rat hole. Abilities would be wasted, under pretense of development. Democracy demands that we have universal education, but nature and the exigencies of the times demand that it really be education. Youths readily let laziness keep them from intellectual work; besides, the movies, radio, and television, each of them a possible excellent educator, have combined with lack of school discipline to delete homework and destroy reading habits. We never did have general reading habits in America; we were too busy as pioneers, making land, founding a new nation, building railroads and factories, fighting wars. In most families in the United States only comic books and newspapers are read; many rarely read a magazine, and only a small percentage read a book a year.

Though speed, machinery, and an uncriticized democracy leave us somewhat illiterate, we have, through radio, television, and the daily paper, a lively superficial intelligence. Think of all the

"I-Q programs" on which a person reaps a fortune by a right guess or by knowing offhand who is bishop of Afghanistan. Think of a large, strong man, with a "college education" and plenty of charm, day by day dialing random phone numbers and saying: "This is the XXX Horstalman program on VBQ. We give away 'oodles' of our nice-as-pie products to the person who can give the right answer to . . ." Such programs do not enlighten either the unfortunate announcer with "a good job" or his startled clients. Do democracy and free enterprise require us to encourage such programs?

In short, what is the morality of doing work which you cannot respect, of selling things that you feel are oversold and dinning honied words all day long into the nation's ears? Have "our patrons" any responsibility to the cultural life of America? The association of women broadcasters has declared for "intangible spiritual qualities" in radio programs, and said there is a malnutrition of mind as well as of body.

What is the morality of publishing, distributing, and reading the 60,000,000 comic books devoured by Americans, mostly children, each week? Morality or immorality in a direct and ordinary sense is one question; another, hardly less vital, is what a perpetual diet of comics does to minds and the national cultural life.

Is the press helping youth to love goodness when it exploits divorce and sex crimes? Is this "telling the truth" worthy of editors? Ought we to boycott the programs of multiple-divorce "stars"? Would we thereby unwarrantably invade freedoms? If so, which freedoms and whose freedoms? Where do people get the right to tell children that immoral conduct is glamorous and beautiful? Was the nation immoral in its reaction against Rita Hayworth's conduct?

Or must homes keep doing their level best against the press, against the movies, against radio, against television? In that case education certainly is a race against catastrophe.

Fortunately we have many favorable winds. Programs, movies,

schools, books, and the press are generally fit for adults and children.

Much good work is done in schools, and it is remarkable what a great teacher can do in the grades or in a high school. Within a generation the high schools have placed music in the forefront with fine orchestras and bands, which evidently require ideals and discipline. We have heard a high school do incredible choral work, and have heard accomplished products in speech which, as a rule, is a neglected art. On the higher levels, picked students—who would be any good unless picked?—do splendid work in biology, physics, and mathematics; the problem in this regard is that neither they nor their teachers have a basic general education or know how to integrate science with theology, philosophy, and humanistic learnings.

We also have promising informal developments. One is the CIO schools set up in Midwest industrial cities. Another is the somewhat correlative growth of Catholic Labor schools which, sometimes tied to college or high school and often to the ACTU,[7] are adult groups of laboring men studying the problems of the laboring man; these exist in many centers, though not in half enough (a list is given in Cronin's *Catholic Social Action,* Bruce Co., Milwaukee, 1948). The third is the body of people, mainly youths, in and out of school, engaged in Catholic Action, which always supposes study of the given situation. A team of these workers has established in a small industrial city a Catholic bookshop and cultural center where till now there was not a ghost of such a growth. Another unit maintains a press for Catholic Action pamphlets and books; another, in a large city, makes known the really liturgical Christmas cards and Mass cards; and many units, each composed of a few families, study the problems and possibilities of a fully Christian family life.

Catholic bishops have said for over a hundred years that Catholic schools must be established, and some bishops require that schools be built before churches. The reason is that children

[7] Association of Catholic Trade unionists.

need the integration of religious practice and religious doctrine with the study of arts and sciences. The completely "lay," "neutral" or "mixed" school is difficult to effect and where it has been effected, in the United States and in France, for instance, such a school defeats itself by turning automatically into the non-neutral school of secularism. To many besides Catholics it is profoundly unsatisfactory.

Whatever the cost, therefore, Catholics have felt an obligation to build Catholic schools. To date, justly or not, they have been required to pay taxes to support public schools while paying a separate tax to build their own. Nobody supposes this a delightful task for families most of whom are poor.

Among moral obligations to the intellect are these. The teacher is obliged in justice to give his time and effort and his life to teach; it is not permissible for him to be unprepared or to do mediocre work. The administrator is bound in justice to do his work, and see that others have equipment, be on the job, and do their work.

Gilson's saying is the best on this matter. He says [8] that it is conceivable that we should never have had Christian schools, but if we are to have them we are bound to have good ones. Nothing, he says, requires a man to be a scholar, but if that is his chosen work, no height of goodness can cover his failure to master his technique and his matter. Who is bound in advance to be a poet or scientist, or to teach? Probably nobody. But once a man goes into the work, he is morally obligated to do it.

Catholic and other church-related schools continue to carry a terrific financial burden. In view of the work done, is the State bound, in distributive justice (that is, State-to-man justice), to offer financial aid to church-related schools? Some referendums, some courts, and some local school officials refuse to let the school bus, passing the Catholic children's door, take them to school. This is evidently discrimination, as the Supreme

[8] Etienne Gilson, "The Intelligence in the Service of Christ the King," *Christianity and Philosophy*, chap. 7.

Court decided; it is an act against distributive justice, which binds the State to treat all citizens with impartiality.

Documents show that when Catholics have built schools, the save-the-faith and save-the-morals idea has ruled. It is time for Catholic colleges and universities to take a more positive view of learning. A Catholic learning, based primarily on the Scriptures, exists, and to teach this Catholic and "adequate" learning is specifically the work of all Catholic schools on the higher levels.[9] It is time for the Catholic schools of higher learning to discover their own standards and ends, and in the light of these try to accomplish what they alone presumably can accomplish for their students and the good of the nation.

A somewhat similar learning is doubtlessly the ever-increasing inheritance of Jewish people and of Protestant people, and only the creation and transmission of this learning would (the author holds) strictly and properly justify the existence of Jewish and Protestant schools.[10]

Some Protestants have gone on the assumption that public schools are Protestant and the remote assumption that this is officially a Protestant country with a union between State and Protestant Church. Real estate men advertise property as near "both Catholic and Protestant schools." Events have done something to jar this un-American idea.

A more basic issue was settled in the twenties by the Supreme Court. In the postwar excitement the one-language law was passed in Nebraska requiring schools to teach only in English, a law set aside by the Supreme Court in the case of Meyer vs. the State of Nebraska. Then Oregon passed a law, to become

[9] See Leo R. Ward, *Blueprint for a Catholic University*. St. Louis: Herder, 1949; especially chapter 5; also D. von Hildebrand, "The Conception of the Catholic University," in *The University in a Changing World*. Ed. by W. Kotschnig (London: Oxford University Press, 1932).

[10] Cf. Arnold S. Nash, *The University and the Modern World* (New York: Macmillan, 1944), chapters 6, 7; A. J. Coleman, *The Task of the Christian in the University* (New York: Association Press, 1947); Gaebelein, *Christian Education in a Democracy* (New York: Oxford Univ. Press, 1951).

effective in September 1925, requiring children from 8 to 16 to be sent to public schools only. This law also was invalidated by unanimous decision of the Supreme Court which, granting "the power of the State reasonably to regulate all schools, to inspect, supervise and examine them, their teachers and pupils; to require that all children of proper age attend some school, that teachers shall be of good moral character and particular disposition, that certain studies plainly essential to good citizenship must be taught, and that nothing be taught which is manifestly inimical to the public welfare"—which makes Communist indoctrination unconstitutional—also said:

"The fundamental theory of liberty upon which all governments in this Union repose excludes any general power of the State to standardize its children by forcing them to accept instruction from public teachers only. The child is not the mere creature of the State: those who nurture him and direct his destiny have the right, coupled with the high duty, to recognize and prepare him for additional obligations."

In the light of that decision the totalitarianism of those who hold that only public schools are American and that all must attend public schools is heretical to good Americanism.[11]

Catholic colleges and universities are not prepared to offer to all the best Catholic applicants graduate work in all fields, nor perhaps in any field. Many must go to other schools or give up graduate studies. It is certainly unethical to direct a student to a school unprepared to do the work. If the student is really fit to undertake such rigorous work, we may direct him to a school where it is offered; also we can, as we barely begin to

[11] See the competent article, "The Supreme Court on Educational Freedom," *Survey*, July 1, 1925, pp. 379–81, by Robert W. Bruère who says: "The avowed purpose of the law . . . was to buttress patriotism in the young and to insure single-minded allegiance to the Flag and the Constitution . . . The Oregon law was one of a recent series through which attempts have been made to do by indirection what could not constitutionally be done directly . . ."

do, create on a high and worthy level graduate schools of our own.

Today we cannot nearly fill our own teaching posts with Catholic scholars, above all in physical science and mathematics. Yet it is hard to see how schools can be Catholic if heads of many departments and most professors in some impressive departments, are not Catholic, and if the student body, in graduate work and in downtown city schools, is non-Catholic. How does one create a Catholic university when non-Catholics form a large part of the students and the staff? [12] The Catholic graduate school is obliged to search for high-rating and promising Catholic entrants and to seek Catholic mentalities for its faculty.

Some Catholics in the United States formed, in June, 1946, a "commission" on the intellectual life. A chief purpose is to find and encourage the Catholic lay scholar in Catholic and non-Catholic schools and research institutes, and help him see and do his work precisely as a Catholic scholar. The present writer holds that three points are strictly required for the Catholic scholar and for the Catholic school. The Catholic scholar, as any other, must be master of his matter and of the methods proper to his field; his life must be profoundly Catholic, as a sine qua non of his being a Catholic scholar; lastly he must know the relation of his special study to theology or the highest theoretic Christian wisdom. It is a considerable accomplishment for the scholar to manipulate these requirements, particularly in a non-Catholic school. So far the commission mentioned has moved on a high level and is one of the promising events in recent Catholic intellectual history.[13]

Why all this shouting about Catholic learning? One reason is that people, including some in this country, have tried to sell the

[12] The writer is happy to know three Protestant professors who left "big" posts to return to more Christian surroundings, one of them at a cut of $4,000 a year in salary.

[13] Catholic Commission on Intellectual and Cultural Affairs, 3900 Harewood Road, Washington 17, D.C. Other nations have followed this lead.

world a communistic totalitarianism which is as opposed to Christian life and learning as darkness is to light. The other is the positive good in Christian learning. Many groups have moral obligations in relation to learning for their members: the NAM, the Farm Bureau, the AMA, the CIO and AFL, the ALA. But administrators, deans and professors have the first and greatest obligation. We cannot exempt from this obligation the schools of Catholics, Protestants, and Jews, and any learning specific to them as Catholics, Protestants, or Jews.

Each of these groups is morally obliged to work with scholars from each of the other groups and with scholars from the often richly endowed nonsectarian schools. No school can live by itself alone; each needs to borrow experts on many subjects. Besides, the Hebrew and Christian schools badly need the stimulus both of the ancient pagan learning and of learning won in modern universities outside the church-related types. Think how inadequately a particular Hebrew school, out of touch with 17th century learning, wished to educate Spinoza. All men of learning need cross fertilization of their learnings with those of other schools and other fields. The day of isolation is passing, and learning demands unification and integration. Christians and Jews must break intellectual bread continually with men and women from nonsectarian universities, on occasion attend their schools, confer with them, make one membership in academic societies with them, and learn what it is to be pure of heart toward knowledge wherever found.

Science is a light and in modern times the chief discoverer of truth. It also leads to many useful goods; if it leads to evil, the trouble is in man's will and not properly in dynamite or bombs. Modern man in the West will have more and more science, since the method of science is progressive. We may not say he needs more science in order to survive, since our use of present or future science may lead to every kind of destruction.

Nevertheless, the schools are morally obliged, so far as their means will stretch, to be engaged in scientific research. Otherwise a school's learning is scarcely modern, and an outmoded learning, whatever its earlier goodness, is on the road to death.

A moral obligation in this regard is to labor to find out, if possible, the relationships of science to all other learnings, its place in schools and society. Merely to say as such men as John Dewey did from the 1880's to the 1930's, "Ah, the scientific spirit! Scientific method!" is no reply to real questions, and to say with them, "Science will solve our problems, science will furnish standards: we must go on with a pragmatic, fideistic trust; this is best," is to ask man to be an ostrich.

An obvious duty of Americans is the reform of the vocational idea. Two generations ago this idea penetrated schools and was in many ways needed. We have little evidence that it was, as it caught on and was written into books on vocationalism, more than individualistic and secularistic. It meant in practice that youths in high school or college would be steered toward well-paying jobs. What was to become of the social good that we might presume the school was bound to serve and youths were being trained to serve?

In going through a dozen works on "vocations" for youth I have found hardly a dozen lines relative to the social aspects of vocation. Vocational directors may be given twenty questions to ask a youth, and one or no question be included on whether the youth wishes to, or has an obligation to, serve society.

The youth's new training makes him slick and efficient for serving himself, but about his serving society, about his taste for doing this, his need to do this if he is really to be a man, hardly a word is said. About the youth's learning to know and act as a Christian, about his coordinating his "vocation" with a vital social Christianity, there is even less said.

Several developments, already mentioned, toward a vital social Christianity, in new schools and in dependent units within schools, are a criticism of the dechristianized, anti-social vocationalism mentioned. Among these are the CIO schools, the Catholic Labor schools, Friendship House, the Grailville School, the Catholic Worker development, and Catholic Action units. Such schools and units, whether Catholic, Jewish, or Protestant or in fact antitheist, seem to ask a serious question. In terms of a vital social Christianity,[14] how long have the high schools and colleges been asleep?

[14] See Emmanuel Cardinal Suhard, *Growth or Decline? The Church Today*. Tr. by James Corbett. South Bend, Ind. and Montreal: Fides press, 1948. John Julian Ryan, *Beyond Humanism* (New York: Sheed & Ward, 1950).

## CHAPTER 15

# THE STATE AND HUMAN FREEDOMS

WE CONSIDER "the State" in the sense of the people living together and forming a *convivium*. They have territory and the other wherewithal so that they can live, and have a relative independence. However, if we take Aristotle's autarchy as a complete self-sufficiency and an absolute independence, no state or people has this in practice or in good theory. State depends on State in many ways; they complement each other and need each other. Each should give up some of its sovereignty, for its own good and for world good.

The old notion of the State as totally and absolutely sovereign is at least moribund if not passé. We live in a modern world. God is absolute sovereign by right. Mussolini is not; Stalin is not; Japan is not; England is not.

The State operates through a government of some kind, relatively good and satisfactory. But a government is not good and is non-existent if it has not authority to make laws and enforce them. What good would the United States law-making body be if it could not make laws, its law-adjudicating body if it could not adjudicate them, its law-enforcing body if it could not enforce them? Through its government the State is in fact a dictator. It has authority and is necessarily authoritative.

A basic point about philosophy of the State is that the State exists by nature. This is the famous doctrine of Aristotle's *Politics,*[1] that man is by nature a political animal. Man is naturally a "polis-forming" animal; men form some kind of political set-up.

[1] 1253a.

The State in this view originates in the bare needs of life and continues for the sake of the good life.

With nearly all Greeks, Aristotle overemphasized the rights of the State. For instance, he says [2] the State is to decide which knowledges shall be pursued and how far they shall be pursued, and according to Jaeger's *Paideia* (volume 1), the Greeks at their best perpetually tended to take State law or nomos as the standard of human goodness. Possibly Jaeger, not friendly to democracy, exaggerates the point; but we agree that most Greeks, not only the Spartans, subordinated person and family to the State.

Granting this, we still hold that men naturally need the State for life and the good life, that the State responds to an excellence as well as a need of our nature, and that men naturally, and therefore always, set up some kind of political society, with authority and power. In Maritain's remarkable formulation, as human intellect has a quasi infinite character, so the human will has a radical generosity, a power and need to give itself in love to the community "according to the law of superabundance."

If we say the State does not exist by nature, we are romantic with Rousseau and see the State as an imposition, or cynical with Hobbes, and hold that antecedently to the State-by-compact it was every man for himself, with nothing good or evil, and then the State-by-compact came to be and since that day the State decides good and evil, just and unjust, merit and demerit.

What the State declares to be good, is therefore good, says Hobbes: it is good because the State says it is good. It is in a totalitarian position. To challenge it in an effective way would be impossible, because of its power. But where would anyone get the right to challenge it, since the State is the source of rights and of just and unjust?

What the State decrees and does is bad, says Rousseau. Only

[2] *Ethics,* I, 1.

what the individual does, in the pre- or post-State condition, is good. It is good because he wishes to do it.

In Rousseau's view, man is naturally without the State and fell when he formed the State. In Hobbes' view man is naturally without the State and was saved when he formed it. One says he fell up, the other says he fell down. Each says the State is not always, not natural. Rousseau says it is antinatural, and Hobbes is tempted to say the same. Hobbes desires to oppose Aristotle and be vigorously royalist in the struggle of political royalists versus the political democrats. More than a century later, Rousseau goes to the other extreme and declares for individualism and anarchy.

If the State exists in some way by nature, the question then is, For what does it exist by nature? Everyone holds that a particular state, such as China or the United States, is set up by particular men under particular time-place circumstances. Still, it may be a demand of nature that the Chinese or the Americans establish some tolerable kind of State, and that when they fall out of one such as the English colonial, they fall into another such as American democracy. Chateaubriand came to America after 1800 to see Rousseau's pretended pre-State condition among the Indians, and said it was a let-down for a follower of Rousseau to find that the Indians in upstate New York had government and law.[3]

Rousseau is a common type: the State exists by force and by no right and the thing to do is to get rid of it, a position with which Quakers, Mennonites, Amish and a few of the Catholic Worker people have sympathy. On that view, the individualist, who wishes at least to bypass, if not destroy, the State is the just man. In America, where pioneers were running away from religious, economic, and political tyranny and where men were far from their European roots and from the law of the land, we acquired a taste for and a defense of anarchism: that govern-

[3] See Irving Babbitt, *Rousseau and Romanticism.*

ment governs best which governs least. That dictum still seems to many Americans true and eminently sane.[4] The State is our enemy, said Nock. We tend to allow to government merely negative functions: it may merely check crime; and even this may be disallowed, since sentimentalists say that freedom of speech has no bounds. Rugged individualism, my independence in economics, religion and morals; what I wish to do; myself alone; I will make my own decisions, lead my own life, form my own beliefs: such are some of our ruling notions.

Individualistic, anarchistic views get a jolt in practice. The State has in fact many positive functions in providing for health, for education, for religion; the old anarchic views hold, but to some extent are a consoling myth.

If the State in no way naturally exists, then what the tyrannos or the demos State does cannot be checked by man's rights or needs, because everything is determined by power. What it does cannot be checked against nature, since this is irrelevant. The antinatural State exists by its own power and for its own good and aggrandizement. Any man, any group may be ground to powder. We stand aghast at the things done by Hitler and by the Bolshevists-Soviets-Stalinites. However, in their view what they do is perfectly right, since what the tyrant decrees is right. The State is absolute and ultimate, and it is nonsense to say it can do wrong.

Freedom means an absolute and divine freedom, says the ultraindividualist. To be free, we must be against government, against law and order in politics, against morals, unless on our plan. A god to be worth a revivalist whoop would have to see that we were absolute. So says individualism.

The totalitarian says that to be under law, we must have no

[4] See Carl Becker, *Freedom and Responsibility in the American Way of Life* (New York: Knopf, 1945), chap. 1, especially pp. 5, 6. These anarchial views are defended by Clarence Manion, *The Key to Peace*. A formula for the preservation of true Americanism (New York: Garden City Books, 1951).

freedoms and must make an absolute of the State. It is remarkable how consistently the secularist falls into this trap.

Our position is that of liberty under law, liberty within bounds; the position that the State is of nature and also of men. The State is demanded by nature whatever men's condition, and will be established by men. Hence it is a work of "nature" and, concurrently, any particular State is a work of "man" or "will." At the same time, we hold that nature exists and sets limits to any man's or group's rights and to the State's rights. Each one has rights: State, person, groups; but nature sets limits to rights. It is so difficult to get this matter of limits to the State's rights that Aristotle missed it, though he was a master of "limits": limits of words, logic, conduct, art, and nature.

If the State is to exist at all well, i.e., to serve its people well, some persons must have the direct daily task of being public servants; e.g., the President, the Senate, the House, and justices of the Supreme Court. In war, men must be ready to expose their lives along with various already deferred freedoms. That is the only way the State can exist for our good, if we serve it and protect it, not for its good and aggrandizement, but for the common good, for the good of the remnant that may be left when and if the State survives. Such is the common Christian view, expressed by St. Thomas [5] when he says that "man is not subordinate in all he is and all he has to the political community."

The State may take a guilty man's life and expose the innocent to danger so great and imminent in some cases (as in battle) that it is almost exact to say the State then exposes men to death. It must do such things, but in doing them it meets limits that it must respect. It meets personality, as people say; it meets the human person who, even when the State is taking his life or exposing him to death, has rights and freedoms that the State may not touch.

The State has no right to invade conscience, though it often

[5] St. Thomas, *Summa theologica,* Ia IIae, q.21, a.4 ad 3.

does so, under the guise of public welfare: when it applies the "third degree" to force confessions. The State compels a man to say white is black; it tortures things out of him. Such extortionate ultra vires conduct is common in a war and, doubtlessly, the Nazis used it, and the Americans, after World War II, used it on Nazis and putative Nazis. A person has the right from nature and God not to have conscience and will forced and broken down. A person also has a right to some freedom of speech; to a just trial before being condemned of any crime; the right to worship, and, within limits set by nature, to worship as he will; the right to be respected as a human person whether or not he is old, of ignoble origin, beautiful, clever, or economically solvent and competent. These rights, says Maritain,[6] are rooted in nature and in the calling of the human person to an order of absolute values and a destiny beyond time.

Maritain has kept [7] to the Christian and properly natural position that man as a person has rights and freedoms not justly touched by any political community, a doctrine clearly relevant to the generation following 1917. Government is always in danger of falling into absolutism and of making man a State slave; Bolshevism-Sovietism, Fascism, and Nazism are victims of that danger. The person, Maritain explains, is not exactly the same as the individual, and in overdoing the individual's place we have hurt both the State in its rights and the person in his rights. ". . . One of the problems against which the modern mind beats in vain . . . the problem of *individualism and personality*. Look at the Kantian shrivelled up in his autonomy, the Protestant tormented by concern for his inward liberty, the Nietzschean giving himself curvature of the spine in his effort to jump beyond good and evil, the Freudian cultivating his complexes and sublimating his libido, the thinker preparing

[6] J. Maritain, *The Rights of Man and Natural Law* (Tr. by Doris Anson; New York: Scribners, 1943) pp. 79 ff. Also *Man and the State* (Chicago University Press, 1951), chapter 4, "The Rights of Man."

[7] See Maritain's many works on social philosophy listed in chapter 9.

an unpublished conception of the world for the next philosophical congress, the superrealist hero throwing himself into a trance and plunging into the abyss of dreams—with what religious pomp the modern world has proclaimed the sacred rights of the individual . . . Yet was the individual ever more completely ruled by the great anonymous powers of the State, of Money, of Opinion?"

Person, Maritain continues,[8] stands for the authentically autonomous; the person is free and can choose among means and, by use of his freedom, introduce new events into the universe; in the whole of nature, the person is the most perfect being. Individual is common to man, brute, and stone. Personality rests on the subsistent soul, whereas individuality is based on the needs of matter.

"My independence! My freedoms! My individuality!" In such expressions we reveal confusion. It is man as person, and therefore as possessed of freedom, who has inalienable rights. Man the individual is to be respected, yet not because he is individual but because he is man, and therefore a person. Of course a man can only operate as both individual and person, but he can so overwork either as practically to cancel the other and do injustice to man and society.

The State must protect minorities, religious, racial, national, occupational, and all those whom wealth or power would tend to crush. That is the way it protects freedoms. It always has tasks, with problems of the Klan in Alabama and New Jersey, of General Motors in the automobile belt, of Labor racketeers. In the face of many claims its officials must hold the middle road of nondiscrimination, but any good law enforced will hurt some persons and groups. That is why the ruler must have the virtue of "prudence" in an eminent degree, so as to be able to help and encourage persons and groups to direct their freedoms toward the good of man. The man with "prudence" has the ability to direct himself toward truly human ends, and, to some extent,

[8] Maritain, *Three Reformers* (Tr.; New York: Scribners, 1929), pp. 19 ff.

to direct those near him, such as his wife and children. The ruler needs this virtue in a comprehensive sense; he must know means and ends for society and break down these means in terms of valid groups and minorities; he must be able to judge when legislative or other political action is demanded; he must decide which matters may be left to private, nongovernmental action, and which matters, though possibly far from satisfactory, are in the circumstances advisedly left alone. With the growth of socialism he must know how to encourage people to help themselves by such seasoned techniques as savings and private ownership, unions, cooperatives, credit unions, and small business. In our conditions he must lead people to love private enterprise and private property and he must love to see enterprise and property widely diffused. He is required to know when he is to protect giant business and perhaps protect monopoly.

The State is to protect and encourage agriculture, trade, and business. Yet the State has, at times, taxed some expressions of these out of existence and at times entered into competition with them; thus it has chilled what we might suppose it was to warm and hearten. The result is that we see Western states competing for power with private economic interests. The outcome is a conflict, the State trying to control and, eventually, to run economic life, and economic life attempting to dominate politics. As the modern third power, labor jockeys with each. European experience suggests that the political power is superior in fact, regardless of right, to labor and economic power.

The rule of Pius XI in *Quadragesimo Anno* is that when private persons or groups are competent to do what must be done, say in medicine, education, or the production and distribution of goods, it is better that these persons or groups do it. It is better in the light of the "human-nature" standard. Men are freer, and men are supposed by nature and by God to be free. What chokes freedom is not necessarily bad, since man's freedom is not absolute; but what unnecessarily chokes freedom is to some degree bad.

The other main way, often used, to show the rightness of the principle is the fact that political powers wading into civilian functions have repeatedly shown themselves inept, notoriously inefficient, subject to bribes and corruption, and let us see that it must belong to man as person and as member of the economic or other non-State group to undertake what the government can only so unsatisfactorily do. Freedom to undertake and to do within the law of the common good is justified free enterprise.

In practice, many freedoms are helped or hindered by government and by the citizens' views and practices relative to freedoms. We mentioned the tyrannical assumption that this is a Protestant country and that members of other religions ought to be discriminated against: in schools, in matters of public policy, of employment, of national and state offices. Consider the Ku Klux Klan whose members persecute people claiming the right to a dissident religious faith and practice. Think how seldom we have had or are likely to have a Catholic governor of such states as Indiana and Iowa. Think of the fact that in Indiana, not noted for discrimination, till almost 1940 the state university (they say) never had on its faculty any Catholic except the football coach. Think of the condition found in Springfield, Mass., by a non-Catholic superintendent of schools born and trained in the Midwest and of Norwegian ancestry: the personnel in the schools represented an outmoded clique.[9] Notice the purely Hitler-Stalin statement reported as made in the Community Church, New York, in 1949: "The time has come to decide whether it is desirable to live alongside what is best termed 'the parochial feeling,' a separateness that is inculcated by Catholic schools."

The demon of the absolute gets us all. We wish to turn our nation or creed into the world; all must conform to our desire. We discriminate against other creeds, color or national groups,

[9] J. W. Wise, *The Springfield Plan* (New York: Viking, 1945); Chatto and Halligan, *Story of the Springfield Plan* (New York: Barnes & Noble, 1945).

other levels of society. We deny to others the freedoms we demand.

More particular obligations of the citizens to the State and of the State to the citizens are the following.

Unless citizens remain alive to current problems the State cannot well serve the common good. We must know all the time what the major parties take as ends and as means; we must make them declare themselves constantly. To a degree they are our rulers, and it is a duty as well as a right to know how they rule us, and at what cost. We must know what the American Federation of Labor intends, what the Congress of Industrial Organizations plans, how each is ruled, how much racketeering each suffers, the means each uses: education, oratory, political promises made and received, force, intimidation, bribery. We must know how Big Business rules us, how it manhandles legislatures, schools, churches, how it blackmails, bribes, perjures. We must know, as we certainly do not know, what the lobbies are doing, lobbies for farmers, for labor, for business, for churches, and for parties. We found out too late that we needed to know what foreign infiltration does to national safety. We have the duty, in homes, movies, schools, and churches, to teach youth that people may not take the political structure as something given to serve them without any question of a *quid pro quo*.

As citizens and as a nation we are bound to observe, judge, and act on what the schools, the press, the radio do, and what new devices and inventions promise or threaten to do. The work of these may never be taken for granted, any more than may the work of Congress, the President and his cabinet, and the courts. Citizens are the watchdogs of democracy, and vigilance is the price of liberty. If we will not perpetually study how to judge and act in the light of Christian principles, we can succeed only as a result of tradition and by luck, and not as free intelligent members of democracy. Generally, we will not succeed.

Our business as local groups, in churches, occupations, and schools, is to see what is going on. We first exercise freedoms and rights at the local level. If we muddle things here, the loss, multiplied by many communities, is national and is also ours. During World War II it was wonderful to see how the English, exercising their traditional freedom of speech, gave it to the Prime Minister and his cabinet.[10]

John A. Ryan said [11] that though it is greatly ad rem for a citizen to be a good father, a good workman, a good employer, in order to be a good citizen he must have specific knowledge of the citizen's power and responsibility and a reasonable acquaintance with political institutions, personages, and policies, a knowledge considerably more mature and realistic than that learned in a civics course. Citizens must be able to make a prudential judgment regarding party platforms, candidates for office, and campaign oratory.

The citizen, said Ryan, has these obligations: to obey the law, to respect authority, to be loyal (i.e. to be faithful and constant in allegiance and service), to be patriotic and yet avoid jingoism and the nationalistic spirit, to pay taxes, to serve in the military, and, if his services are needed, to run for public office.

Taxes bind in conscience and strict justice, and the tax evader is bound to restitution. However, a citizen is bound to pay only his share, and if the prevailing custom is to understate taxable property by twenty-five per cent he would pull more than his part of the load in declaring more.

Deliberate sin on the part of officials is more common than on the part of citizens. Many officials take bribes under various guises and continue to favor their family, their friends, and their party. They reward those who have helped them to be elected, a step not necessarily immoral, so long as persons rewarded (given certain preferments at public expense) are fitted to serve the public. To put incompetent people into well paying positions is immoral. Often this is done in order to preserve a person's party

[10] See the letters published during that time in the *Manchester Guardian*.
[11] John A. Ryan and Francis J. Boland, *Catholic Principles of Politics* (New York: Macmillan, 1941), chap. 15, "The Duties of the Citizen."

and probably himself in office. Such an act could be justified only if a person's party were *the* party and oneself truly *the* man to serve the public welfare. With respect to the party, this could happen pro tempore though not for any considerable time in a two-party or a multiple-party system. Some man may be convinced he is the man for office, otherwise government will deteriorate. Possibly Roosevelt was the essential man for a third and a fourth term, but it is not likely that he was or that any other was, or will be, the absolutely essential man.

Graft is sure to occur in a large nation and within states and cities, but we are not allowed to take part in it, and it may not be blest or exonerated in view of any custom or principle. Some people say: "That is what the other party would do if it were in power. If we do not, others will. We are in today and out tomorrow; so today is our only chance."

It is not difficult to see the principles used in such statements.

The policeman has a responsibility to public order, and is not morally allowed to line his pockets with bribes. So, naturally, of the judge, and of any public official. Francis J. Connell says, "The clergy of our Church, if they view the matter sincerely, must admit that as a group they are not taking a sufficiently definite and outspoken stand on dishonesty in civil office." [12]

[12] Francis J. Connell, *Morals in Politics and Professions* (Westminster, Md.: Newman bookshop, 1946), p. 65. See chapter 6, "Dishonesty and Graft."

Chapter 16

# THE ETHICS OF ONE WORLD

We see man against man, social conflict everywhere, even a gospel of conflict; Negro against white, and his efforts well reciprocated; nation against nation; communist against the world; capitalist facing labor, and for better or worse meeting his match; the religions, not on fire with love for each other, standing their grounds in a kind of truce sporadically broken on the State-and-Church question or in the form of KKK bonnets worn by men of this or that religion.

We are born to hate, evidently. We are born to misunderstand and misinform. Man is born to be a wolf to man, to eat him alive if he can. *Homo homini naturaliter lupus est.* Let every man think, work, love, hate for himself alone. Let every man's hand be raised against every other man's hand. Man is by nature to get what he can, and to keep it while he can.[1]

This antihuman, man-eating doctrine is in Hobbes and the pessimist Schopenhauer. Something like it is the principle of the ultra free enterpriser: that is mine which I can get and hold, so long as State law is on my side, and I will try to get State law on my side.

That is nature, say Hobbes and Schopenhauer. That is nature and iron law, says the old die-hard capitalist.

War is in our bones and we must get it out, say the militarist and warmonger: the sooner the better, since war is inevitable.

Black with white, Protestant with Jew or Catholic or vice

[1] For an excellent summary of these antihuman views see chapter 1 of Saul D. Alinsky's, *Reveille for Radicals* (Chicago Univ. Press, 1946).

versa, capital with labor, one world—ugh, it's nonsense and against nature; a peace plan, the popes for peace, a world community, a workable UN: all this will do for the Pollyannas. We realists are tougher; we announce war of every kind; ours is the Realpolitik.

The assumption of the "war-always" people is that man's nature is to hate and mistrust man, to waylay man whenever possible. The first law of nature is self-preservation, and, on this view, to preserve is to destroy. One world, yes; but it is inhabited by me alone, a solipsistic juggernaut. Lion and lamb will lie down together when the lion has swallowed the lamb.

This pessimistic doctrine has a considerable grain of truth. People are known to have fought people, to hate people, make things difficult for them, steal from them, use them in the light of expediency as standard. What helps me and my people—the Jews, the English, the Blacks—is good because it helps me and my people. What hurts my clique is evil. Wars go on and on. They have gone on throughout history. The presumption is in favor of the view that they will go on and are inevitable. Self-seeking will never end, and two can play at this game, can wish to be first, to obtain trade and markets, to have colonies. Aristotle told his pupil Alexander that lust for world empire would ruin Greece; but Alexander would go, whatever the risk. He was not the first, nor the last, to desire power and to sacrifice truth, virtue, and resources, and to handicap others for generations in order to satisfy his lust for power.

Let us say—and no one can certainly disprove it—that the lust for power is in every man. In some it is dominating; these use every wile and, in modern times, machinery and pressure propaganda. The danger is perpetual. Not perpetual peace, as Kant promised, but war.

Perhaps, however, man demands peace and is headed naturally for peace. The Hobbists notwithstanding, perhaps man in himself, in relation to nature and in relation to other men and to God, on an objective historical view, is more at peace than at war. Animals fight, but Tennyson's "nature red in tooth and claw" is a time-conditioned reading of nature.[2] So too of man defined as the warrior.

"Man-eat-man" is out of date. Not that it does not happen, but that on the pragmatic as well as the human view, it is more intolerable than ever, and is seen, better than before, to be unnatural. Circumstances will not let us think it God's will. Today we must in many matters give up antiquated ways and take into account modern conditions. Physically, geographically, commercially, we are being forced to be one world. "One world or none" is an expediency appeal, but is not therefore unjustified. Since on this one-world question, politics has not led commerce and communications, it must follow them.

At present, it seems that only two large forces go ungrudgingly and naturally with the "do-or-die" demand for an international view of the world. These two are the alleged old enemies, science and religion, and, it seems, especially the Catholic religion. Science by nature is universally the possession of mankind, not of Galen or Einstein, not of chemists or biologists or mathematicians or of our nation, but the possession of anyone who can make discoveries or of anyone who can assimilate scientific findings, and then the possession of any nation that knows how to use scientific products. The nature of science is to be universal. The Catholic Church has the extraordinary advantage of a generally common language, a liturgy and ceremonial fairly common everywhere, as the military experienced in world wars, and a universally common doctrine. It is not the Missouri Synod, excellent as this may be, but the Catholic Church. Yet each of these, science and Catholicism, suffers in relation to world unity. Science suffers from political brakes and controls and economic brakes and controls, on the national and the international level.

[2] See Wallace Craig, "Why do animals fight?" *Internat. Journal of Ethics* (now *Ethics*), XXXI, 246 ff.

The Catholic religion is hobbled by the fact that its members are men, with the old divisive habits, traditions, and prejudices, many of them anti-Jew and anti-Protestant. Every good tool for unity, such as commerce, religion, and science, must be carefully handled.

The basic factors, nevertheless, are for the most part in our favor. Allowing the individual to be individual, and the nation both to be and to be individual—which, of course, is the only way the individual or the nation could be at all—still, the demand of our time is for breaking down division walls, political, economic, scientific, cultural, religious; consider the friendliness of Pius XII to men of all faiths, and his unaccepted offer to send observers to the 1948 Amsterdam council of Protestant Churches.

World trade has in a measure led the way. It is true that commercially the nations make war, but despite import duties, patent rights and copyrights and trade rivalries, commercially the nations in many ways get together. Despite prejudices, merchants of the United States trade with Argentina and Spain; this is done on a profit and expediency principle, but it is done, and the principle is not necessarily bad. Japan learned to trade with China, and each, even if discriminated against, managed to trade with England and the United States.

That is not much, but it is something in the direction of a possible one world. Bad as trade is in this regard, it is politics or trade leagued with politics that produces trouble.

Is it merely expediency and profit, however, that bind nations together and tend to effect unity? On the commercial-plus-the-political-expediency basis could we ever make a success of international unity? Do not all of our international political acts suppose we somehow could?

We have stronger, more basic reasons. Let's review them. They are a stellar case of going with our standard of "human nature" and with the somewhat shocking fact that all are men. These reasons are as radical as our nature, and are our nature. With Aquinas [3] we break them down as follows:

Love is the major unitive force as hate is the major divisive force in us. We should love all men because all are men. We have the same nature as other persons and other peoples, and "nature" is deepest and most radical in us. The destitute is ourself with accidental, relative differences; none of us could be that man, because each is irreducibly individual, but essentially we are one with him.

The color and shape of our eyes, the color of our skin, the contour of our noses, the traditions and language proper to us, the culture we have through centuries created, are, as it were, our flesh and bone. But they are not our nature, but accidents of our nature, even though proper, inevitable accidents. They are of us, in us, belong to us, but what we are precisely as men the people of other nations, other climates, other faiths also are. In important minor matters, we are different; we are Oriental or Occidental, black or white, English or French, Protestant or Catholic, men or women, owners or workers. Important and unchangeable as some accidents are, they are not the nature and essence which we have with the Chinese, the Italians, the Germans, and the Protestants.

It is strange and doubtlessly somehow in accordance with divine economy that we should make more of what is less and less of what is more. It may be due to circumstances, to our insularity, to the fact that it is difficult for man to get a balanced and total view.

All one in nature: that is the radical ground of one world. Man is man whether tall or short, Jew or Gentile. This is our first and central natural reason for loving all men. *Homo homini naturaliter amicus est.* We are queer if we love cats, dogs, cars, the sea, or canaries. But unless short on human quality, we actively love all men or stand prepared on occasion to love

[3] *Contra Gentiles,* III, c. 117; cf. c. 128.

all; it is a terrible thing to hate or so much as despise whole groups such as Gentiles, whites, or Germans. Nearly all of us love most the people close to us, close in blood, in religion, occupation, race, nationality. Undoubtedly our own kin may be loved most. But we must love others.

This means two things. First, we must learn to love them, or, as a bare minimum, we must try to learn. Secondly, we look to their good; if they needed us we would without hesitation make sacrifices for them. Thy people are my people. Born together in the same excellent and rotten human world, we accept our destiny with them. Negatively, "one nature" means that we give up hurting people in their goods, their feelings, their freedoms; no pilfering and stealing, no enslaving in an economic, political, or any other sense, no name calling: no "niggers," no "perdifious Jews," no "fish eaters."

Charity begins at home, but my mother and my brothers are all these people: the Japanese, the Indians, the monks, the Masons, the Klan; not precisely as Klannites, but as people.

Possibly only a St. Francis goes with such a tough-hided program. St. Peter had a difficult time at first to accept this principle and required a vision from heaven to bring him to his senses.[4] "The apostles and brethren, who were in Judea heard that the Gentiles also had received the word of God. And when Peter was come up to Jerusalem, they of the circumcision contended with him, saying: Why didst thou go in to men uncircumcised, and didst eat with them?" To put it mildly, it was not the custom of Jews to "visit and eat with" uncircumcised men. To St. Peter it was scandalous. St. Paul was the first to learn that Christ came for all, and that all belong together in Christ. No Jew, no Gentile: this was a new doctrine and life. Just as if now a new Peter and a new Paul were to say: "Germans, yes; Irish, yes; Negroes, yes; but basically the unity of all." The Little Flower's new way was an old and fundamentalist way: the way of the child. We are bound to find another new way that is an old and

[4] Acts, chap. 11.

fundamentalist way: the way of love for all. God, nature, and the times will not release us. Many nominal Christians could learn from Gandhi. The new Rome, the new Jerusalem will not be built in a day. People have been brought up on another diet. They have sucked in hate almost from their mother's breast, they have been taught, quite contrary to nature, that certain families, certain colors, nations, nationalities, religions are inferior. Youths at Oxford University from the "best" families were ready to knife one who suggested that, over recorded time, possibly the Italians are, considering all things, the greatest Western people; these youths had learnt another doctrine; their minds were closed; *nosotros,* with plenty of vengeance. In short, persons, families, nations, all kinds of groups have learnt to balk nature on this matter of human love and unity.

This is evil. This is precisely what we mean by evil, things essentially snarled and fouled, things as Whitehead said "at cross purposes," nature headed one way, and we jauntily going another way.

"It's sentimental to preach love and ask people to love one another! Nations to love one another!"

In view of our ingrained habits, which are second nature, the doctrine of love and unity is romantic. As a man is, so he does. As a man does, so he is, and things like himself and his habitual way of acting he judges to be good and defends as good and natural. Time out of mind we have been difficult with the neighbors. That is true. But basically the romantic sentimentalists are those who, not willing merely to allow for the psychological, historical fact of division, try to erect division, hate, and fear into a principle. Hobbes, a remarkably poor Christian, if one at all, tried to do that. As A. E. Taylor says in his *Thomas Hobbes,* here was this brilliant and influential man Hobbes who had no genuine or realistic concern for the spirit and for morality. The doctrine is essential pessimism.

The story is that at home, in Scotland, Scot and Scot fight like cats and dogs, yet if abroad anyone says "Boo" to a Scot, no other Scot will tolerate the affront. But it is evident that between Scot and Scot there is a radical homogeneity; there is human nature, and on that ground, at least as much as on the ground of our being Scots or English or Catholics or Lutherans or Negroes, at last we can—it is reasonable to hope—by sacrifice and fear of the Lord, build into one world what God and nature have in the first place made one world.

A second way to express the truth of man's natural unity is that, whatever our origin, whether or not from nature and God, and whether by design or by cosmic accident, we all have the same origin. My ultimate origination is your ultimate origination; we belong to one family.

That is what the Bible teaches us. It is what the anthropologists tell us. It is what Darwin said in a remarkable passage at the end of his *Origin of Species*. He said that this is a grand view of life: the Creator breathing life into a first form or a few first forms, and then under the constant laws of nature all the other forms, so wonderful and beautiful, "have been, and are being evolved."

Some of us wish not to think of it, because in our estimation we are so much superior; nevertheless on this basis of common origination all are brothers.

Again, whatever the destiny and end of man, there is, properly, one destiny and end for all men. If we are to enjoy a personal immortal life with God, it is not merely you or I, not merely Jew or Gentile, not merely Oriental or Occidental, who is to enjoy that life, but all men. If our destiny is the grave, the destiny of all is the grave; no supercolossus can escape it. If nature or God in any way sets any temporal end for us, such as the building of a kingdom of order and goodness, truth, and beauty, this end is set, not merely for professors or scientists or priests, but for mankind.

How unnatural it is for us who are one in nature to be tearing each other to pieces. How unnatural and cannibalistic it is for us to devour one another if we are one in origin and ultimately one family. How unnatural it is for us, struggling for one common end that presumably has room for all, to despoil, malign, and wound each other on the way.

One common nature, one common origin, one common destiny! These truths should be taught at home, at church, at school, in movies, in books, on the air. We should use every honest device to help people to begin, even if generations are required, to understand such basic truths.

In "A Free Man's Worship," Bertrand Russell is as usual, whether on congenital or other grounds, a pessimist, but he is consistent; he has man appear on the planet by accident, struggle meaninglessly for meaningless goals. The merit of this eloquent essay is that Russell makes all of one piece—all is accidental, meaningless, useless: he says all are in the same boat and the boat is sinking: man comes to be catastrophically, meaninglessly; he lives cynically, he perishes hopelessly.

In a sense we must go with Russell; we must keep origin, nature, destiny all of a piece.

At least, whatever man is, all men radically are. Whencesoever man is, all men are. Whithersoever man is headed, all men are headed.

For these reasons among others we are morally bound to show consideration, to show respect, to sympathize. If a man or a nation in some terrible way falls, it is not for us to throw stones; if any succeeds, it is for us to rejoice and be glad to offer congratulations.

All this is on the "human nature" standard and not on an expediency standard. *Nihil humani a me alienum,* and certainly not *odi vulgus profanum.*

Because we are one in nature and one in origin and destiny, we have the same basic needs, the same basic sufferings, the same fears, hopes, loves, and hates. Shakespeare's Richard II says that a king, after all, is a man, and Shylock says a Jew is a man.

It would get us nowhere to try to dodge facts. The Jew is in a score of ways different: in visage, in backgrounds, traditions, in religion—see how he cracks up, religiously and politically, in our times if he loses his religion: "how shall we sing the song of the Lord in a strange land?" He is different in secondary and relatively trifling ways, in fears, hopes, loves, and hates and, as everyone knows, in abilities. So of the Irishman, the Greek, the Pole, the Catholic. Fortunately the Irishman cannot turn into an Englishman, nor vice versa; the Frenchman and the German can trade hats, perhaps, but have traits they cannot exchange. This may or may not be all to the good, but we must accept it.

It is shocking to see the narrowness and clannishness of many deported, imported European scholars in the United States. We notice this because we are scarcely in a position to see our own nationalistic reactions and partly because we have been exposed, in most American communities, to people of every national origin. It suggests how great will be the problem of deflating the nationalistic spirit, while allowing for healthy nationalism in every country.

The Christian view makes the doctrine of unity stronger and more persuasive. All are born of Adam. All come from God and go to God. All have sinned, both in their ancestry and in their own freedoms. All, redeemed in Christ, are brothers of Christ and therefore human-divine brothers of one another. All are sons of our Father. For white to despise black, discriminate against black, or vice versa, is contrary to our nature. It is a denial of common family relationship, a common temporal end, and a common immortal destiny. It is a denial of our common relationship to God, our common lot of sin, our redemption and brotherhood in Christ.

Since people tend to hold that what they do is the thing to do, re-education is difficult. However, among practical steps we suggest the following to aid in community building. First, playing with people, and as occasion offers with people of different colors, different religions, different occupations, different social strata, different national backgrounds; secondly, eating and drinking with people; thirdly, working with them on tasks such as washing and ironing, spading the garden, putting up screens, taking down storm windows. It is hard to suspect and despise people if we work and play, eat and drink with them. We recommend the Martin de Porres Club (South Bend, Indiana) half of whose membership is white and half is black, and Friendship House which, in Toronto, New York City, and Chicago, brings whites and blacks together on common problems, to discuss, eat, play, and pray together. Also, we recommend the popular old-fashioned dances.

Fourthly, in negative fashion, we are bound not to hurt people by thoughtless, inconsiderate, nagging word or gesture. The "Our Father" is a farce unless we mean it. "Give us this day our daily bread" is a prayer for me and my family and for mankind. Snobbery must be lived down, whether social, financial, theological, or academic.

Fifthly, as Cardinal Newman said, it is good for priests and laymen to meet, learn to allow for each other and understand each other. The same holds true for teachers and students, employers and workmen, Protestant and Catholic. Every Christian family ought to have some Jewish families as friends, and vice versa: how that practice would reduce the tension in New York City! Relatively few, even among leaders, now work to reduce it. The Negro family should have white families as friends and vice versa. The priest in a Michigan town worked with every good cause, turned down no nationality, color, occupation, or faith; the St. Patrick's day program was mostly by non-Catholics, most of the audience was non-Catholic.

On the international question, we have farther to go. We have to get beyond the expediency standard; e.g. beyond the notion that what helps my nation is good for mankind. Two English political philosophers independently of each other have said that England knows on which side her bread is buttered. This kind of cancer, affecting every nation, wrecks peace and order. But many minor steps will help to build them.

For instance, we could learn about the good in every nation, learn to appreciate and cultivate the music and literature of foreign nations, to share science with mankind, as we will have to do, anyway. We could learn to love through knowledge and communication. It is a shame how intolerant and misinformed many Catholic, Protestant, Jewish pastors are, how intolerant and uneducated many scholars are. Before some pastors are for goodness, they are vigorous, outspoken "anti's," and before some alleged scholars are for truth they are against this or that man. It will help if more people live in other countries for a year or two; of course, live with the people and not isolated in hotels, where the people do not live.

A wider vision therefore, a more objective version of other races, other social groups, other faiths, other nations. A long way to go, and God help us!

Cecil Rhodes wished to sell English imperialism to the world, but Rhodes scholarships have done much towards unity. Rotary's program of bringing foreign students to America can be a positive move towards unity and peace. People might go to other nations, not as spies or salesmen or propagandists, but to learn and to iron out the troublemaking spots in themselves and their nations.

Would war then cease? Perhaps, but more probably not. Would war never occur, however, in a world where people began to learn about the goodness of peoples? In a nicely arranged ideal world, war would not occur. But we do not live in an ideal world, though the standard by which we judge conduct must be an ideal, a ne plus ultra; only accomplished saints reach the ideal in practice. Still, not to have the ideal and not to try to reach it, is to revert to pessimism and defeatism.

Will war occur in the real world, and, if it does, can it be justified? Can any modern war, no matter how provoked, be justified? Was the United States justified in entering World War I or II?

To say the least, wars are likely to occur. They have intermittently and in that sense "always" occurred, though we might claim that because peace has been intermittent it has always been. Wars have been recurrent and probably will be recurrent. But a modern war, destroying everything wholesale, goods, lives, virtues, standards: how can it be morally justified?

E. I. Watkin in his *Men and Tendencies* argues that no modern war can be justified. His basic reason is this. War can be justified in the abstract: a nation has the right to defend itself and its goods and people; some wars possibly were justified on that ground. But with Vittoria, the father of international law, Watkin says that though a war may be justified in itself, yet because of collateral circumstances it may be unjustified. Vittoria (writing in 1532) says that a war, up to his time at least, might be justified as follows: If a nation is invading my nation, the latter may defend itself. But my nation may also wage offensive war to avenge a wrong and to take measures against an enemy. Without war for a due cause, society could not hold together. But everything needed for the government and preservation of society exists by natural law.

Vittoria admits that it is hard to say when our nation's cause is just; it takes careful inquiry, since each prince thinks his own cause just. Carelessness and error, with all kinds of calamity in the balance, would be inexcusable. It is a matter of moment, involving many, "and they our neighbors, too, whom we are bound to love as ourselves."

A war may then be just and lawful "in itself," but owing to collateral circumstance it may be unlawful. He gives two possible instances. One is that some scandal would follow in retaking a city or province; then the war, otherwise lawful, would be unlawful. His bigger case is: "inasmuch as (according to what has been said before) wars ought to be waged for the common good, if some city cannot be recaptured without greater evils befalling the State, such as the devastation of many cities, great slaughter of human beings, provocation of princes, occasions for new wars to the destruction of the Church (in that an opportunity is given to pagans to invade and seize the lands of Christians), it is indubitable that the prince is bound rather to give up his own right and abstain from war. . . . When, on the contrary, great ills would befall each side by the war, it could not be a just war." [5]

In view of that principle, it would generally be difficult to justify a war, but Vittoria thinks it would not be impossible. If we followed that principle could we justify modern war, any war since 1914 and in any likely future? Watkin thinks we cannot. Therefore to wage World War I and World War II was, on the part of each side and each party to each side, immoral.

Standing literally by Vittoria's principle we must say that no recent and no likely future war can be justified. Do we have to stand literally by his principle?

Referring to World War I, G. K. Chesterton has an interesting reply. In his autobiography [6] he says we must not pretend to do too much in a war, not set out on a war to end all wars, an end perhaps that we could not accomplish, or to make the world safe for democracy. We set out to save something if possible and are bound to try to do this. "It is all nonsense to say that in such a struggle defeat would not have been destruction, merely because it probably would not have been annexation. States so defeated become vassal states, retaining a merely formal independence, and in every vital matter steered by the diplomacy and penetrated by the culture of the conqueror. The men whose names are written . . . died to prevent it and they did prevent it."

We do not ask whether England was justified in fighting that

[5] Franciscus de Vittoria, "On the Right of War" (edited by Ernst Nys, Carnegie Institution of Washington, 1917), pp. 163 ff.

[6] 1936, chap. 11.

war, or the next war. We say only that in spite of colossal destruction, greater than Vittoria writing in 1532 could well conceive, it could still be that nation X has a right and also a duty to fight. It may be that invaded Belgium and France and invaded Poland had such right and duty, and it may be that invaded England in 1939, and practically invaded England in 1914, had the right and duty. It is not heroic Christian charity to stand by when the nation is invaded or has been robbed and plundered.

Man's law is to be and as fully as readily possible to be, in himself and his communities. But this he cannot do without a good healthy State. But the State cannot exist at all and much less in good health if invaders are allowed to do as they please. That is why war may sometimes have to be fought.

If some virtues are fostered by wars, all kinds of losses are suffered: loss of materials, of men, of morale in many ways, loss of virtues. No war leader or fighter may seek these losses. What he must seek is preservation and peace for his nation. He forsees the evils and would if possible prevent them. A person or group may sometimes pursue a good although sure that evils will result. These follow as a byproduct which, try as we will, we cannot forestall.

Chesterton's argument for England's just cause in World War I supposes the victory that her losses helped to achieve. But she or any nation could be justified in fighting, win or lose.

It is harder than formerly to justify a war; the tonnage, the waste and losses, the breaking down of standards seen by Thucydides (born about 460 B.C.) are much greater. But the principles are the same. It is the old question, for man and communities: To be or not to be. God has ordered us to try to be, an effort which, war or peace, costs much.

Can the bombing of open cities be justified? Sometimes, yes. Suppose that we describe war as the attempt of one nation or group of nations to impose its will on another nation or group of nations. To use bare fists is to use force; to use propaganda, a step which can be moral or immoral, is to use force; to use guns, ships, submarines, air warfare, is to use force. The essential nature of the procedure has not changed, and the best understanding of modern war is still to be found in Thucydides' *History of the Peloponnesian War.* To use bombs is to use some more of the same thing: force. The kinds and amounts of weapons have changed, but not the nature of the thing done. Even to use the "A" and "H" bombs is not, in itself, to do an evil thing. Our own use of the bomb at Hiroshima is another question, of course, and Stimson's defense of its use [7] by no means makes it clear that its use was justified.

It is terrible to use shillelaghs, arrows, guns, bombs, gas, germs; because war is terrible. To secure an effective truce relative to any of these would be a good thing. Still, degree and amount cannot change nature.

What are we to think of our entry into World War II? The reply depends on many factors. We were applying pressure to Japan, to keep her from effectively helping Germany. We may not say that our action was necessarily immoral, though our national leaders, for example Presidents and Secretaries of State, have likely long been immoral in not seeing that we have trained diplomats in all foreign capitals. If Roosevelt sought war for glory, his desire was terribly immoral. If we did not know what propaganda we were fed, perhaps by the English or by Roosevelt and the English, each with ulterior purposes, the immorality rests also on us, on our press, our professors, clergymen, legislators: our "town meetings" were not realistic and courageous enough. If in spite of all reasonable care, locally and in our national and international leadership, Japan went to war anyhow, our cause was just and our terrific losses during the war and postwar were justified.

Are propagandists, entering the United States, immoral? By

[7] Stimson, "The Decision to Use the Bomb," *Harper's Magazine,* February, 1947.

no means. That seems to be the only way that the English, for instance, can hope to survive into any considerable future; possibly the English have a duty to propagandize, in peace and war. It is for our "town meetings" and our professors, legislators, rulers, and all leaders to know about any propaganda we suffer. We ought to have good jokes and songs about it, to follow closely those who subject us to it; we ought to fingerprint every foreigner reaching our shores, our FBI ought to keep track of his mission.

Look at these principles. Man is born to be, and the nation, to be any good at all and to be justified in being, is (we may say) born to be. Man is inevitably an individual, *sui generis;* and so is the nation. Man is born selfish and never does or can get totally over self-seeking: being is like that, being in God, or a man, an angel, a fish, a rat, a tree, or a log. Man is often cheated in fact and can hardly survive for want of goods; and so of his nation. To complicate matters, at least some persons inordinately desire power; so do some nations. Those with lust for power get the "swell head" and upset things. Thus wars may again result in spite of everything.

Made for peace and order, we can learn that so long as persons will not sacrifice much, peace and order cannot be. Nations can learn that so long as each seeks its own end, there will not (says Aquinas) be peace. *Meum* and *tuum,* Plato is eternally right in saying, make trouble. And yet whatever the outlook at any time, we are bound to seek the good of peace. Perpetual peace is a hope. But we must perpetually try for a world community. The case need not be all white or black; if the United States has to give up some sovereignty for the good of the United States and other nations, then let her do it. Only God has absolute authority and sovereignty. Nations, like persons, must give up something for the common good, in this case the international common good of peace.[8]

[8] See Robert M. MacIver, "Sovereignty means the right to resort to war." *The New Leader,* Jan. 4, 1947.

We conclude this point with Sturzo, Christian democrat and patriot who labored forty years for peace. He says[9] modern war is an irrational custom, but until the social elements making it possible are modified it is "rendered rational" in terms of "right, justice, social necessity." Disputes continually arise, and the effort to settle them short of "diplomatic ruptures, economic reprisals, and war, has been such as to show that mankind has made real moral progress seeking to free itself from irrational trends, and to seek a more comprehensive rationality. In the midst of the grave problems left unsolved by the last war and complicated still further by postwar policy, the consciousness of an international community has been and is still alive, even during the Second World War."

Postwar conditions always raise problems of unity. The "enemy" has been maligned, called whatever were then the bad names, and seen in an hysterical light. One group of nations now is at the bottom of the pile, and theoretically the other has won. Practice shows that the latter is open to all kinds of immorality. After World War II, the plan of dismembering and "dismantling" Germany was enacted with a kind of religious fervor. Bernard Baruch fathered the Morgenthau Plan, which, looked at in the light of facts, appears to justify the judgment made in 1945 by the *Economist*[10] on Baruch's plan before Morgenthau's name was attached to it. That journal said Baruch's plan was bad economics, bad politics, bad morals. The plan was to destroy German industry and in that way make future wars impossible, and concurrently reduce Germany to a pastoral nation. The Allies acted on this plan, taken to the Quebec Conference by President Roosevelt, though Stimson and

[9] Don Luigi Sturzo, *Inner Laws of Society*. A New Sociology (New York: Kenedy, 1944). Pp. 18–19, 135.

[10] "Mr. Baruch Has a Plan," the (London) *Economist,* CXLVIII (June 9, 1945). For Baruch's fathering the plan see also the *New York Times,* June 1, 1945, 1:7 and 7:1; June 9, 12:6; June 23, 1:4; August 6, 3:6; also the 1945 volumes of *Business Week, Newsweek, Commonweal, Time,* etc.

Hull say [11] they tried to restrain him. The Potsdam Declaration, signed on August 2, 1945 by Stalin, Truman, and Atlee, did not weaken the Baruch-Morgenthau plan. Texts of the Declaration and of the Plan are easily obtained and are brief and simple.

It is immoral to paralyze the economy of any nation; it is economically bad for neighbor nations and the community of nations; it is politically bad for a nation to have its economy destroyed, to have its political life cut to pieces, rendered pro tempore nonexistent; we have not the right to destroy a nation's political life. The forced migrations were to be, but could not be, "orderly and humane." Of course, after a war it is inevitable that much suffering will result. The question is whether the suffering is in any instance unnecessarily increased.

Russia's conduct after August, 1945, was clearly immoral, unless we are to say that world communism is a good thing, that imperialism at any cost is a good thing; and to destroy nations, prevent peace, and make international order impossible are good things.

[11] Henry L. Stimson, *On Active Service in Peace and War* (New York: Harper, 1947, 1948), pp. 565–82; Cordell Hull, *The Memoirs of Cordell Hull* (New York: Macmillan, 1948), pp. 1616–21.

CHAPTER 17

# MAN AND THE WORSHIP OF GOD

OUR claim is that man as person and member of society is to worship. His nature, seeing "nature" in "Nature" and in himself and society, demands it. He is to worship if he is freely and intelligently to be man. At least on occasion he is to worship.[1] The penalty for nonworship would be severe; man would be perhaps strong in many ways and yet seriously cheated and a man only in part. By his nature and if he is fully to be, he is bound to worship.

Proof of this statement rests on three grounds. First, on the logic of man's position in nature. Secondly, on a body of psychological data. Thirdly, on a wealth of anthropological, historical, and sociological data.

We begin with the logic of man's position. Religion is the moral virtue that consists in man's giving God the honor due to Him; this is the highest honor, and we give such honor by any of a hundred inner acts and outer acts; the totality of the inner and outer acts by which we freely honor God is worship. Our argument is that man is bound to worship God, to give by any appropriate means the highest honor to God. Man is bound because he knows that he is to give honor where honor is due, and in some vague, dull way or with relative clearness he knows indeed that God exists and is worthy of the highest honor. He knows that God is, but only with some vagueness or at best a relative clearness what God is. To rise to his manhood, man

[1] We like what appears to be the strict Mennonite view; people are always "in church" (therefore a woman always keeps her head covered).

ought to honor all men, as St. Peter says; to pay a tribute of honor and praise to all persons. The only persons, so far as we know, are human, angelic, and divine persons. If man knows persons, he ought to recognize the excellence of their being, and their greater or lesser excellence according to their levels of being. If angels exist and are known by man to be greater than man, it is man's business, supposing he desires not to deflate himself, to recognize the fact. If God is, and is known to be superior to man and angel, it is man's business, since he does not wish to deflate himself, to recognize God's existence. This recognition by any appropriate means is called worship, and the habit and virtue of worshiping is called religion.

To refuse to worship is to treat ourselves unfairly, to let our being suffer a hollowness where there should be manhood. Besides, it is unjust. What the virtue of justice requires is that we give persons their due, whether the "due" be labor, money, or honor. If God exists and if we know this and yet do not recognize God, we dishonor ourselves and leave the universe underdone at a point where we could bring it up in a vital and conscious way. So far we are not, and the universe so far is not; but God remains in His totality.

When we are irreligious we commit what the Greeks called *hybris,* the sin of getting out of place in relation to any known higher being or beings. The point is important because, so far as we know, we are the only ones throughout the planets able to know and worship God and thereby declare in an intelligent, free way the relationship of man and lower nature to any higher being or beings. In our freedom we are able to personalize and thus "save" an otherwise subpersonal universe, and in the act of worship make intelligent and free within ourselves a basic relationship that otherwise would remain dumb and necessitated. Of necessity, things seek God, says St. Thomas, but the act of man's freedom is not right (straight, *rectus*) until man consciously seeks God.

Many object that it is hard to know even that God exists and especially hard to comprehend the meaning and nature of God; the unthinking, they object, think they know; they take some one's word for it; and the businessman and politician either take people's word or merely go through the ritual of worship on Machiavellian grounds, for profit and votes; but people who try to think it all out are mystified and almost stupified by uncertainty.

Truly, it is hard to know at all well what God is; and the most confident of the theologian-philosophers, such as Thomas Aquinas, proclaim that fully to comprehend what God is, in the totality of His being and meaning, is not possible for finite intelligence: God is for us *"quasi ignotus";* we know God, and yet in a way God is the unknown God encountered by St. Paul among the Athenians, and the unknowable of Herbert Spencer. At least on the Thomistic theological-philosophical view, the full comprehension of what it is to be God is too much for man, and confronted by reality man does well to be mystified and semistupified.[2]

Yet man does not need either to go around in primal nescience or to fall into agnosticism. The common man can, and commonly does, know that God is. He can know that man is not the highest being, that he is dependent on some higher being. Honesty, humility, and justice require him to recognize God as superior, not only in strength and knowledge, but in kind.

I suggest (a) that every man recognizes that man is not the highest being there is, and (b) that every man worships; i.e., pays the highest tribute to something. Man knows that he is a subordinate being, and that the biggest man or colony of stars is dependent and subordinate. Men are at best second-raters. Vaguely or clearly they know this, and know also that ours

[2] Contemporaries are impressed by this relative impotence in man; e.g., Charles Hartshorne in *The Divine Relativity* (Yale Univ. Press, 1948) holds that if God loves or if man knows God, God as so related to us must be nonabsolute; H. N. Wieman's philosophy of religion, in *The Source of Human Good* (Chicago Univ. Press, 1946) sees God as the humanitarian totality of developing human goods.

is a personalistic universe; the greatest and first being is some person or body of persons. To recognize this truth in any inner or outer way is, so far, to be a religious man, and, if the irreligious man exists, we may say with Christopher Dawson [3] that he "is precisely the man without roots who lives on the surface of existence and recognizes no ultimate spiritual allegiance."

Religion may be described as it is by Schmidt: "Subjectively, it is the knowledge and consciousness of dependence upon some one or more transcendental, personal Powers to which man stands in a reciprocal relation. Objectively, it is the sum of the outward actions in which it is expressed and made manifest, as prayer, sacrifice, sacraments, liturgy, ascetic practices, ethical prescriptions, and so on." [4]

So much for the logic of man's position. The psychology is nearly as simple. To refuse this allegiance is a good road to ill-adjustment. In chapters one and two of *The Return to Religion,* by no means an exhaustive study, Henry C. Link says that a person who refuses allegiance to God will wonder why things go badly with him, why his job, his home and wife and neighborhood are unattractive, why games are colorless, why he fails to find normal happiness in private and public functions, why it is so hard to meet crises, why life has to be forced. Dr. Link says his work does not mean to show how psychology solves people's problems, but "to point out the conditions and the course of life which create these problems. How to avoid the unhappiness of a misshapen personality is certainly more important than the belated devices by which it can be remade."

What creates these problems? The commonest causes, Link says, are two. One is failure to live one's religious life; perhaps not failure in all instances to believe, but failure to integrate faith and works; at best one has a comfortably believed religion,

[3] Christopher Dawson, *Enquiries into Religion and Culture,* Introduction.

[4] Wilhelm Schmidt, *The Origin and Growth of Religion* (Tr. by H. J. *Rose;* New York: Dial Press, 1931), p. 2.

not a socially lived religion. The second is failure to live for other people, to be considerate and self-sacrificial for their happiness, their pleasure, their needs, and aspirations.

In fifteen years, Dr. Link examined and advised or helped to advise over four thousand ordinary cases whose condition may be regarded as the ordinary toll demanded by life in an American city. As Link proceeded he saw that he required and was using the language and teachings of religion and the Bible, and though he himself had, as he at the time thought for scientific reasons, discarded religion, he found that it was the truth and works of religion that many persons needed. It was by way of a science that he made his return to religion. "And now, a mathematical and quantitative science, applied to people rather than to things, without any conscious awareness of the process on my part for a long time, has completely revolutionized my ideas and values. . . . The fact that the results of these studies confirm certain fundamental religious beliefs will inevitably become more generally recognized."

In a word, what people need is "a more effective attack on life and society and yet an attack inspired by a truer and more practical set of ideals. The religion I speak of, therefore, is not the refuge of the weak but the weapon of those who would be strong"; it includes belief in God as the Supreme Being, in a divine moral order as given in the Ten Commandments and the life of Christ, and the acceptance of the Church as the main though imperfect vehicle of truths greater than science.

Link says he has had to tell persons in case after case that their problem is a religious one and that the solution is to live their religion. In terms of our own standard, man or human nature adequately considered, it seems clear, on psychological as well as on logical grounds, that religion if lived helps man truly to be man, to become at least something of what nature desires him to be. Dr. Link's problem-cases might appear negative or at most only quasi positive, but are backed and completed by the positively lived religion of myriad persons and societies. Crude as some religions may be and inadequate as any of them may at times be, religion goes with man's nature, and the person or society defaulting in religion defaults relative to human nature as the basic norm of human life.

A task modern man has found difficult is that of assimilating the data of primitive and comparative morals, including religion. We have just said, "Religion and worship, or defaulting as men." A generation or two ago, people would not so readily have said this; they were still overpowered by the tremendous body of data dug up in the realms of religion and ethics. In America, people were hardly able to take comparative religion and ethics in an objective way till at least 1900, and some of them not till 1920 or after. Some dogmatically tight-laced people were too busy or too narrow-minded to face the facts or to consider the possible truth in doctrines on the evolution of religion. Besides, many people who loved aristocracy could not believe that the ceremonial and devotional life of primitives or even of mankind at large was basically anything but a mass of errors. "Good-bye to all that! Man is coming of age!" Such was in many cases the precritical response. It was thought that religion was superstition, and that people, swamped by fear and sentiment, were at the mercy of ignorance and credulity, if not of gullibility; their priests, who were at once their political rulers, patriarchs, medicine men, sorcerers, soothsayers, and rain getters, were seen as fakers and mere lovers of power. Superstition and idolatry, the people paying divine honors to the sun or stars, to woods and waters, a goat or a bull, the ancestral spirits, the people possessed of and by fetishes, amulets, and totems and a host of taboos: that, in sum, was religion.

Thus the earlier evolutionary anthropologists and comparative religionists reported that all was superstition and idolatry. Fear on one side, and love of power on the other; and ignorance on both.

A result was that for many persons not only primitive religion but all religion came to be taboo and declared an opiate and the degradation of the people. Religion was the open field for practical untruth; it was a Moloch, shameless in its demands and profligate in its practices.

An interesting sidelight on this interpretation of the data is that, though it amounts to a condemnation of the people's practical wisdom, it occurred at a time when we had, after a setback following the French Revolution, resumed the Western struggles for economic and political democracy, and our own social democracy was as vigorous as any has ever been. The verdict was that, after all, the voice of mankind on this serious practical question was wrong, and that the voice of an elite was right. Some few men had discredited man.

Almost anything had at some time and place been judged right, and the same had also been judged wrong. Hence morals were seen as relativistic only; "*tempora et mores*" summed up all. So for religion. Every kind of action had some time or other by some people been taken as the liturgical expression par excellence, and any and every object as the object of devotion. Good modern Christian and scientific people were shocked at the lively variety of evil deeds that were commanded and blessed in the name of religion.

Many theories arose to say what religion universally is. It was seen as originating in some kind of nature myth or star myth, as fetish worship, or by Spencer as founded on beliefs in ghosts, by Tyler as based on animism, or as totemism, by Frazer as magic or not to be separated from and differentiated from magic. All these theories, unless that of nature myths, assumed evolution and progress; religion was supposed to have begun with lower forms, and its higher monotheistic forms were thought to have come latest. Liberalism and socialism were not friendly to religion, and were unable to grasp religion's deeper meaning.

Schmidt continues by saying that primeval man was not as ignorant as we imagine. "The prehistoric tools and weapons and those of the ethnologically oldest peoples of today are alone enough to show that he was a vigorous and daring man of action. To begin with, his mental powers made their way through nature and analyzed her phenomena; his synthetic activities mastered her by forming generalizing and classificatory ideas; he grasped the conception of cause and effect, and then adapted that to the relationship of means to end. His means, to effect the ends he desired, were his tools, which he invented and used. Now all this sufficed to lead him to a real religion, to the recognition of a personal Supreme Being; for he was able to apply these same mental powers to the contemplation of the universe as a whole."

The question is one of ethnological fact and not of theory. It is at the beginning of history, says Schmidt, that we find, in a remarkably clear form, belief in a supreme cause and a personal God, not in a mere "something holy," but in the Lord of life and death, the judge of man's actions, and among the most primitive tribes a belief in God as Father and Creator. Schmidt keeps steadfastly to the democratic view: "I content myself for the present with emphasizing the fact once again, that we must begin with power, not impotence; with the positive, not the negative; with effort and efficiency in the search for a cause, and not with 'primeval stupidity.' "

The assumption of the evolutionary position was that the clearer affirmations of God must have come later and that early beliefs were in a god of low order, so that "hardly anyone found courage to oppose it and to draw attention to the quite frequent examples of this exalted sky-god appearing among decidedly primitive peoples, where not the least trace of Christian influence was to be found." What we discover through wide investigation are "high gods of low races" with strong support in known fact, a thesis that Schmidt has reached through a study of religion among the most primitive and isolated peoples in many parts of the earth. "It is self-evident how interesting a knowledge of their religions must be; for in them we meet, naturally, with the oldest forms of religion we can hope to find." Working out the elements common to these religions, we come as close as possible to primeval religion. Here we can only refer to Schmidt's study, covering first the Pigmy tribes of Africa and Asia, among the latter of whom was found "a nocturnal liturgy addressed to the Supreme Being and couched in a sacred language no longer intelligible to the natives themselves"; secondly, the Southern primitive culture; thirdly, the Arctic primitive culture; and fourthly, the North American primitives. "If it is clear that wherever remnants of the primitive peoples are still discoverable over this huge area, they show belief in a Supreme Being, then it is likewise manifest that such a belief is an essential property of this, the most ancient of human cultures, which must have been strongly rooted in it at the very dawn of time." [5]

The same report, from a carefully scrutinized base, is given by Alexander Le Roy in his *The Religion of the Primitives*.[6] When Le Roy went to Africa as a missionary in 1877, he says he went with all the preconceptions of his time; the blacks were supposed to be "fetichist peoples, without religion or morality, with no family life, stupidly adoring animals, trees, and stones." In a generation with the natives and sympathetic study of them, he learned much. For instance, the emotions used to express our relations to the supernatural being are the same emotions the natives use: submission, veneration, adoration, grief, joy, purification, the desire for imitation, and a human aspiration for a material idol as god. Their prayers are petitions, as ours mainly are, since nearly every one remains primitive in this matter; prayers for rain, crops, health, victory in war, the means to kill enemies. Offering is often a first step; something is offered to the supernatural being; then commonly it is sacrificed, with the aim that the object sacrificed "will in its turn furnish the means of contracting or renewing a more intimate alliance with the invisible world if one incorporates himself with it." Here we have communion, in which Le Roy feels we discover the basic notion

[5] Wilhelm Schmidt, *op. cit.,* chap. 2; pp. 136, 150, 153, 170–71, 217, chaps. 15, 16, 17.

[6] Translation by Newton Thompson (New York: Macmillan, 1922), Preface and chap. 6.

of primitive religion, including prayer, sacrifice, morality, and the taboos. "It seems to me that this fundamental idea, which is so simple and which harmonizes with all these manifestations, should be regarded as the basis of the religious conceptions and practices of primitive man."

In this connection we recommend, as more philosophical but less ethnological than the work of Schmidt or of Le Roy, the highly readable *Religions of Mankind* by Otto Karrer.[7]

As a summary relevant to ethics, we note that aristocratic and "better-than-they" prejudices must be kept out of our way, so that in the first place we can see and understand the religions of the primitives. We must, no doubt at considerable cost, re-educate ourselves on the primitives' religion and all religion, and see that religion, as the habit of worshiping God, is proper to mankind; see in short that man is the worshiping animal. We do not ask which is the true religion in the sense of being the purest and the least overrun by errors so likely in this difficult matter of knowing what God is and our relation to God. We must allow for scores of odd and interesting variations; we should be mature enough not to let factual variations scandalize us. Besides this duty to intelligence, we should in practice carry out, more generally than we now do, the whole liturgical worship of the Church. Primitives naturally have their own liturgies, traditional and ritual ways of expressing their beliefs in God. We should not readily let ourselves be outdone by primitive men, though we may not assume that it is we who are not primitive.

Society suffers without religion is the central point made by Christopher Dawson in all his historical and sociological works.[8] Dawson's thought may be expressed thus:

[7] Translation by E. I. Watkin (New York: Sheed and Ward, 1945), Introduction and chapter 1.

[8] See Dawson's *Enquiries into Religion and Culture* (New York: Sheed and Ward, 1933), Introduction and the chapters on "Religion and the Life of Civilization" and "Religion and Life"; and his Gifford Lectures, *Religion and Culture* (New York: Sheed and Ward, 1948); *Religion and the Rise of Western Culture* (New York: Sheed and Ward, 1950).

Major. "The society or culture which has lost its spiritual roots is a dying culture, however prosperous it may appear externally."

Minor. But our society, especially in the West, has long been progressively losing its spiritual roots.

Conclusion. Ours is a culture and society in process of dissolution, or at least on the downgrade.

This view is not popular, because we have long assumed that religion is not needed at all. "The liberal thinkers and statesmen who were the makers of nineteenth-century civilization regarded religion and culture as entirely independent phenomena. Religion was entirely a matter for the individual conscience and it had nothing to do with social and economic life." The split between religion on the one hand and cultural and social facts and institutions on the other, a split encouraged by the supposition that religion is faith only, resting on private interpretation of the Bible, has been serious. The resulting secularization of Western European culture brought its own nemesis: it discredited a religion with no power over culture, and a culture with no spiritual sanctions; and Marxism, instead of this halfway liberal step of forgetting religion, ousted it altogether and opened the way "for the complete re-absorption of the individual in the social organism," and for seeing society as an economic machine. The practical conclusion is: "If our civilization is to recover its vitality, or even to survive, it must cease to neglect its spiritual roots and must realize that religion is not a matter of personal sentiment which has nothing to do with the objective realities of society, but is, on the contrary, the very heart of every living culture. The desecularization of modern civilization is no easy matter."

Dawson says this state of things has always marked the dissolution or weakening of a culture. We must recover our spiritual roots, and not merely for the comfort of souls or their salvation, but for the health and salvation of Western society. A dying religion results in a dying society, and we must regain openness of mind toward spiritual realities and carry through an application of religion to cultural and social life. As early as 1922 Dawson said: "The great task of the coming age is to promote that spiritual unity without which material unity and control over external nature become merely the organs of a world tyranny or a complication of machinery crushing out true life."

Our conclusion is that man is capable of knowing his basic relationship to the Supreme Being and of living that relationship. He can and ought to do it, if we believe in a man-length democracy known through anthropology, history, and psychology; and he ought for the good of human society. Privately in his own cell he ought to be religious, and in his family life through family devotions, shrines, and liturgy, and also in a wide social way in his labor unions, farm granges, legislative operations, his wars, his political life, and his struggles for peace, as well as in his Church doctrines and churchgoing. He and his societies ought in some way to kiss the dust, acknowledging fealty to God. Not religion here, and life there; but religion in all his life, and all his life in religion. Man need not be scared because religion, as every activity of human and animal life, is emotionally toned, though of course it is evident that emotion can overrun and dehumanize religion or any human activity. For the freedom and general good of persons, their intellectual development, the good of families, nations, and the community of nations, we must mature on the religious question and outgrow the stage of the "bad-boy" professor indoctrinating youth and assuring it that religion is superstition and an opiate. Concurrently the religions must welcome an uncompromising intellectual and critical life in their ministers and their members, and the basic starch that can come only from dogma founded on metaphysics and history.

Some concrete steps to be taken are these. First, let every man practice his religion and every group learn to keep its people religiously alive: we see how bad it is for society and international life when young intellectuals lose their faith.

Secondly, to practice the Catholic religion means study and sacrifice to know and to do, it means a sacramental and liturgical life at home and with the community; it means a perpetual reincarnation of social Catholicism based on Christ's brotherhood with men.[9] Thirdly, it is my business as priest and teacher to encourage people to worship God, not only Catholic people, but all people; this means that I am on occasion to encourage Lutherans to be good Lutherans and Jews to be good Hebrews: these people, commanded by God and nature to worship, we assume are sincere; pro tempore they are likely to worship only in the Lutheran or the Hebrew form, and sincere worship is something fundamentally right in the universe; one recalls that Cardinal Newman did not wish Protestants to become religiously decadent. Each of us is to be all things to all men, though by no means convinced that one religion is as good as another.

Fourthly, men of all faiths might slow up, gradually for fear of the psychological jar, on old habits, often uninformed, sometimes unjust, always uncharitable, of persistent recrimination. Relative to others' religions, our words and actions must conform with knowledge and at times turn to silence and inaction, since charity is better than a bitter zeal.

Fifthly, persons, occupational and fraternal groups such as labor and ownership and the Shriners, and professional groups, as well as religious groups must learn silence, honesty and justice, charity and only the good word. The religion of others may seem ridiculous to me, but is a matter of life and death to them and I may not hurt their convictions or feelings. The captious, inconsiderate word at others' expense is nearly always immoral. Religious and other groups must learn to build up the local and the national religious edifice.

Sixthly, religious leaders and scholars must perpetually reexamine the grounds of their religion and of all religion. How to make seminary education much more vital than it is and yet

[9] See this point in Cardinal Suhard's *Growth or Decline* (South Bend, Ind.: Fides Press, 1948).

not make it thin and jittery is a question that demands attention. In this connection, aids toward realism are the teaching of orphans, "reformees" and poor children, helping with street-preaching in Oklahoma or elsewhere, study and action tours in the deep South, seminarians' and young priests' working where and as poor people work in factories, in mines, and on farms. Also helpful are Catholic Action forums and practices, leaving seminarians much on their own, to observe, judge, and act in the light of Gospel principles; and Catholic Action is best when integrated with the liturgy and contemplation.

In other words, says Maritain, we urge "a truly, and not a decoratively, Christian society"; it is not by granting the Church favors and temporal advantages "paid for at the price of her liberty" that the State would give her help in her spiritual mission, but "by asking more of the Church—by asking her priests to go to the masses and share their life so as to spread among them the Gospel leaven and so as to open to the working world and to its celebrations the treasures of the liturgy; by asking her religious orders to cooperate with the social service and educational agencies of the civil community; by asking her more zealous laymen and her youth organizations to assist the moral work of the nation and develop within social life the sense of liberty and fraternity." [10]

[10] Maritain, *The Rights of Man and Natural Law* (Scribners, 1945), pp. 54, 28–29. In this connection we cannot too often recommend Perrin's *Priest-Workman in Germany,* Bishop's *France Alive* and Michonneau's *Revolution in a City Parish.*

Chapter 18

# TEST CASES ON THE MORAL ORDER

Often a person assumes fifty per cent of his argument. Suppose he assumes that we can know something for certain, or that the senses do not ordinarily mislead, that reasoning holds water, that the basic standard is the mores, that what counters communism is bad, that man is good or that basically man is evil. The assumption, of which he is perhaps unaware, makes a difference to his whole argument. The difference is so great that in many cases the man could not argue what he argues if he did not assume what he assumes. The assumption then is more decisive than anything he is conscious of and that he explicitly says.

T. E. Hulme (English philosopher killed in War I) shows in *Speculations* how the conscious or unconscious assumption commonly works. The typical procedure is as follows: You argue that A is so; I wish to know why. It develops that you hold that A is so because B is so. Why do you hold that B is so? Because you hold that C is so. You take C to be self-evidently so, or to be so because you hold that D is so. In this way the argument may have to be run a long way back; let us say to X. It is only on this final ground, final so far as we are now concerned, that we can profitably argue. It is here that we disagree, and "A is so" depends for its truth value finally on the truth of this presumably much more basic X. If X is so, and if the logic holds, A really is so. Whether we begin with a value rather than a truth does not matter. Then we would say, "A is good because . . . X is good."

At the level of X we have left the particular and have come to what, at least for us, are first principles. These are true and count, or everything falls. Hulme says the French revolutionaries used "liberty, equality, and fraternity" as the ground on which they stood, the principle in the light of which they fought and killed, that in the name of which, at whatever cost, they freed people. So they thought, says Hulme, but a deeper ground was prompting the leaders' action. It was the more abstract, general plane that, as Rousseau had said, man is good. (We would say that if Hulme has reached their fundamental principle, possibly he has not fully stated it.)

In this chapter we put down statements, often quite incomplete arguments, on particular ethical matters. The reader is asked to complete the argument in each instance. To do this he must ordinarily supply the missing premise or premises or even the conclusion. Often the argument is tersely and more than summarily stated, as is the way in conversation, but somewhere in the argument or back of it, is a standard. The argument possibly assumes the mores as standard or the hedonistic, the pragmatic, or the religious standard, or the person's own interests as standard: what defends his interests is good. The reader has to try to find which standard is the one likely used; still this standard is—let us suppose—not named, not mentioned, much less overtly stated. Besides the standard, which is a principle immediately relevant to one's position on an ethical question, the person arguing has a particular view of man, of knowledge, of man's relation to society, of the best type of government, of man's relation to nature and to God, of man's origin and destiny; and it is likely that one or more of these may supply premises in his position, principles thus absolutely, though less immediately, relevant. To understand a man's position on euthanasia or on birth control or on abortion or on power politics and dictatorships, it may be needful to know, not merely the formal ethical principles he employs, but to know that he is a communist, or that he takes the universe to be in the hands finally of Providence, or that, contrariwise, he holds that all is finally meaningless.

The completion of a man's argument on matters ethical may comprise several steps. First, discovering his standards, or formal principles. Secondly, discovering his theology and philosophy of nature and of society. Thirdly, checking his overtly alleged facts and principles. These may be invincible, or be as vincible as a rusted tin can. One last step, by no means the first step, is then required. Having checked on his alleged facts and principles and on his assumptions relevant to both cosmic and to ethical matters, we still have to check the validity of the logic he has employed. The four steps are these:

1. Finding his assumed standards, in case any are assumed.

2. Finding his possibly assumed position on questions of nature, man, society, God, knowledge.

3. Finding the true value of his overtly claimed facts and principles.

4. Finding whether the logic of his statement holds. Logic as well as metaphysics is at times assumed.

The unfinished statements used below are taken from many sources: from common experience, from radio and press, from popular articles, from loosely stated positions overheard in conversation, from students' oral and written declarations, and from both current and old-time philosophers and other scholars. Some statements may be complete, some are justified when fully tested, and others have all kinds of incompleteness and invalidity, which the reader may wish to examine. As the reader completes and investigates any proffered statements, he should make up others or adduce for investigation some that he hears or that he gathers from the papers, from movies, from ads, and from books, popular or scholarly. It is of little use to refute a man's overt statements if they represent less than half of his meaning. Readers are asked to work out the logic of each statement, and, if refutation is in order, to refute the statement, in terms of the basic standard. Some statements or parts of them are alleged, not as arguments, but matters of fact, and possibly this is what some of them are. Valid matters of fact, or principle, or logic, must be picked out of the confusion in which they occur. In this book they may be more terse than they are when buried in discussions on sex, labor, ownership, the comics, and freedom.

## I

### On Economic Goods

1. Every man has his price. After all, we're all after the same thing: "to get into the big money."

2. He's doing well; you'll see: he's going to be well off.

3. What we need is to gear our production up 25 to 40 per cent, and we can do it and make the country safe from attacks and wars.

4. "The freebooting, rugged individualist, whose vigor, imagination, and courage contributed so much of good to the building of our country . . . we must now recognize, where his activities destroy resources, as the Enemy of the People."—Wm. Vogt.

5. "Labor, like flour or cotton cloth, should always be bought in the cheapest market and sold in the dearest; the sole legitimate condition that regulates wages is the demand for service and the supply of workers. If the demand diminishes, wages decrease; if the supply diminishes, wages increase; the wage ordinarily paid is determined by an automatic division of the whole amount which the community is willing to pay for the specified sort of work, by the whole number of persons willing and able to do it."—"What Rights have Laborers?" *Forum,* March 1, 1886.

6. Why not go into the small loan business? It is legal in Indiana to collect a minimum of 20 per cent and a maximum of 42 per cent; in Illinois and Iowa a maximum of 42 per cent; in Minnesota and Nebraska 36 per cent. Why not do it? People needing the money are willing to pay, and the law OK's it.

7. If I don't, some one else will—and perhaps outsiders: Wall Street invading Main Street.

8. "How hard it is for a rich man not to lean upon his riches . . . it is so hard for us to give up our high hopes, and willingly encounter poverty, ridicule, and discomfort!"—Trollope in *Framley Parsonage.*

9. The economic system which has been dominant in America belongs to the people, and not exclusively to financiers or NAM, nor to the few men, families and corporations that control industry. Nor is the system sacrosanct.

10. Congress should require full and open financial reports from the National Tax Equality Association and other powerful class organizations set up to weaken agriculture and labor; they propagandize small businessmen, hire so-called experts to spread their "one-sided, and often false, contentions," furnish speakers free to churches, to the C. of C., and to patriotic bodies, and "plant their stooges" from coast to coast.—Reported Speech by Senator George D. Aiken, December 9, 1947.

11. "Overnight mechanical invention has relieved us of the haunting fear of starvation. At one bound the harnessing of power has made our society rich beyond the dreams of any that went before. With our resources it is easily possible for every man to enjoy comforts and luxuries the Caesars could not command; and in America at least most of us do. In this world of incredible devices for the easing of life, what can remain of the moral ideals of those centuries of destitution? Where is there room for resignation and humility and patience? Who can preserve a righteous and contrite heart?"—John H. Randall, Jr. (1929).

12. Business is Business. That is the first law of finance and of trade.

13. We need just two basic studies: religion for the soul and commerce for the body; all else is subsidiary in education.

14. "If we believe, as we must, that humanitarian action is the essence of the American spirit, we will give to the Com-

munity Chest."—Firestone, in a broadcast: October 4, 1948.

15. The standard in the industrial and commercial world seems to be profit. It appears to be the only reason why men enter these activities, the driving force for all their actions. The whole structure and force behind it seems to be based on profit as standard. The criterion of success in this field is money. The richest are the most successful.

16. "For value received, the undersigned promise to pay to X Loan Co., at its office in Y, Nebraska, the sum of $ . . . together with interest at the aggregate rate of 3 percent per month on that part of the unpaid principal balance of the loan not exceeding $150 and 2½ percent per month on that part . . . in excess of $150 and not in excess of $300 and ¾ of 1 percent per month on any remainder."

## II

### On Work

1. Workers are not given a say in running industry, a condition contrary to human nature and to the function a man is to perform.

2. The production in a plant, the morale, and the quality of work improve through the cooperation of the company with the employees; therefore plants should have such cooperation.

3. The American laborer, equipped with electricity, baths, central heating, a car, radio, refrigerator, the daily paper, and the movies, is better off than any other laborer in history. It is time to let good enough alone!

4. The revolution of the proletariat is a fact, most of all in Russia; it promotes goods and freedoms lacking in the present system.

5. Labor has had to fight its way every inch against almost every capitalist-employer. Its only hope is in an all-out fight, in revolution and its own triumph.

6. Cases make it clear that capital yields when it must; that

is why labor is justified in using pressure methods, sit-down strikes, hunger strikes, picketing, political action committees, intimidation, and in some cases property destruction.

7. We are watched, and they get what they can out of us. That is why sabotage and loafing on the job are justified.

8. We will do what we are paid for, no more, no less. Workmanship and quality are no concern of ours.

9. Many labor affiliates, such as the Transport Workers Union, have been dominated by communists; in fact, Walter Reuther and his brother went to Russia to study the system. It is evident then that the safe and sane thing for Christians is to bypass labor.

10. "The CIO? I have nothing to do with those fellows! Not me!"—Graduate of a Catholic law college.

11. "The modern apostolate, without overlooking anybody, must be based primarily on the working class."—Cardinal Suhard.

12. Capitalists are steeped in the spirit of capitalism, the spirit which dominates an age whose chief desire is profit and ever-increasing profit with the aid of theoretically free labor. Their standard seems to be: the more profit and the more freedom to seek profit, the better. On the other hand, labor is probably using the pragmatic standard when it employs strikes. Its standard is: "If it works, it is good."

## III

### On Politics

1. The men just out of office took the spoils for themselves and their friends; the next group will do the same. The present officeholders have their chance now.

2. The English have been accused of guiding their diplomacy on the basis of expediency, or what is best for the English in the case.

3. The new M.P. says to the old M.P.: "Ceteris paribus,

I believe it's all right to give the plums to my friends." The old M.P.: "Ceteris paribus, be damned!"

4. From the communistic doctrine of revolution has arisen the standard of expediency. Attempting to eradicate evils of maldistribution, they use the theory that the end justifies the means.

5. When it was asked whether it was right for certain nations to tie in with the Soviets in War II, an Englishman (the story goes) said, "Any stick will do to beat a mad dog."

6. Using the Christian standard of human nature adequately and objectively considered, bombs may conceivably, at some time and place, be used. The cases would be much restricted.

7. A nation is justified in killing to save itself; so we were justified in using the A-bomb to end the war; it was a question of thousands of lives against hundreds of thousands, as Secretary Stimson (*Harper's,* February, 1947) said. That thousands died is regrettable, but all war is regrettable. It is a shame that the power of the bomb was first used to kill, but it does not follow that atomic power is evil. Even in its role as a bomb, it is a just means to a good end.

8. Bombs may be considered merely another weapon, a jump from high explosives similar to the jump from bow and arrow to gunpowder. If the common good is best served by the bombs, men may use them. It takes greater reason to justify their use.

9. If you say the use of bombs is bad, be consistent and say that the use of any appliance or instrument is bad.

10. We should develop a rational principle in the use of bombs. We should ask whether we would wish them used on us. Is the gain won by their use going to develop a better and more unified world? Will their use bring about peace and security; lead to respecting the dignity and rights of man? Will their use bring about a wholesome democracy built for the common good?

11. In a war, the killing of innocent civilians, unless merely accidental and not intended, is never justified.

12. Society must be strong in order that man may achieve

his natural desire to live completely as man. Therefore good means, techniques and institutions, good government, a good economic life, work, arts, science, and education must be developed so that this good of man may get a chance.

13. Plato is wrong in saying that it is better to suffer injustice, bad as that is, than to do it. We must fight fire with fire; sometimes it is the only effective weapon we have. If due to a whispering campaign you were losing an election which you had a right to win, why not turn the tide by using a counter whispering campaign?

14. Governments have enabled man to live on a rational plane rather than on an animal, or subsistence level. As transportation and communications have developed, peoples are drawn closer together, and governments have spread in area. War at the same time has become more deadly and has involved more nations. Some sort of international community, involving some sacrifice of sovereignty on the part of individual nations, appears to be the only hope of a solution.

15. To respect the dignity of man, we must respect all men and strive to preserve the rights and liberties of all. The realization of this fundamental duty would seem to call for an international community: all men of all nations united to preserve the rights, liberties, and dignity of man. This agrees with Maritain's pluralistic character of the social, temporal order; he says men belong together for the full development of man. Such a community would be the natural end for Christians: a Christian social democracy recognizing the dignity of all.

16. The standard applied at present to the problem of an international community or a united world seems to be individualistic; each nation is more concerned with its own gains and the race for power than with world peace. A one-world community would be required to have a formal principle, something, for instance, like the UN Charter; but to be effective it must have the support of all.

17. No modern war can be ethically justified.

18. Hitler was the cause of World War II. But the German people were responsible for Hitler's rise to power, for letting him go to war, and for the concentration camps. The Germans were collectively guilty and deserved punishment.

19. The "vae victis!" slogan of the Romans was not merely a description of fact, but a summary of the rights of conquerors, in any war, over the fallen.

20. Just as a person may not anticipate the attack of another on him, so neither may a nation anticipate another nation's attack, but must wait at least until attacked.

21. "Because wars ought to be fought (only) for the common good, if some one city cannot be recaptured without greater evils befalling the nation, such as devastation of many great cities, great slaughter of human beings," widening the area of conflict, "occasions for new wars to the destruction of the Church (because a chance is given pagans to invade and seize Christian lands), it is indubitable that the prince is bound to give up his own right and abstain from war."—Vittoria (1532).

22. The Nazis persecuted all Jews and many Christians and started two world wars in a generation; therefore Germany should never be allowed to become a strong nation again.

23. The Morgenthau plan, backed, at its origin, by the great name of Baruch, was originated for the good of nations, and was free of sectarian interests.

24. The Morgenthau plan was bad economics, bad politics, and bad morals.—"Mr. Baruch has a Plan," London *Economist,* June, 1945.

25. A memorial was set up at Beaconsfield, England, to commemorate the fact that out of World War I, Beaconsfield was saved, not an ideal or perfect Beaconsfield, but Beaconsfield: "A certain social balance, a certain mode of life, a certain tradition of morals and manners. . . . The men . . . died to prevent Beaconsfield," and England, from "being so immediately

overshadowed by Berlin. . . . They died to prevent it and they did prevent it." Therefore England was justified in taking part in the war.—G. K. Chesterton, *Autobiography,* chap. 11.

26. If England had not succeeded, her entering the war would not have been justified; this case shows that the pragmatic standard is basic.

27. Law is what the people prescribes for its safety, convenience, and prosperity: in general, for its welfare.

28. Americans "acknowledge no principle by which a government can prescribe a bill of duties along with a bill of rights, duties under our system being a matter between the individual and his conscience."—John K. Jessup, in *Life,* June 21, 1948, p. 56.

29. Man was once without government and law, a condition in which his life was nasty, brutish, and short, in which there was no just or unjust, no property, no merit or demerit; each man took and kept what he could: a war of every man against every man. Then the State arose by agreement among men, and with the State came just and unjust, merit and demerit, and private property.—Hobbes, *Leviathan,* Book I, chap. 13.

30. Why should men be equal? Because humanity is common to all. Where and how be equal? In the life of the spirit, and in the coexistence of rights and of duties assured by an ethico-juridical order. Still, one element is wanting, to overcome the ill will and egoism "with which we are all imbued," and to cause the order of justice to be willed and respected. This element is mutual love, not a sentimental but an effectual love, not limited to our circle, but extended to all men, and this love "can be realized only through a luminous religious conception."—Sturzo, *The Inner Laws of Society,* p. 238.

31. Liberty and democracy are spiritual goods before being the forms of political regimes: people must know, love, and defend them. Truth and love are the soul of social life in any political regime.

32. "Democracy requires the continuous development of in-

dependent thinking and criticism of the prevailing order."—Attributed to Charles A. Beard.

33. The people are the end of democracy, its subject and its foundation. But the masses are the greatest enemy of true democracy.—Pope Pius XII, Christmas message, 1944.

34. "The democratic contention is that government (helping to rule the tribe) is a thing like falling in love, and not a thing like dropping into poetry."—G. K. Chesterton, *Orthodoxy,* chap. 4.

35. My country: may she ever be right, but my country, right or wrong!

36. After World War II, England, France, and America desired peace and order for all, and therefore felt obliged to dismantle German factories. But if dismantling cost too much in dollars and if England's and France's share in the Marshall plan were thereby reduced, the factories should not have been dismantled.

37. Often the national elections offer us no great leader for President. Therefore democracy in this regard is a failure, and young people of ability and of leadership quality are ethically obliged to serve in political posts, locally, regionally, and nationally, whether or not their income would thereby be decreased.

38. ". . . Report by Justice Robert H. Jackson on the Nuremberg trial. Last Saturday the state department released the report, a thick volume containing the minutes of the negotiations between the various members of the International War Crimes Tribunal, preliminary to the Nuremberg trials. The justices were laying down the rules of procedure and defining the nature of the crimes. On July 25, 1945, at a session of the Tribunal, the members were discussing a draft defining violations of the rules of war, for which violations they were unctuously preparing to try the German leaders. But, at the last moment, Justice Jackson apparently discovered that 'judging in our cause' might involve some embarrassments. So, (page 380 of the Report) we

find him saying: '. . . we have left out of our draft the destruction of villages and towns, etc. I have seen the villages and towns of Germany. I think you will have great difficulty distinguishing between the Military necessity for that kind of destruction from some done by the Germans, assuming the war to be legitimate. It seems to me those subjects invite recriminations that would not be useful in the trial.' We leave to our readers the privilege of examining the rich implications of such a statement.

"Fortunately, we find one happy instance where the example of Nuremberg is not followed. Nuremberg sought to give the odious ex post facto principle international sanction. It is reassuring to note that the Jews who suffered so much from 'Kangaroo justice' have taken heed of one principle which our Constitution upholds and which a Supreme Court justice dishonored. In the new proposed Constitution of the State of Israel appears this section. 'No one should be convicted of any infringement of the law which did not constitute an offense when it was committed.' "—Frank C. Hanighen, *Human Events* (supplement), VI February 16, 1949.

39. Political crime is far worse than private crime, and homicide for political reasons, worse than murder for money or jealousy or personal revenge; no political crime may be condoned or palliated because of time, place, circumstances, or motive.—Attributed to Lord Acton.

## IV

### On Life: Right or Responsibility?

1. The doctor is a friend, counselor, and protector of the family. That is his profession. Never may he be a party to killing a human being. Every man's conscience must rise in revolt against the idea of intentionally killing an innocent person.

2. If a man does not wish to live, that is his business. If a second man is willing to help him fulfill his desire, that is the second man's business.

3. "Patricide is a horrible crime. Matricide is a horrible crime. Fratricide is a horrible crime. But infanticide by abortion or by contraceptives is a crime that cries to Heaven."—Arthur Hebert, in *Extension,* November, 1948.

4. "Nowhere in his profession does a doctor's ethical sense have more direct bearing than on therapeutic abortion. He recognizes the fact that the unborn child is a human being, that its destruction is justifiable only in the most extreme circumstances when continued pregnancy is a direct and imminent threat to the mother's life."—*Newsweek,* June 21, 1948; p. 54.

5. We have many great virtues to exercise: mercy, truth, justice; but the greatest is mercy, above all when accompanied by charity. That is why mercy killing can be such a virtuous act.

6. Scobie in Graham Greene's *The Heart of the Matter* was a man full of kindness and pity: for his wife, for a sick girl who had lost her husband, for a servant boy, for a Syrian money-lender. Of course, he told lies to his wife, was guilty of adultery, treason, and misfeasance, and at last of sacrilege and of suicide. But his compassion and pity counterbalanced all.

7. "Life means nothing to me."—Attributed to a woman doctor charged with killing her daughter-in-law.

8. Life: "Right or responsibility?"

9. Ugh! those surgeons who make from one to three thousand a week and yet enclose with their bills propaganda against socialized medicine!

## V

### On Principle

1. Man as the standard means that every good thing is good so far as it is applied to man and because of its relation to him. Man is the head of creation, and raises things to his level; he does not descend to theirs.

2. Why bother? It will all be the same a hundred years from now.

3. It must be all right to "go overboard," because it is the common thing at parties among the educated and the wealthy.

4. "The essential things in men are the things they hold in common."

5. Only men who have the Chrstian outlook and understand Christian principles know that man should be treated as a human being and be granted rights.

6. An exclusively economic development tends to dehumanize man.

7. Academic freedom is inherent in the American credo that the teacher be free to teach and the pupil free to learn; we must have no Iron Curtain in the realm of knowledge.

8. Knowledge is power, and all power inflates, and is bad.

9. (a) Without science, more moral problems would arise than we now have. Therefore its development is a moral good.

(b) Science won the war and should therefore be developed.

10. Natural law is a "participation in God's eternal law." Since man is not eternal and not divine, the statement has no foundation.

11. Pleasure debases man.

12. "The view that all nature is somehow thoroughly corrupted and that mankind is collectively and individually in a fallen estate is the only ground upon which there can be urged the necessity of redemption by extranatural means."—Y. H. Krikorian, *Naturalism and the Human Spirit.*

13. "Hire the handicapped. It is good business."

14. Read chapter 1 of *The Good Pagan's Failure,* by Rosalind Murray, and state its "A, L, V." [1]

15. Read George Dunne, "Blanshard Charges," *Commonweal,* March 12, 1948, and state the A, L, V.

16. Read John Dewey, "What I Believe," in *Living Philosophies,* and the *Forum,* LXXXIII, March 1930, and state the A, L, V.

[1] Assumptions, logic, and validity will be referred to as "A. L. V."

17. Dewey's article appears with articles on this subject by others in the book, *Living Philosophies*. Read any chapter of this book and state its A, L, V.

18. State the A, L, V in G. K. Chesterton's "The Sceptic as Critic," in the *Forum,* LXXXI, 1929; reprinted in *The Thing*.

19. State the A, L, V in Paul E. More's "Revival of Humanism," *Bookman,* LXXI, March 1930; reprinted in *On Being Human.*

20. *"Odi vulgus profanum."*

21. The more I see of man and man's inhumanity to man, the more I honor dogs and monkeys.

22. Man is supreme, and morals are made by man, and may be made over, depending on times and circumstances.

23. Man has a nature; the basic law for him is his nature.

24. "Nature" is worth zero as a principle, since anyone can claim that he appeals to "nature."

25. If we cannot ostracize everyone with Jewish blood in him, we should kill all Jews.

26. The person who is not pro-Zionist is anti-Semitic.

27. You can fool some of the people all of the time and all of the people some of the time, but you cannot fool all of the people all of the time.

28. If we are going to say there is nature and natural tendency, we are right back at "natural law" and Providence and design; and modern progress means nothing to us.

29. For the first time in the history of man, we have a chance at a real civilization.

30. Science can brook no external authority or curtailment of publicity.

31. "We, even we fortunate Americans."—Wm. Vogt.

32. What has posterity ever done for me?

33. If human nature is the standard, man is the measure; but this is an old-time secularistic and individualistic fallacy.

34. The assumption that there is a generic "human nature" is counter to our heterogeneity and universal individuality, and

would, if followed, make us robots and subject to Fascism. Besides, the assumption is that human nature is static, unprogressive, and that evolution has not occurred; in brief, it is medieval.

35. The (St. Louis) *Post Dispatch* platform: "I know that my retirement will make no difference in its cardinal principles; that it will always fight for progress and reform, never tolerate injustice or corruption, always fight demagogues of all parties, never belong to any party, always oppose privileged classes and public plunderers, never lack sympathy with the poor, always remain devoted to the public welfare; never be satisfied with printing news; always be drastically independent; never be afraid to attack wrong, whether by predatory plutocracy or predatory poverty."—Joseph Pulitzer, April 10, 1907.

## VI

### On Sex and Marriage

1. We have too many people now; this is a world problem and not an insular one; food supplies and the means to live cannot keep up with an unrestricted birth rate. That is why Planned Parenthood must preach birth control, and government, church, and school must help in the campaign.

2. People have the right to live their own lives, with which marriage often interferes; it interferes with freedom and a person's career. Married couples on occasion should get divorced.

3. Business could not survive if two out of five business contracts reached the courts; but two marriages in five in the United States end in divorce; our divorce rate has increased six hundred per cent since the Civil War and is still going up. Are Americans polygamous?—Read entire article, "Are Americans Polygamous?" by David L. Cohn (*Atlantic Monthly,* August, 1947) and state its assumptions, logic, and validity.

4. State the A, L, V of "Too Many People," *Harper's,* February, 1948.

5. People are not to be dictated to by any church. That is why they may get divorced if they wish. It is only the dictator-ruled Soviets who have (since 1935) made divorce more difficult.

6. What we need is a uniform national divorce law and support of the Capper fight for this end.

7. Catholics emphasize marital stability and permanence. But their preaching fails. What they really need to emphasize is intelligence, freedom, and maturity.

8. Artificial insemination is scientifically possible, and people who are unable to have children, desire them, and have the right to get them by the new insemination.

9. Standards used today in regard to marriage and sex are the hedonistic, "the more pleasure the better," and the individualistic, "What I want, that is good." The hedonist sees only pleasure in marriage, and is not willing to deny himself and make sacrifices; the individualist uses any standard any way at any time to suit his fancy. He makes his own rules about relations and about the use of contraceptives in or out of marriage.

10. It is possible for everyone in the United States to have a high standard of living, social insurance, vacations, a career, a full social and human life, in a word, to live. But not if people have big families and old-fashioned ideas about home and marriage.

11. We cannot have children and maintain the standard of life we are used to.

12. Mr. and Mrs. "GI" already have two babies and are borrowing money. They must practice contraception.

13. With shortage on food and shelter for the present world population, and the population, even of India and China, increasing, it is a duty to practice birth control; besides, it is a matter of health for mothers and babies, and the quality of the whole population.

14. In order for married couples to be and fully to be, they must have children if possible. Any parents or grandparents

soon impress you with that fact. Married couples without children feel a definite lack of being.

15. If the Mack Jones's are poor it is their own fault: they shouldn't have so many children.

16. If it is made difficult to have a family, most people just will not have one. Speaking in dollars and cents, it is just not worth it.

17. "Biological instincts and appetites exist not for the sake of furnishing pleasure, but as activities needed to maintain life, the life of the individual and the species. Their adequate fulfilment is attended with pleasure. Such is the undoubted biological fact."—John Dewey and James Tufts, *Ethics* (1908), pp. 270–71.

18. "Marriage is the social consecration of biological function."—Read "Christianity and Sex" by Christopher Dawson, *Enquiries into Religion and Culture.*

19. Bone of Contention

Tell me not in mournful numbers,
Life is but an empty crib.
Adam works to feed and clothe
An unproductive rib.—*Integrity,* November, 1948.

20. During War II and after 1945, the United States, without suffering, poured billions into foreign countries. The people of the United States cannot afford food and shelter, and simply are forced to reduce their population.

21. Marriage vows reading "so long as you both shall live" should be changed to "so long as you both shall love." The former is antiquated and does not conform to the "present cultural pattern of society." Marriage is a civil ceremony and its basis is love.

22. "In general we are unfortunately forced to admit that birth control is urgently demanded by the present state of the world, and will be even more urgently demanded in the future. It *ought* not to be, but that which will come about without it ought to be still less; this is the apology for it. It is better that

the unborn be destroyed than that those who are born kill one another consciously later."—Hans Driesch, *Ethical Principles in Theory and Practice* (Tr.; London: Allen and Unwin, 1930), pp. 121–22.

## VII

### On Religion

1. Religion, a hang-over from medieval superstition, is harmful in an age of science.

2. The axiom that "business is business" is a bad guide in morals, because, in fact, business is just a part of the great business, which is that of saving souls.

3. Study of arts and sciences is a nuisance in a world where we are not commanded to be learned, but to be good, and where the final examination will not be on what we have known, but on what we have done.—Thomas à Kempis.

4. In this age of power and the machine, some force must be found to spiritualize man's nature and not destroy it. The enemy today is not the humanitarian naturalism and liberalism of the nineteenth century, but the much older iron law of power, with many new implements, wielded over men's souls. It seems that total organization of power is a necessary condition of social survival, "until today in the totalitarian states, and only to a slightly less degree in the democratic ones, social control extends to the whole of life and consciousness." In such a world of total power, how can religion continue to be a main spiritualizing force?—Dawson, *Judgment of the Nations,* pp. 8, 26, 106–7.

5. Many elements in the primitives' religion are false and superstitious; many points in medieval theological philosophy are also false, and this philosophy was passing into a metaphysics and was sure, sooner or later, to become merely a philosophy. We are in the age of science, and it is no longer possible, logical, or necessary to believe in religion.

6. "We have abandoned what was once a widespread notion:

that to be 'good' is faithfully and without regard to consequences to obey a code of set rules revealed by a 'God' through a sacred book and through His 'Laws of nature'; or to cultivate the traditional virtues and duties as if they were valuable just in themselves. No: the rules, the virtues, the duties are now thought of as merely the *means to an end* to be achieved. It used to be said that 'The end does not justify the means.' Now we say 'If the true end of man does not justify the means, what does?' "—Jay Wm. Hudson, in *Religious Liberals Reply* (1947), p. 64.

7. "Any activity pursued in behalf of an ideal and against obstacles and in spite of threats of personal loss because of conviction of its general and enduring value is religious in quality. . . . The opposition between religious values as I conceive them and religions is not to be bridged. Just because the release of these values is so important, their identification with the creeds and cults of religions must be dissolved. . . . There are values, goods, actually realized upon a natural basis. . . . We need no external criterion and guarantee of their goodness. They are had, they exist as good, and out of them we frame out ideal ends."—John Dewey, *A Common Faith* (1934), pp. 27–28, 48.

8. "Could religion, as a concern for man's existence and the human situation, shift from the perspective of supernaturalism to that of naturalism? Could it candidly accept the full import of modern knowledge about man and the cosmos and set itself human objectives, personal and social, with a naturalistic world view as a background? . . . He who acknowledges, and wishes to further human values, cannot be said to be irreligious or unspiritual."—Roy Wood Sellars, *Religious Liberals Reply* (1947), pp. 156–57.

9. Religion is faith in the conservation of values.

10. "The irreligious man is precisely the man without roots who lives on the surface of existence and recognizes no ultimate spiritual allegiance."—Christopher Dawson, introduction to *Enquiries into Religion and Culture* (1933).

11. The fool has said in his heart: There is no God.

12. Blessed is the people whose God is the Lord. Go to church Sunday.

13. What do those people worship who do not worship God?

14. If a person has compassion and mercy and is decent toward other people, it does not matter what his religion is. Complete honesty and charity! What more may be demanded?

15. There is no sin unless our neighbor is injured or scandalized.

16. Read Pascal's "Wager" and state its A, L, V.

17. Religion is the opiate of the people.

18. Opiates are the religion of the people.

CHAPTER 19

# ETHICAL PRINCIPLES AND EQUIVALENTS

WE PUT down first some of the principles common to all persons and groups in their moral life and their thinking on moral problems.

1. The first principle of ethics is that good is to be done. This may be put: Only good is to be done; or: if anything is to be done, good is to be done. Good or nothing: this is the first principle of the practical order and therefore holds for making things as well as for ethical action. It means that the end is to be sought and that the means are, if possible, to be discovered and used, a principle which holds in housebuilding, in carmaking, in cooking and all "fine" and rough arts, as well as in personal living and community building.

2. The other side of this is that evil is to be avoided. Evil is never to be done. Good; no matter what.

3. Restatement: Since we have designated human good in terms of our being and human evil in terms of our nonbeing the first principle is a strictly existentialist principle. This is easily seen in the double negative, Evil is never to be done.

4. There is an end, a consummation set by nature for human life. We cannot, says Joseph Buckley in *Man's Last End,*[1] state the common temporal end in concrete terms, such as: Man is to win war X; man is to raise a family; man is to be a monk; but only in some such terms as Aristotle used when he said that man is to live as man. This no doubt gives limitations within which and only within which, but not concreteness.

[1] St. Louis: B. Herder, 1949.

5. Man's desire as person and as member of society, his great and never-obliterated desire is to be and fully to be. Man finds and accepts this law of being.

6. The law of self-preservation is a first law of life and of nonlife.

7. Whatever of minerals, plants and brutes, man cannot come at all fully to be unless he gives his life for others, according to the law of super-abundance.

8. As a man acts, so he will become. At first he has no virtues or vices, but by acting, under many social influences, he picks these up. His way of acting leads to an acquired state of character, a complex of virtues and vices.

9. As a man is, so he will act, and things like him and his actions will in time seem good to him; he will tend to rationalize his own conduct, good or bad. What he does he will tend to lay down as law for all. The same is true of the group.

10. Whatever his goodness or badness, a man uses standards in judging the acts he is to do, the acts he has done and others' acts: some standards, "get-away-with-it" standards, the human-nature standard, and so on. He cannot judge and act as man if he tries to live in a standardless vacuum.

11. Man cannot come fully to be as man or even preserve his present relative fulness of being, unless he acts as man: (a) in his thinking and wishing for his individual, private life; (b) in relation to other persons and groups; (c) in relation to lower beings, and (d) in relation to any known higher being or beings. That is, at all times in the use of his freedom, man must respect human nature. This is the standard and guide for him and may be called the natural human law. The Christian or Hindu has no right to try to pretermit it, and the crown prince has no such right.

12. In all matters of action, the last end is the first principle, a principle which holds for brief series, such as winning a race or a ball game, or for the series that seemingly is set by nature toward some ultimate end of human life.

13. Unless I have reason to doubt it, my conscience is in almost all instances to be followed; my conscience is subjectively and individualistically right, but it can be objectively and socially and cosmically wrong. A man has to follow such guide as he has; relative to something here and now to be done, using as well as he can such standards as he has, he judges that X is to be done and Y avoided. He should therefore do X and avoid Y. That is the natural line of the prudential judgment. Using such and such standards he judges and "forms his conscience."

14. Each man is inevitably a person and an individual person. A stick or a stone is an individual, and so is a man. A person has intelligence and freedom, is responsible; open to him is a whole world of values not open to a mere individual, values of truth, of autonomy, of giving himself freely and generously to the community.

15. The complex of family life and civic life, including national and international life, frequently requires person and group to do good though accompanying evils, neither done nor desired, are foreseen. Hence the principle of the double effect.

16. Animals and human persons have a bias for pleasure. The inference appears to be that pleasure is a good. That it is not the chief good follows from the fact that as enjoyed in certain contexts pleasure is far from good. It seems that it would be an accompaniment of the chief good. To control pleasures is a task for the virtue of prudential living, and Plato says that for children to learn from their youth up in which things to take pleasure and at which things to be pained is education.—From Aristotle's *Ethics*.

We can go far toward finding an equivalence among law and end and good; these are equivalent realities. Consider this list:

"to be good and virtuous" equals
"to choose the right means," which equals
"to go on effectively towards the end," which equals
"to live according to rational nature," which equals

"to do one's duty; to fulfil one's obligations, to do what one ought to do," which equals

"to be effective, practical, efficient in human living," which equals

"to practice the intellectual know-how virtue of *prudentia,* supposing the moral virtues," which equals

"to follow (a right) conscience," which equals

"to observe the natural law or the human *ratio operandi,"* which equals

"automatically to get the benefit of the 'sanction' working from the inside," which equals

"to 'qualify to be qualified' on the supernatural level," which equals

"to live according to the eternal law," which equals

"to live as man," which equals

"to do the will of God," which equals

"to respect and develop our personal and community life," which equals

"to go with the root principle in all matters of action," which equals

"to avoid evil," which equals

"to observe the basic principle of the moral law; *bonum faciendum,"* which equals

"to square with objectivity," which equals

"to accept the universe," which equals

"to do what, most deeply within itself, the human being desires to do," which equals

"to be thereby what, most deeply within itself, the human being desires to be."

This is our answer to the fact of creative conflict in man and life and possibly in all nature, to the fact of moral evil and the sense of tragedy and frustration in human lives, to the fact of human limitation. We are not asked to hate bearbaiting mainly because some people possibly enjoy it. We are asked to do something much more native to us and elemental in us. We are asked by our nature to respect our nature. If our doctrine were mainly a deontology or a duty-ethics, it would still be miles from Durant Drake's statement that "duty is doing what you don't like to do." Duty is doing exactly what man most radically wishes to do. It is miles from an old statement (1909) by Ralph Barton Perry that "morals is the massing of interests against a reluctant cosmos."

God is not offended except at what we do against our own good.[2]

[2] St. Thomas Aquinas, *Contra Gentiles,* III, c. 122.

BIBLIOGRAPHY

# MORAL STANDARDS

Which standards men use is seldom clear to them, and often they are unaware that they use standards at all. In chapter one we said they make judgments relative to any matter on which they exercise their freedom. Hence the wide variety of fields and divergent philosophies represented in the following reading list on standards. First a brief sample is given in an editorial, since editorials from almost any journal could serve as reading matter, as well as the columns of Eleanor Roosevelt, Walter Lippmann, or Pegler or anyone available; or campaign speeches, court records, news and magazine articles, town meeting or other radio discussions. The editorial cited is from the *Labor Leader* for October 20, 1949:

"The New York department store field continues to provide interesting—and disturbing—examples of the close cooperation that can be worked up between management and communist unionism.

Just a few days ago Stern Brothers signed up with Local 5, Department Store Union (unaffiliated). This was done despite management's knowledge that the AFL Retail Clerks Union, which had lost a close election to Local 5 last March, was still awaiting Labor Board action on its appeal for a new election on the score of intimidation.

Two reasons can be attributed for the Stern management's action. One was fear—fear that the extreme pressure tactics used by Communists in this field would interfere with "business as usual."

The second was the lure of a "cheap deal." The general raise negotiated was $3.00. It is significant that the starting wage is now set at $33.50. This is the best that could be achieved after ten years of left-wing unionism!

With the Stern's settlement most of the major stores are now back under the old Communist control. Loeser's, Gimbel's, Saks-34th St. and Hearn's signed up last Fall with wage clauses subject to further negotiations. The workers in all these stores are still waiting for an increase. Macy's and Bloomingdale's followed, with Stern's bringing up the rear.

It is enlightening too to recall that last year, when a House committee investigated Communist activities in the distributive trades, New York department store management was loud in denunciation. Louis Broido, executive vice-president of Gimbel's and Saks-34th St., shouted loud and long. But when the test came Mr. Broido signed on the dotted line. His employees are still waiting for a raise.

We are looking forward to the day when management groups generally will awaken to a realization that their fate is being decided in the world-wide ideological battle now raging. If they want an example of what happens to 'free enterprise' when the battle is lost they might with profit investigate what has happened to the Check people, and particularly its middle class, in the last year and a half. There are things on this earth more important than the dollar."

What standard or standards does the editor accuse Stern's of using, and what standard or standards does he use in his stand against Stern's? What assumptions are made by Stern's, and what by the editor? Questions such as these may be asked about any of the following readings such as those from Plato, St. Augustine, or Edmund Burke.

### Books of readings

Clark, Gordon H. and Smith, T. V. Readings in Ethics (New York: Crofts, 1931).

Leibell, J. F. Readings in Ethics (Chicago: Loyola Univ. Press, 1926).

Rand, Benjamin. The Classical Moralists (Boston: Houghton Mifflin, 1909).

### Reading list from many fields

Acton, Lord. Inaugural Address on the Study of History, 2nd ed. (Macmillan, 1896); also with other materials in Essays on Freedom and Power (Boston: Beacon Press, 1948).

Adams, Henry. The Education of Henry Adams, chap. 10, "Political Morality."

Alinsky, Saul D. Reveille for Radicals (Chicago Univ. Press, 1946); chap. 1.

Altgeld, John Peter. On Municipal and Governmental Ownership, Labor Day speech, 1897.
Aristotle. Ethics, Bks. II–IV; Bks. VIII, IX on friendship.
Politics, Bk. I, 4–7 on slavery; Bk. II, 1–5 on Plato's proposal to abolish the family and property.
Atlantic Charter and the four freedoms.
Babbitt, Irving. Democracy and Leadership, chap. on Democracy and Standards.
Literature and the American College, chap. 1.
Essays toward Definition, in Humanism and America, ed. by Foerster.
Belloc, Hilaire. The Servile State, Introduction; chaps. 1, 4, 7, 8, 9.
The Restoration of Property, chaps. 2, 3, 4.
Beecher, Henry Ward. Antislavery speech in Liverpool (1863).
Berdyaev, Nicholas. The Bourgeois Mind.
The End of Our Time.
Russian Religious Psychology.
Bible, the. Job. Chapters 10, 12, 14, 21, 23, 24, 26.
Psalms 143 and 144 (in King James version, 144 and 145).
St. Matthew. Chapters 5–7: sermon on the mount.
Acts of the Apostles 10, 9–43; 11.
St. Paul: to the Romans 3, 29–31; 15, 7–12.
I Cor. 12, 13–27; I Cor. 7, 1–35.
Ephesians 5, 21–33.
Bill of Rights, the.
Bradley, F. H. Ethical Studies. Chapters: "Why Should I Be Moral?" "My Station and Its Duties," and "Selfishness and Self-sacrifice."
Brandies, Louis D. The Curse of Bigness.
Business—a profession.
The Social and Economic Views of Mr. Justice Brandies.
True Americanism (an oration).
Briefs, Goetz. The Proletariat, chaps. 1, 7, 8, 12, 14: "A challenge to Western civilization."
Bryan, Wm. Jennings. The Cross of Gold.
The Prince of Peace.
Burke, Edmund. On Conciliation with America (1775).
Trial of Warren Hastings (1778).

Carlyle, Thomas. On Heroes and Hero-Worship, "The Poet as Hero."
Past and Present, "Aristocracy of Talent," "Gospel of Mammonism."
Sartor Resartus, "The Everlasting No," "The Everlasting Yea."
Carnegie, Andrew. The Empire of Business.
The Gospel of Wealth.
Carnegie, Dale. How to Win Friends and Influence People. "6 ways to make people like you; ways to win people to your way of thinking."
Chandler, Albert. Clash of Political Ideals, 2nd ed. (New York: Appleton-Century, 1949). We find these well selected readings.
Chesterton, G. K. "The emancipation of domesticity," in What's Wrong with the World?
"The ethics of elfland," in Orthodoxy.
"The Sceptic as Critic," in The Thing, Why I am a Catholic (also in The Forum, 1929).
"The Shadow of the Sword," in Autobiography.
Cicero. On Duties. On Friendship.
Cooper, John M. Birth Control, chap. 4.
Court decisions. E.g., Dred Scott decision.
October term, 1922 in the cases of Adkins v. Children's Hospital and Adkins v. Willie A. Lyons (261 U.S. 525): on minimum wages for women: majority decision by Justice Sutherland; dissenting opinion by Chief Justice Taft, and by Justice Holmes.
Everson v. Board of Educ., 330 U.S. 1 (1947): New Jersey school-bus case.
McCollum v. Board of Educ., 333 U.S. 203 (1948): "released time" case.
Meyer v. Nebraska, 262 U.S. 380 (1923): the one-language case.
Pierce v. Society of Sisters, 268 U.S. 510 (1925): the Oregon school case.
West Coast Hotel Co. v. Parrish 1937 (300 U.S. 379): Congress has power to establish minimum wages for women. (See Harold W. Metz, Labor Policy of the Government. Brookings Inst. D.C., 1945).
D'Arcy, Martin C. Christian Morals, Part 1, chaps. 1, 2.

Dawson, Christopher. Enquiries into Religion and Culture, Introduction and pp. 106–15; chap. "Christianity and Sex."
Day, Dorothy. House of Hospitality.
Union Square to Rome.
Declaration of Independence.
Demosthenes. On the Crown.
Philippics, or against Philip king of Macedon.
Dewey, John. Human Nature and Conduct, Part 1, chap. 5, "Custom and Morality."
Experience and Nature, chap. 10.
The Influence of Darwin on Philosophy.
The Quest for Certainty, chaps. 4, 10.
Reconstruction in Philosophy, chap. 7.
Dostoievsky. The Possessed, Part 3, chap. 5, "The Wanderer."
Douglas, Paul H. Social Security in the United States, 1936.
Emerson. The American Scholar.
Ewing, Oscar C. The Nation's Health.
Franklin, Benjamin. Poor Richard's Almanac.
French Declaration on the rights of man.
Gandhi. Autobiography, 1948.
Mahatma Gandhi at Work, 1931.
My Appeal to the British, 1942.
Gill, Eric. Art and a Changing Civilization, 1929.
Art-nonsense, 1929.
Autobiography, 1944.
Sacred and Secular, 1940.
Work and Culture, 1938.
Gilson, Etienne. "Intelligence in the Service of Christ," in Christianity and Philosophy.
Gladstone, Wm. E. The Bulgarian Horrors (London, 1876).
Hayek, F. The Road to Serfdom (Chicago Univ. Press, 1944).
Hildebrand, Dietrich von. In Defense of Purity.
Liturgy and Personality.
Marriage.
Hippocrates. The Oath and the Law of Hippocrates.
Holmes, Oliver Wendell, Jr. The Dissenting Opinions of Mr. Justice Holmes (New York: Vanguard, 1929), Sections on: Natural Law;

Hampering Social Experiments; Infringing on Freedom; Escaping Taxes.
Representative Opinions of Mr. Justice Holmes (New York: Vanguard, 1931).
Law and the Court (a speech).
Hueck, de, Catherine. Dear Bishop.
Friendship House.
Hügel von, Friedrich. Essays and Addresses (London: Dent, and New York: Dutton, 1931).
Hull, Ernest R. Why Should I be Moral? (Bombay: Examiner Press, 1923).
Hutchins, Robert M. The Higher Learning in America.
Autobiography of an ex-Law Student.
I'll Take My Stand (New York: Harpers, 1930), Introduction.
Ingersoll, Robert. At his Brother's Grave, 1879.
Jefferson, Thomas. First Inaugural, 1801.
Leo XIII. *Rerum novarum.*
Human Liberty.
The Christian Constitution of States.
Lincoln. Emancipation Proclamation.
First Inaugural.
Gettysburg Address.
The Lincoln-Douglas debates, 1858.
His Speeches and Writings (New York: World Pub. Co., 1946).
Livingstone, R. On Education (New York: Macmillan, 1944).
Locke. Civil Government.
A Letter Concerning Toleration.
Some Thoughts Concerning Education.
Machiavelli. The Prince. The Discourses.
Manning, Henry Edward. The Eternal Priesthood.
The Four Great Evils of the Day, 1883.
The Grounds of Faith.
Maritain, Jacques. Antisemitism, 1939.
Education at the Crossroads (Yale Univ. Press, 1943), Part 2, chap. 3, "The Fundamental Norms of Education."
The Rights of Man and Natural Law.
The Person and the Common Good.
True Humanism.

Marshall, John. Maryland v. the U.S. Government.
Constitutional Decisions of John Marshall (Putnams, 1905).
The Federal Constitution, June 10, 1788.
Malthus. Essay on the Principle of Population.
Marx. Capital.
Mencken, Henry L. Prejudices, e.g., ser. 3, chap. on Education, or chap. on Memorial Service.
Mercier, Louis J. A. The Challenge of Humanism, chap. 8, "Naturalism or Humanism?"
Milton. On Liberty of the Press.
On Education.
More, Paul Elmer. On Being Human, chap. 1, "A Revival of Humanism."
Newman, John Henry. Apology. On "Lying," Part 1, chap. 7; Appendix 8.
Idea of a University. Part 1, discourse 5, "Knowledge Its Own End"; Part 2, "Christianity and Scientific Investigation."
Letter to the Duke of Norfolk.
Nuremberg Trials.
O'Connell, Daniel. Speeches.
Ozanam. The Letters of Frederick Ozanam.
Parnell, Charles Stewart. Speeches.
Pascal. Thoughts: "The Mean."
Pericles. Funeral oration.
Perrin, Henri. Priest-Workman in Germany (New York: Sheed & Ward, 1948).
Peterson, Elmer T. (ed.). Cities Are Abnormal (Oklahoma Univ. Press, 1946).
Pius XI. Atheistic Communism.
Christian Education of Youth.
Christian Marriage.
Reconstructing the Social Order, 1931.
Pius XII. Christmas message of 1944.
Darkness over the Earth, 1939.
Plato. Republic. A. Standards used by Thrasymachus, and by Socrates against him. B. Standards used in arguing for community of wives and of property.
Problems in American Civilization (New York: D. C. Heath Co.).

(Useful readings; most problems featured are political and economic.)

Rights. Bill of Rights. French Declaration. U.N. Bill of Rights.

Roosevelt, Franklin D. Selected addresses and papers.

Roosevelt, Theodore. American Motherhood (oration).

Rowntree, Benjamin Seebohm. The Human Needs of Labor (Longmans, 1937).

Ryan, John A. A Living Wage.

Moral Factors in Economic Life (with Francis J. Haas) (NCWC, 1931).

The Norm of Morality, NCWC.

The Supreme Court and the Minimum Wage (New York: Paulist Press, 1923).

Smith, Adam. Wealth of Nations, Part 1, chap. 7, "Of the Natural and Market Price of Commodities."

Steinbeck, John. Grapes of Wrath, chap. 15.

Stimson, Henry L. On Active Service in Peace and War, chap. 22, especially pp. 565–82.

Suhard, Cardinal Emmanuel. Growth or Decline (Tr. by James Corbett; South Bend, Ind.: Fides Press, 1948).

Tawney, R. H. Religion and the Rise of Capitalism.

Thomas, St. On the Governance of Rulers.

*Contra Gentiles*. III, cc. 114–17; 141.

*Summa theologica,* Ia IIae, q. 18–21, 90–95; IIa IIae, q. 23, a. 6–8; q. 26.

Thucydides. History of the Peloponnesian War.

To Secure These Rights. Report of President's Committee on civil rights (U.S. Gov't Printing Office, D.C. 1947).

Victoria (Vittoria). The Rights of the Indians.

The Right of War and Peace.

Watkin, E. I. Men and Tendencies, chap. "Peace and War."

The Catholic Centre.

Webster, Daniel. Speeches.

Whitman, Walt. Leaves of Grass.

Magazine articles

Adams, James Truslow. "The Mucker Pose," Harpers Magazine, November, 1928.

"Why be Good" and "How be good," Forum, May and June, 1930.

Barr, Stringfellow. "The Liberation of the Mind." Free America, September, 1939; reprinted in Frederick and Ward, Reading for Writing, 1941 edition.

Bowie, W. R. "Protestant Concern over Catholicism," American Mercury, September, 1949.

Briefs, Goetz. "Trend in Population," Commonweal, February 25, 1938.

Carnegie, Andrew. "An Employer's View of the Labor Problem," Forum, April, 1886.

Cenerazzo, W. W. "How to Lick Class Struggle," Readers Digest, September, 1949.

Cohn, David L. "Are Americans Polygamous?" Atlantic Monthly, August, 1947.

Dawson, Christopher. "Catholicism and the Bourgeois Mind," Colosseum, II (1935).

Hook, Sidney. "Should Communists be allowed to Teach?" N.Y. Times, magazine sect. (February 17, 1949).

"I Live with the Ku Klux Klan," Negro Digest, April, 1949.

Lloyd-Thomas, Rev. J. A. "Lambeth and the Wider Outlook," Hibbert Journal, 1930.

Lynd, Robert. "Why Literature Declines," Atlantic Monthly, September, 1928.

Mace, Robert David. "Is Chastity Outmoded?" Woman's Home Companion, September, 1949. See also Margaret Culkin Banning, "The Case for Chastity," Readers Digest, August, 1937.

Maritain, Jacques. "The Meaning of Contemporary Atheism," Review of Politics, July, 1949.

"Marriage and Free Thought," Fortnightly Review, 1871.

Martin, J. B. "Hickman Story," Harpers Magazine, August, 1948; Readers Digest, October, 1948.

Michel, Virgil. "Ownership and the Human Person," Review of Politics, April, 1939.

Murray, John Courtney. "The Catholic Position," on church and state, American Mercury, September, 1949.

Oesterreicher, John. "The Catholic Attitude Towards the Jews," Orate Fratres, July 24, 1949.

Pieper, Josef. "The Christian Idea of Man," Review of Politics, January, 1949.

"The Penny and the Gingerbread," Harpers Magazine, October, 1928.

"Should the State Teach Religion?" Forum, 1886.

Shulberg, Budd. "Movies in America: After Fifty Years," Atlantic Monthly, November, 1947.

Stimson, Henry L. "Decision to Use the Atomic Bomb," Harpers Magazine, February, 1947.

Sturzo, Luigi. "Modern Wars and Catholic Thought," Review of Politics, April, 1941.

Sutherland, Arthur E., Jr. "Due Process and Disestablishment," Harvard Law Review, June, 1949.

White, Wm. C. "These Russians," Forum, May–September, 1930; Readers Digest, July, 1930.

Williams, Ruth. "Revolution in a City Parish," Integrity, June, 1949.

# INDEX